THE
AMERICAN SECRETARIES OF STATE
AND THEIR DIPLOMACY

Volume XV

THE AMERICAN SECRETARIES OF STATE AND THEIR DIPLOMACY

ROBERT H. FERRELL, *Editor*

SAMUEL FLAGG BEMIS, *Advisory Editor*

COOPER SQUARE
NEW YORK

VOLUME XV

GEORGE C. MARSHALL

by

ROBERT H. FERRELL

PUBLISHERS, INC.

1966

MANUFACTURED IN THE UNITED STATES OF AMERICA
NOBLE OFFSET PRINTERS, INC., 400 LAFAYETTE ST., NEW YORK, N. Y.

For Lila

VOLUME XV

TABLE OF CONTENTS

PREFACE TO VOLUME XV

GEORGE CATLETT MARSHALL was the only professional soldier ever to become Secretary of State. As a military strategist he had no peer in American history. It was his strategy which guided the great American field commanders MacArthur and Eisenhower, during the Second World War; in fact, he steadied the combined strategy of the Allies once the United States entered the war. This military background proved to be a valuable experience in later dealing with the realities of Russian, if not of Chinese communism. His first diplomatic experience, that of the mission to China for President Truman in 1946, turned out badly. Hindsight compels us to say that in candor: it was impossible to unite the undeviating purpose and fervor of the Chinese Communists with the nationalistic patriotism and efforts of Chiang Kai-shek, handicapped as he was by an inefficient and imperfectly honest government, to hold off the Communists. Marshall's failure in China, however, was not his failure alone; it was the failure of the whole United States Government and its credulous inexperience with communism in Asia.

General Marshall owed his appointment not to that dismal adventure in China, but rather to the continuing confidence which President Truman had in the man. "You can always count on George Marshall," said the President. "He is steady as a rock."

It was Marshall's experience with the inveterate character of Russian foreign policy, at the Moscow Conference of 1947, at the very beginning of the general's incumbency of the Department of State, that annealed his appraisal of the Communist Revolution. It was with the initial phase of this immitigable conflict that the Secretary principally concerned himself during the short but decisively important period of his term of office. His confrontation of the Cold War in Europe, and soon again in China, apparently distracted his attention from the communist conspiracy in Latin America, which first erupted at Bogotá in 1948.

After Marshall had recovered from the serious operation that compelled his resignation in 1949, the President again called upon him to become Secretary of the Department of Defense during part of the Korean War emergency.

This great American, "the great one of the age" in President Truman's vocabulary, deserves well of his country and of this Series.

SAMUEL FLAGG BEMIS
Advisory Editor

New Haven, Connecticut
VI.15.1965

ACKNOWLEDGMENTS

Many individuals have eased the task of research and writing, and my thanks especially must go to the able group of scholars, including some high officials of the Truman Administration, who attended the Conference on the European Recovery Program held at the Harry S. Truman Library on March 20-21, 1964. The present writer and Jerry N. Hess edited a transcript of the sessions, recently published by the Library's Institute for National and International Affairs. May I also acknowledge the help of Philip C. Brooks, Director of the Library, and his colleague Philip D. Lagerquist, Research Archivist, for assisting my work, and reading and criticizing chapters on the Marshall Plan. Thanks also to friends and colleagues —Eugene Davidson, Louis L. Gerson, Howard H. Quint, Thomas J. Roberts, Barbara Stevens—who read chapters, argued about them, forthrightly suggested change.

The Advisory Editor of this Series, Samuel Flagg Bemis, pointed out avenues of research, and was of extraordinary help, preventing a great many foolish errors of style and substance when he read and criticized the entire book in galley proof.

The Honorable William L. Clayton, Undersecretary of State in 1946-47, kindly read a draft of pages on the Marshall Plan; Brigadier General Frank L. Howley the chapter on the Berlin blockade; Forrest C. Pogue, Marshall's distinguished biographer, the first chapter on the general's early years; and Richard G.

Hewlett, Chief Historian of the United States Atomic Energy Commission, the chapter on atomic weapons.

I am indebted also to: Rear Admiral William H. Leahy, U.S.N. (Ret.), for permission to quote from the diaries of his father, Fleet Admiral William D. Leahy; Ellen Clayton Garwood for use of interviews she undertook during work on her biography of her father, Undersecretary Clayton—Mrs. Garwood deposited records of the interviews in the Oral History Research Office at Columbia University; the James V. Forrestal estate for permission to quote from the Forrestal papers in the Princeton University Library; the Oral History Research Office at Columbia for use of its collections; the Librarian of the British Library of Political and Economic Science (London School of Economics and Political Science), and Lady Dalton, for allowing quotation from the diary of Lord Dalton; and William M. Franklin, Director of the Historical Office of the Department of State, and E. Taylor Parks, Chief of the Research Guidance and Review Division of the same Office, for much good advice and assistance.

Finally I do want to thank David Nelson Rowe of Yale University, who originally undertook the work on George C. Marshall for the present Series but whose many important responsibilities forced him to withdraw. He most helpfully allowed me to use notes he had accumulated for the project.
June 15, 1965

                                    Robert H. Ferrell

GEORGE CATLETT MARSHALL

GEORGE CATLETT MARSHALL

1947-49

CHAPTER ONE

THE SOLDIERLY YEARS

GEORGE Catlett Marshall, Jr., seldom looked like anything but a soldier—he did not have appearance of a diplomat—and so when the White House in January, 1947, announced his appointment as Secretary of State the country's newspapers showed him in his wartime portraits: left shoulder turned toward the camera to reveal his five circling stars, the military face with the tightly brushed graying-white hair, straight eyebrows, staring eyes, round nose, firm mouth, carefully shadowed double chin. He was the first professional soldier to occupy the Secretary's office at the Department. He had served in the Regular Army all his adult life, since the year 1902, and was on the active list in 1947.

The general was a fine choice. In the power-crazed postwar world, where such phrases as cold war and protracted conflict were gaining currency, there was need for a Secretary who understood the connection between diplomacy and military power. Secretary James F. Byrnes who had served from June, 1945, was an able Southern politico and an attractive Irishman who stood for American rights, and some-

1

times for his own Cabinet rights as against the free-wheeling foreign policy speeches of Secretary of Commerce Henry A. Wallace. To some people Byrnes did not seem the steely sort who could take on the Russians. President Harry S. Truman once received a semiliterate letter which, referring to the fact that Byrnes often had been abroad at conferences, caught some of the feeling about him: "Mr. Burn's might be very smart man but we need something powerfull, somebody big and strong stern voice. . . . He's been over there so many times and still comes back and over again."[1] Byrnes' predecessor Edward R. Stettinius, Jr., (December, 1944-June, 1945) had been a successful executive at General Motors and United States Steel, and had become a United Nations man. An enthusiastic and even effervescent individual, Stettinius once on the spur of the moment asked Sir Alexander Cadogan to explain the work of the Dumbarton Oaks Conference of 1944 to the "rockettes" of Rockefeller Center, backstage after their show. To his countrymen Stettinius seemed too bland a person to oppose the Russians or even his superior, President Franklin D. Roosevelt. Marshall had other qualities. He knew about power. As Chief of Staff from 1939 to 1945 he had presided over the growth of the United States Army from a size of perhaps the Portuguese Army to a force larger and far better equipped than any other in the world. Moreover, he had attended all the major wartime military-diplomatic conferences. He could pass easily from the role of soldier to that of diplomatist.

Marshall had the confidence of President Truman.

The President's preceding Secretaries, Stettinius and Byrnes, had not been so fortunate—Stettinius never had Truman's confidence, and Byrnes may have lost it. Truman worshiped Marshall. During the war when the President had been Senator Truman of the Special Senate Investigating Committee he had begun to describe Marshall as the greatest living American, an interesting description from a Democratic politician when another great American was alive at 1600 Pennsylvania Avenue. Throughout 1946 the general was in China seeking to bring the Nationalists and Communists together, but Truman could not forget Marshall's stature and availability. He suggested Marshall's name for important government posts as they became vacant, and the regularity of presidential suggestion became a matter of cautious amusement among the White House staff. The President trusted Marshall as he did no other individual in public life.

1

Marshall was born on December 31, 1880, in Uniontown, Pennsylvania, into a fairly well-to-do family. His father was a plunger in business, doing well for a while, gaining a modest fortune in the coal industry then so important for steel-making in Pittsburgh; but he made some wrong business moves and his latter years were pinched and difficult, leaving the family almost in straits. At least for the youth George it was a pleasant life. Marshall's early years passed in the usual round of boyhood experiences and it is

difficult to draw much from them. In old age the veteran soldier and statesman did recall a few episodes such as reading the adventures of the dime-novel hero Nick Carter in, of all places, the loft of St. Peter's Church at odd moments of organ-pumping; once the story took his attention so that he failed to pump at a solemn moment. Another time he spent a day in a blacksmith's shop, having decided to learn that trade rather than attend school; his sister discovered and reported him whereupon his father gave him a licking.[2] There was a creek nearby, in which Marshall sailed matchstick vessels representing the White Fleet of the 1880s, that first squadron of steel-protected sailing cruisers that heralded the building in the 1890s of a new American Navy. Marshall built a small ferry boat in the creek, and took girls across the dangerous waters; once when some customers refused to pay the necessary penny or pin or what you will, the youth reached down and pulled the boat's plug, sinking everything.

Almost the sole observation of any importance one can make of his first years was that tradition must have marked them. He had a tradition to live up to— he descended from the Virginia and Kentucky family of illustrious Marshalls which included the Chief Justice. There was also Humphrey Marshall, a distant cousin, now forgotten, an early American envoy to China, who served in the uneasy interim after Caleb Cushing, from 1852 to 1854, prior to the Treaty of Tientsin of 1858 and appointment of the first American Minister to China.

Tradition's influence could have appeared when the

future Secretary of State went to the Virginia Military Institute in September, 1897: tradition of the Civil War, of Stonewall Jackson. One of Marshall's first biographers, Robert Payne, gave much attention to the influence of the great Confederate strategist on the supreme American strategist of the Second World War.[3] As Payne explained, by the turn of the century the onetime Professor of Natural and Experimental Philosophy and Artillery Tactics had become a legend for students and faculty of VMI, much as General Lee served as patron saint for that little neighboring institution, Washington and Lee College. Jackson's spirit dominated VMI. Young Marshall, so Payne surmised, picked up from Jackson the devotion to duty and precision in performance that marked his later career. No matter that Jackson like Lee had been on the side of disunion and, as the government in Washington said, rebellion. General Lee lay buried in the chapel of Washington and Lee, and his memorabilia included the taxidermic remains of his horse "Traveller" in a glass case in the chapel basement where they are still to be seen. VMI had no stuffed horse to show, but the cadets venerated Jackson and his statue dominates the campus drill ground. One of Marshall's traits in after-life which almost everyone would notice, his selflessness, might have come from youthful meditation on the life and death of General Jackson. Unfortunately for the surmises of Marshall's biographer Payne, while similarities did appear between General Jackson and General Marshall there was little or no conscious connection on the part of Marshall. The men Marshall

admired most in the history of his country were Robert E. Lee and Benjamin Franklin.[4]

As a student at VMI, Marshall did not shine. He was dogged rather than brilliant, a bit mechanical, no flashing intelligence or wit. Academically mediocre in his classes, he excelled on the field. In his final year he was cadet first captain, first in military proficiency among the few dozen students at the school.

After graduation his father pulled strings, and young Marshall in a daring maneuver put himself at the end of a White House tourist line and secured an impromptu interview with President William McKinley, all to obtain appointment as second lieutenant in the US Army. The goal proved not too difficult. The Army was expanding, for there was trouble in the Philippines with the insurrection.

Early in February, 1902, Marshall married Elizabeth Coles, a young lady who lived near the campus of VMI. They spent their honeymoon in Washington, and a few weeks later Marshall, alone, was on the way to Manila to join the Thirtieth Infantry.

To chronicle Marshall's life in the years 1902-16, before his career took a sharp turn into importance, is of value only to show the interminable waiting, the patience, necessary for officers of the old Regular Army who stayed in service between the Spanish-American War and the First World War. There were to be two such periods in Marshall's life, one from 1902 through 1916 and the other from 1919 to 1936, but the second period of waiting was under the authority and friendship of a General of the Armies, John J. Pershing.

Duty in the Philippines began on the island of Mindoro, where the lieutenant joined a detachment of men of Company G at the island's capital, Calapan. From there he passed on to Mangarin at the head of Mangarin Bay, a miserable place, a post mainly for guarding a convent of the Recollect Order together with its lands and cattle. Life in the Philippines in those days, apart from amenities available in the Islands' capital, was squalid and pestilential. Over a year passed before he was shifted to Manila.

He went home to a different sort of wild environment, a stint in 1904 in the American West, at Fort Reno, Oklahoma Territory. There the young lieutenant did some map work under difficult circumstances, most of the time afoot, often for long stretches without water, but he gained firsthand appreciation of the West before it passed into civilization. It was on this tour of duty that he met a young captain of cavalry, Malin Craig, who became Chief of Staff in the latter 1930s and brought Marshall to Washington in 1938.

In these early days the future general slowly acquired a professional reputation. He attended the Infantry and Cavalry School at Fort Leavenworth where he showed ability, and became first lieutenant in 1907 just before emerging first in his class at the school. After taking the second-year course at Leavenworth he stayed on two more years as an instructor. Service followed with the Massachusetts National Guard and a brief period, again in the Southwest, with the Fourth Infantry in Arkansas and Texas. Then another Philippine tour in 1913 under General J. Franklin Bell. The latter individual had taken a

genuine liking to the young lieutenant during the Leavenworth days when Bell was Chief of Staff. According to the memory of General Johnson Hagood, Bell now spoke privately of Marshall as "the greatest military genius since Stonewall Jackson." Hagood did not remember aright; Bell said no such thing, if he did think well of him and was willing to do what he could to advance the young man's career.[5] But respect and admiration from even an influential general had little to do with promotion in the army in the old days after the Spanish War when seniority was the largest merit, and Marshall became a captain in 1916 after fourteen years as an officer.

2

When the country entered the World War in 1917 Marshall's chance seemed upon him, the opportunity for service which he had hoped for and courted. He sailed with the First Division—that conglomerate force thrown together to get troops to France if only for display—and was the second American officer to step ashore (after Major General William L. Sibert). He trained with the division, and one day put some troops through their paces for the commander-in-chief of the American Expeditionary Force, General Pershing. The troops were ragged, and Pershing rudely turned on the Major General. Marshall, then only a very junior officer, lost his temper and told Pershing off. There would be another such episode years later, with Franklin Roosevelt. On both occasions friends informed Marshall he was through, finished. In each

case this daring tactic, if one may so describe it, worked to great advantage, for both men, Pershing and Roosevelt, were big enough to take and even enjoy a little disagreement. Pershing sent the outspoken young officer to GHQ at Chaumont and gave him the highest tasks of planning, involving tens of thousands of men. Day and night, seemingly without end, Marshall arranged the transport of men and equipment into the front areas, a trying task because the AEF was so largely an improvised affair. Wonder was that the raw American Army developed so quickly into a machine which could help break the Imperial German Army in the great autumn offensive of 1918. Behind an important part of that triumphant forward surge of the Allied divisions lay the planning of Marshall, poring over his maps. Pershing made higher decisions and engaged in military diplomacy in headquarters and at Paris, but a few key men like Marshall prepared the battles.

During the war Marshall almost—but not quite— made the break from obscurity into a permanent prominence. The war ensured the careers of many of his fellow officers, men not farther or much farther in rank. Douglas MacArthur, also of a class of 1901 but from the Academy and not VMI, became a brigadier and managed to hold general officer rank for the rest of his long life. Marshall's ill luck brought recommendation for brigadier general (he had achieved temporary colonel) on October 17, 1918—too late, for the War Department halted promotions after the Armistice. Marshall reverted to captain in June, 1920, became major in July, 1920, lieutenant colonel in

1923, colonel in 1933, brigadier general in 1936 at the age of fifty-six. As the years passed, he faced the prospect of not reaching high enough rank to secure a top command position before mandatory retirement.

He was a Pershing protégé, a member of the "Chaumont group," a favored clique within the Army's officer corps. He served as aide-de-camp to Pershing from 1919 to 1924, and as such reached an intimacy with the World War commander that few if any of the general's assistants enjoyed. At the interminable receptions and luncheons and dinners and fetes and reviews as Pershing for years after the war moved about the country, Marshall usually stood at his side, making arrangements, helping in the receiving line, standing next to the ferns and flowers and rubber plants, tipping the general off to identities of fading associates coming up the line for introduction ("Argonne," Marshall would whisper . . . "Glad to meet a comrade of the Argonne!" Pershing would bellow). Marshall gave Pershing frank advice when the general wrote his memoirs, which suggestions Pershing largely refused—Marshall wanted the general to stay out of the command arguments of the AEF, not get into recrimination with generals who had been fired or passed over and had written critical memoirs.

The General of the Armies became so fond of Marshall that he designated the younger man as the officer to take charge of funeral arrangements in case he passed on, a weighty contingency, for which meticulous plans were laid, but which failed to come off

because of Pershing's good health (the general died in 1948).

During these years of peace the two men maintained a long correspondence and Pershing tried to push Marshall's career whenever he could. Against the seniority system even he could not prevail.

Had Marshall gotten over the hump of promotion back in 1917-18 things might have gone differently; as it was, assignments had to follow the usual pattern. During 1924-27 Marshall served in Tientsin with the Fifteenth Infantry where he learned some Chinese, gained at least a rudimentary military knowledge of the East which he later would call upon, and met such fellow officers as Joseph W. Stilwell who came to prominence in the Second World War. Marshall's next command was at the Infantry School at Fort Benning, Georgia, in 1927-32. During the first months of the Roosevelt Administration he helped organize Civilian Conservation Camps in the southern United States. Then came assignment as senior instructor with the Illinois National Guard, with headquarters in Chicago, by order of General MacArthur who was Chief of Staff, a duty sounding suspiciously like an exile. Apparently it was not, for there was some danger of riots in Chicago and the Army needed a cool-headed colonel in such a place. Marshall protested to MacArthur, to no avail; the Chief of Staff had jumped the seniority system himself at the end of the war, but was unwilling to let anyone else do so. Chicago was the low point of his military career. His second wife—Elizabeth Coles Marshall had died in 1927 and in 1930 he married a widow, Katherine Tup-

per Brown—wrote in her memoir *Together*: "Those first months in Chicago I shall never forget. George had a grey, drawn look which I had never seen before, and have seldom seen since."[6]

In the mid-1930s it seemed impossible that he could get anywhere in the Army, given its obscurantist tendencies. For a while at the Chicago National Guard headquarters he and his wife maintained a city apartment across the hall from Major General Frank R. McCoy, then in command of the VI Corps Area. McCoy had been an extremely influential man in the Army and in high public service. He had just been to Manchuria with the Lytton Commission and was a strong contender for Chief of Staff in 1935. This new friendship relieved some of the sting of Marshall's inglorious Chicago assignment. Finding the city insufferable, the Marshalls moved out to a cottage near Wayne, Illinois where the colonel could take the train to the office and in summer raise garden vegetables. During these years the Hitler regime in Germany was going, literally, great guns, Mussolini was conquering in Africa, the peace of the Continent and the entire world disintegrating. Pershing generously sought Marshall's promotion and wrote the President about it. One of FDR's memoranda read: "General Pershing asks very strongly that Colonel George C. Marshall (Infantry) be promoted to general. Can we put him on the list of next promotions?" The presidential note disappeared into some War Department file cabinet. Secretary of War George H. Dern visited General Hagood at San Antonio in 1935 and inquired whether there were any good colo-

nels available for promotion. Hagood had been waiting the chance—and one can almost see him pause and look the Secretary of War in the eye.

"Mr. Secretary," he replied, "I have a great many good colonels whom I could recommend, but the best colonel in the Army is not under my command. His name is George Marshall, and he is on some duty over in Chicago."

"Yes," said the Secretary of War, "I have heard that Colonel Marshall is a very good man. But he is too young!"[7]

Eventually in 1935 Douglas MacArthur went to take command in the Philippines, and Malin Craig became Chief of Staff. From that moment onward, Marshall's career rose like a skyrocket. He received promotion to brigadier general in 1936. He was called to Washington in 1938 not for urgent military purposes but because Pershing seemed about to die and the Army would have to hold that well-planned funeral. Marshall went to Tucson where Pershing lay ill. The Army sent a special train to remove the general's body to Arlington for burial. Rumor has it that when word of these activities got to Pershing he swore he would recover if it killed him. A few weeks later the old warrior appeared as best man at his son's wedding in New York. Marshall returned to Washington as Chief of War Plans and then Deputy Chief of Staff. Craig's four-year term began to run out in the summer of 1939 and ended in a fourth-month terminal leave, and Marshall became Acting Chief. There ensued an unnerving period when, still a brigadier general, he had to maneuver for the top post.

He sought support both from Secretary of War Harry H. Woodring and Assistant Secretary Louis Johnson, who were at outs with each other. Both supported him, but he had to avoid letting each one know. His military competitor was Lieutenant General Hugh A. Drum. The latter "beat his drum" too much, so Roosevelt seems to have complained. But some months before this time Marshall had broken up a large conference at the White House by openly opposing a scheme of the President, one of FDR's hare-brained ideas of building ten thousand airplanes when there were no supporting troops, an act that would have thrown the small American military establishment completely out of kilter. Again friends told him he was finished. Then Roosevelt gave him the appointment. On September 1, 1939, a momentous date in history, Marshall became Chief of Staff.

3

From the outset of the Second World War the new Chief of Staff faced a frantic scramble to build forces to confront the deterioration of America's political position all over the world. Often rearmament had to await a favorable political moment or react to an unfavorable one. For many months world politics went so badly—from the fall of France in June, 1940, until the summer, perhaps, of 1942—that the entire outcome of the war became uncertain. Marshall found himself a world strategist, and began to give the extempore surveys of Western civilization for which he later would obtain renown. At VMI on June 12,

1940, he was the commencement speaker, with no time to prepare an address. With wonderful sense of the occasion he stood before the graduating class and spoke with deep emotion of the prospect before them: "It is your graduation day, but it may also be one of the most fearful in the history of the world. No man can predict the outcome of the tragic struggle in Europe. No American can foresee the eventual effect on the Americas. The world we have known may be revolutionized; the peaceful liberty we have accepted so casually may be a hazard in this ghastly game abroad."[8]

A year and a half later Pearl Harbor punctuated his address. Upon General Marshall fell the direction, at first of American military effort, then the strategy of the Allies in the greatest war in history.

As for policies in 1939-45 as Chief of Staff, they are well known and need no recital here. Marshall agreed heartily with the Anglo-American strategy of the war, that defeat of Germany took precedence over defeat of Japan. Like most Americans the initial Japanese victories in the Pacific had shocked him because of their ease and extent; like all Regular Army men he saw some of his oldest associates pass into Japanese prison camps; he would have liked nothing better than to avenge the Philippine disaster. But he knew that the pressing task was to defeat Germany first. Here he held the view of the War Department, that the best way to beat the Germans was by the shortest route, *i.e.*, through France from England. It was not merely familiar territory—he knew all those rivers and rail lines and the rolling terrain; it was the most

practical invasion route, known since the Romans.
He and Secretary of War Henry L. Stimson opposed
Prime Minister Churchill's Mediterranean and peri-
pheral strategy, born, they believed, out of sentiment
for Lord Nelson and for the failure a century later at
Gallipoli, and also for the one million British battle
losses in France in 1914-18. By 1944 the Americans
had accumulated enough troops to carry their own
strategic ideas. In retrospect it was probably fortunate
that British strategy for Europe prevailed in early
stages of the war. If Anglo-American forces had hurried into invasion of France to take pressure off the
Russian front, had gone in there in 1942 or even 1943,
the Germans might have thrown them into the sea
with terrible losses. Such disaster could have led to
catastrophe: either the communization of Europe because of Anglo American inability to muster another
large army in time to meet the Russians in Central
Germany, or a Russian separate peace with Nazi Germany because of failure to receive Western assistance.
Invasion of France in 1944 at last proved a huge success and enabled Churchill and Marshall to believe,
each in his own way, that the tactics of each had been
right.[9]

Although if one looks at the strategic arguments
again he sees another side to the delay to invade
in 1942-43: the Germans gained more months in
which to liquidate Jews and other peoples of Europe. If an invasion would have succeeded two years
earlier, hundreds of thousands, even millions, of persons could have escaped German death camps.

And so on through the long war years until relief

from duty in October, 1945, Marshall maintained a hard driving routine, broken by trips about the country or to military and diplomatic conferences abroad. His wife bought a house, Dodona Manor, in Leesburg, to which he could go on week ends and odd moments. For the most part he lived in "Quarters Number One" at Fort Myer and drove back and forth to the Munitions Building and, in later years, to the Pentagon nearby. He would arise about 5:30 A.M. and ride for an hour—his critics were to upbraid him for this habit, pursued too late in the morning on Sunday, December 7, 1941. He would customarily arrive at the office around 7:00 or 7:30, and would open his mail, marking letters in pencil with "take action," or "no," or "yes," in the manner of busy men protected by secretaries. Routine would give way to conversations and conferences with the President, Secretary Stimson, or the Joint or Combined (British and American) Chiefs of Staff. By 4:30 he was usually on the way back to the red-brick house at Fort Myer.

Marshall's *modus operandi* was striking. He organized everything, so far as he personally could. He told subordinates to take responsibility, and expected them to do so. "Eisenhower," he said to one assistant, "the Department is filled with able men who analyze their problems well but feel compelled always to bring them to me for final solution. I must have assistants who will solve their own problems and tell me later what they have done." According to Ike's reminiscence, the general "looked at me with an eye that seemed to me awfully cold, and so, as I

left the room, I resolved then and there to do my work to the best of my ability and report to the General only situations of obvious necessity or when he personally sent for me."[10]

There could be no political interference with the organization of Army authority:

I was in his office once when he picked up the telephone to answer a call that an aide said came from a senator—the chairman of an important committee. As I watched the General's face, it became flushed; he was obviously more than a little annoyed. Within moments he angrily broke in to say, "Senator, if you are interested in that man's advancement, or that of any other, the best thing you can do is to avoid mentioning his name to me. Good-bye!" Then he turned to me to say. "I may make a thousand mistakes in this war, but none will be the result of political meddling! I take orders from the Secretary of War and the President; I would not stay here if I had to respond to such outside pressures. Moreover, I don't like people who are 'seeking promotions.'" To possible senatorial displeasure he gave not a single thought.[11]

In these times of busyness few persons took liberties with the general. Marshall kept his distance, and relations with both fellow officers and civil officials of the government were seldom enthusiastic. Assistants at the War Department were wary of camaraderie. With few individuals other than Mrs. Marshall was he ever "George." With Secretary Stim-

son, a man of formality, relations were on the plane
of Mr. Stimson and General Marshall. With President Roosevelt there was considerable care. In marked
degree the President possessed the Rotarian tendency
to call grown men by their first names, and in an
early meeting sought to refer to Marshall as "George."
The general did not reciprocate: "I remember he
called me 'George.' . . . I don't think he ever did it
again. . . . I wasn't very enthusiastic . . ." It was a
gingerly friendship between White House and Pentagon. Apart from differing customs of address the general distrusted the President as a man who did not
always keep his word and had a weather eye out for
politics and the smaller chances. Marshall felt that
Roosevelt went along with Churchill on the North
African invasion of November, 1942, because of the
congressional election that year, thinking it would
be impossible politically not to engage American
troops in combat somewhere.[12] Roosevelt also was
an untidy administrator and the general knew it. The
President had Marshall's unflagging support, but no
personal intimacy or excess of admiration. The Chief
of Staff always refused to see Roosevelt at Warm
Springs or Hyde Park. "I found informal conversation with the President would get you into trouble.
He would talk over something informally at the dinner table and you had trouble disagreeing without
causing embarrassment. So I never went. I was in
Hyde Park for the first time at his funeral."[13]

Speaking of the war years, and Marshall's relations with leaders of the American Government, one
might remark an incident early in the war when

Senator Truman called at the general's office on a personal matter. The Senator held a reserve commission as colonel and wished to get into uniform.

"Senator Truman," Marshall said, without tincture of diplomacy, "you've got a big job to do right up there at the Capitol, with your Investigating Committee. Besides, Senator, this is a young man's war. We don't need any old stiffs like you."

"I am younger than you are, General Marshall," said the Senator.

"Yes, but I'm a general and you'd only be a colonel. You stay right where you are."[14]

This encounter may have been the beginning of the great affection Truman was to hold for Marshall.

At last came the end of war, and Secretary Stimson's V-E Day encomium before a select group of generals and high officials: "I have seen a great many soldiers in my lifetime and you, sir, are the finest soldier I have ever known."[15]

CHAPTER TWO

CHINA MISSION

THE MOST controversial episode in Marshall's entire career, military and diplomatic, was his mission to China in 1946. The mission failed; China turned communist. The question at the time and later was why China went to communism and what Marshall had to do with it. On this matter there has been mild disagreement among American diplomats and among scholars. Most of the controversy has been between the Republican and Democratic Parties. The political issue is still living in the 1960s and sometimes comes out of the woodwork for an irrelevant occasion. But it served its major purpose in anticipation of the presidential election of 1952 when troubles of the United States in China linked with other frustrations, notably Soviet explosion of an atomic device in August, 1949; conviction of a former State Department official, Alger Hiss, for perjury over an alleged case of espionage; the appalling revelation in 1950 that the British physicist Klaus Fuchs had been communicating everything he knew about atomic weapons to the Russians, which was a great deal; the victory of the communists on the mainland of China after October, 1949; the Korean War with its ups and downs including the Chinese Communist intervention; relief of General MacArthur from his

21

commands in 1951: all sorts of disparate arguments were rolled together with China into a ball, so to speak, which critics of the Truman Administration then hurled at the most convenient personal targets, President Truman and Marshall's successor as Secretary of State, Dean Acheson. At this time Marshall often became the focus of abuse, with the most vile allegations those of Senator William E. Jenner of Indiana who in 1950 told fellow Senators that Marshall was not only willing but eager to play the role of front man for traitors and that this was no new role because Marshall was a living lie.

As far as concerned China, behind the personal abuse, the whole verbal uproar, lay a fairly simple situation which the record of the time, not to mention all later revelations, fully supported. It is strangely true that American policy toward China in the immediate postwar years was one of the most publicized policies pursued during the nation's history. Both President Truman and Secretary Marshall made it clear, however mistaken it seems as one looks back at it. It was announced when General Marshall had gone to China as Ambassador in 1946: get Communists and Nationalists to give up their war against each other and face the world as a united people and nation.

1

The present narrative is no place to offer the history of China in the nineteenth and twentieth centuries, and yet without reference to that history, or at

least holding its existence in mind, so much of what happened in China after the Second World War, especially during Marshall's mission in 1946, is unintelligible. To put matters in briefest form, one must say that ever since the middle of the nineteenth century the Chinese nation had been in deep trouble; the Tai-ping and Nien-fei uprisings had taxed the resources of the Manchu dynasty beyond all endurance; it was a matter of time until the Revolution of 1911-12 should usher in the Chinese Republic. The latter government passed through several weird incarnations before General Chiang Kai-shek came to prominence in the mid-1920s and established a unified regime in 1927-28, but was never secure, never on solid foundation, before the Japanese began to attack it. Chiang had unified China nominally, buying or balancing his opponents, but his taxing powers reached only a short distance from his capital in Nanking. Then the Japanese began their hammer blows to bring China to her knees, as Prime Minister Prince Fumimaru Konoye so undiplomatically said in 1937. If the occupation of Manchuria in 1931-33 had been a comparatively peaceful business, the fighting that began with the sack of Nanking and other cities in 1937 was soon savagery, so much so that Japanese generals in command of some of those mad troops would hang for their sins after the Second World War. The long years of war stretched almost endlessly until the Allied victory in 1945 crushed Japan.

The truth—so undramatic—is that Chiang's government had come near to collapse during the war,

with coastal areas under Japanese control and the countryside in chaos or under Communist control. The Nationalist Party had become increasingly conservative, as during the war years the students starved or were drafted, coastal businessmen lost their commerce and industry or existed silently under Japanese rule, and landlords by default acquired influence in the wartime capital of Chungking. The poor peasantry of China found the Communist promises of land reform most attractive, and Communists could cut off almost the remaining support of the Chiang regime. The Nationalist armies were a mass of ill-fed, disgruntled recruits who wished to fight no one. The Americans flew in supplies from India over the hump of the Himalayas. Some supplies went to grafters in the Chungking government and much was wasted, and Chiang used some to continue buying and balancing his supposed supporters. Things got so bad that Ambassador Clarence Gauss told Lieutenant General Albert C. Wedemeyer in 1944, when Wedemeyer was taking command of the China Theater, that "We should pull up the plug and let the whole Chinese Government go down the drain."[1]

By the end of the Second World War there was at first some hope of new Chinese unity, but it disappeared after Chiang's greedy governors came into the liberated coastal and other areas and their light-fingered troops set to work for themselves and the officers. By the end of 1945 everything was rapidly setting the stage, paving the road, to use the old academic metaphors, for a Communist victory.

American officials in China found themselves in-

tensely frustrated. Some saw the Chinese Communists, of whom many at least seemed personally honest, as more attractive than the Nationalists. Both sides in China were arbitrary, but honesty did seem a virtue. Bluff old Major General Patrick J. Hurley, then American Ambassador, did not know what to make of the situation. Hurley had grown up in the simplicities of the American West where he applied his own financial talents to the opportunity of pioneer days and made a fortune. He was a big, tall man of action, and once when a mule named Kicking Pete kicked him he seized a two-by-four and brained Kicking Pete.[2] He took these energies to China, with results that became part of American history: he gave a Comanche Indian whoop to the assembled Chinese Communist top hierarchy when he appeared without notice at Yenan and Mao Tse-tung and others came running across the field to meet him; in dinner conversation in Chungking he whooped for his guests; sometimes in loud voice he would pronounce the name of the chief communist of China which in his Oklahoma diction came out as Moose Dung. China was too much for Hurley. He felt that the State Department officials in Yenan and Nanking and in the Department—John Stewart Service, John Paton Davies, Raymond Ludden, John Emerson—were undercutting him, which was probably true: there was confused opinion about proper American policy in China, and career men there and at home had little respect for Hurley's judgment. Hurley came home to report in the autumn of 1945. After promising to return to China he lost his temper and resigned, making wild public accusations and

sending to President Truman a not altogether coherent six-page letter ventilating his charges of personal disloyalty which he said involved public disloyalty.

Marshall's appointment as special envoy (with personal rank of ambassador) followed from the above event. Hurley's blatant charges amused, annoyed, and confused the Cabinet and President, and Secretary of Agriculture Clinton P. Anderson suggested sending Marshall whose appointment would take the heat off Hurley's resignation.[3] Marshall had just driven down from Fort Myer to Leesburg to set up residence in retirement at Dodona Manor. He and his wife had no sooner entered the house when the telephone rang, with the President on the wire. Mrs. Marshall had gone upstairs. The General listened to Truman's explanation and proposal, said "yes" and hung up. Afterward he had to explain to Truman that he couldn't risk Mrs. Marshall's hearing of this new mission after the wartime service, coming exactly at the moment of his cherished retirement. (Mrs. Marshall went to China with her husband during the following year.)[4]

A day or so after the telephone call the former Chief of Staff appeared in the office of his former subordinate, General Eisenhower: "The President is sending me to China; I'll be needing some help from the Army; will you see that my requests are considered?" He asked it all with his customary directness.

"Of course," said Eisenhower. "Anyone you want."

Eisenhower could not help inquiring whether Marshall was to have some rest and vacation. "It seems,"

Marshall said laconically, "that the matter is one of some urgency." Not a word, Eisenhower would recall, of complaint against fate or superiors—"he just set about quietly to do his duty. But this time I knew where his heart lay; and I knew he felt keen disappointment, even though he would never voice it."[5]

With some technical assistance from the War and State Departments the new Ambassador to China virtually drew up his own instructions. In that sense he was his own superior, although he and President Truman saw eye to eye on requirements of the mission.[6] In a presidential statement of policy toward China, released by the White House on December 15, 1945, the general's task appeared without diplomatic embellishment. The President called for the two factions—recognized government and the Communists —to get together. Truman said: "The existence of autonomous armies such as that of the Communist army is inconsistent with, and actually makes impossible, political unity in China. With the institution of a broadly representative government, autonomous armies should be eliminated as such and all armed forces in China integrated effectively into the Chinese National Army."[7] The President sent out a communication to the several heads of government departments or agencies who had possible business in China (including the Reconstruction Finance Corporation and Maritime Commission) asking them to suspend all conversation with Chinese officials "regarding extension of American economic or financial aid to China," and to have no conversation which might look toward this kind of thing except in ac-

cord with recommendations of General Marshall. "All discussions and negotiations with Chinese in this country should be initiated or resumed and carried on only in complete coordination with General Marshall and recommendations in the premises, both from and to General Marshall, should be cleared through the Department of State."[8] It was an end to freewheeling in China, to interdepartment undercutting; the general was to have policy control.

Troubles in China, which had gone on for generations, now became troubles of Marshall, their solution a problem of policy for the United States. If he or policy or both failed there might be the devil —perhaps the Republican Party—to pay. It is interesting that about this time (actually on March 18, 1947) Senator Arthur H. Vandenberg said on the Senate floor that bipartisanship applied only to the United Nations and the European satellite peace treaties, not to policy toward Latin America or China.

2

Why did Marshall fail in China? Much of the criticism of his mission of 1946 has been of his purpose, namely, that he tried to mix completely opposite political systems and, of course, never had a chance. The usual critical metaphor is that he tried to mix oil and water.

Was the design in error? One does not have to investigate this criticism in depth, to employ the phrase of the political scientists, to say that Marshall knew he had a large assignment. Nonetheless, the

President asked him to undertake the task and he was willing to try. And it does seem as if there was at least an outside chance of success. Marshall believed there was one. For some months he thought he had a chance and played it for all it was worth. The chance rested on the fact that the Chinese people were intensely weary of war, civil and otherwise. Coincident with a quick jacking up of the liberal wing within the Nationalist Party—Marshall thought there were enough liberals to form such a group—it might be possible to find some men of good will among the Communists who had not been in the Yenan movement long enough to be doctrinaires; these two groups, he thought, might join to ensure peace for China.

If sheer activity or the enthusiasm of his initial reception could have ensured success, Marshall would have become the savior of China. News photographs of the wartime commander showed him wrapped in his Army olive-drab coat with the general's stripes on the sleeves, regulation officer's hat with its great-seal golden emblem and visor fastened down over his gray hair (none of the jaunty rimless insouciance of the Air Force, the extra braid of MacArthur), a half-smile on his usually straight mouth because of quasi-civilian duty, the interested and interesting eyes, boyishly pugnacious nose. Marshall went from meeting to meeting, flying from city to city. It was hard to remember how many conferences he attended. One reporter's estimate was three hundred formally recorded meetings.[9] Marshall used the figure six hundred which may have included lesser con-

claves.[10] It was a lot of talk, almost all through trans-
lators. Often he traveled with the chief Communist
envoy, Chou En-lai, later to have such a prominent
career in the Peking Communist government. He got
on well with Chou who he thought was negotiating
seriously. He admitted that his several sessions with
Mao Tse-tung were not so easy. "Mao Tse-tung I
could not penetrate. That is a real iron curtain when
you get there. We had some very frank talking but
when he talked I didn't get anything from it at all; it
was just talk. I was reminded of it very forcibly with
Molotov at times."[11] Again, there seemed a chance
of bringing the two sides together, and Marshall
made the most of it. Everything he said was carefully recorded, weighed, commented on. Toward the
end of his initial tour he spoke at Hankow and said
that "Last month and the next two months are the
most critical months in the history of China." This was
overstatement but showed the mood he was trying to
create and use. In the first week of March alone he
flew nearly four thousand miles over North China
with Chou and the Kuomintang General Chang Chih-
chung, visiting a dozen cities. Banner bearers called
him the Savior of China, God of Peace, First Lord of
all Warlords. To prevent widening the war he arranged an embargo of all American munitions shipments to Kuomintang China. Before he left on a
short trip home on March 11 he succeeded in ex-
tending the cease-fire order, agreed to by Nationalists
and Communists on January 10, to cover all Manchuria, and it seemed as if the most dangerous corner of China was under control.

Then everything began to collapse. The cease-fire broke down while he was in the United States, and although he managed another when he returned, lasting June 7-30, peace no longer was possible. Verbal arguments between Nationalists and Communists rose higher and higher as troops maneuvered everywhere. The Communists purchased the new American weapons of individual Nationalist soldiers, a good bargain for the dragooned peasant-soldiers who would far rather sell their weapons than use them. Often it was possible to purchase entire troop units by buying their commanders, triumphs achievable not always with gold but by offering retiring Nationalist generals military or administrative places, equivalent to gold. With the countryside in control of the Communists, the cities began to fall after mock sieges and sporadic fighting.

It was a dreary business for an American negotiator in the latter months of 1946 and Marshall could do little other than give unwelcome advice, threaten to cut off American dollar and material aid, and watch the unfolding disaster. Advice he gave freely, and Chiang Kai-shek knew exactly what the Americans wanted—honest administration in government and army which might infuse will power into the faltering Nationalist cause. To help the task Marshall on July 11 secured appointment of the seventy-year-old President of Yenching University, John Leighton Stuart, as American Ambassador. Stuart negotiated in Chinese, urging American policy with missionary zeal. He was as effective as anyone in such a situation, but by the time of his appearance on the

diplomatic scene matters had passed beyond exhortation. Dollar aid, offered occasionally in 1946, had little effect except to increase bank balances in New York City. Material aid, as in the US-Chinese agreement of August 30, 1946, for sale of surplus property then in the Pacific, gave huge floods of surplus to the Kuomintang and by implication proved the charge of the Communists that the United States while trying to bring the two sides together was favoring the Nationalists. Creation of an American Army-Navy-Air Force joint unit to help construct a broadly national Chinese army out of retained Nationalist and Communist troops (the Joint United States Military Advisory Group, JUSMAG) produced the spectacle of some five hundred American officers and as many enlisted men and their wives and children living ostentatiously and parading through the streets of Nanking, another evidence of American "imperialism." All the while Nationalist troops moving into North China and Manchuria put themselves in impossible military postures and began to think of surrendering to the Communists.

There was no sign of Russian Communist activity during Marshall's year of mediation. "I had officers pretty much all over North China, along the Yangtze and in Manchuria, and I always felt that the reports I got were far better than those the Generalissimo received. . . . Always I was trying to find out anything you could put your finger on that was authentic as to the Soviet influence or Soviet help in all this; I never got anything except the influence of what I would call the spiritual, or something akin to that."[12]

By the end of December, 1946, Secretary of State Byrnes had finished the satellite peace treaties at the series of Paris meetings and was ready to resign, and Truman recalled Marshall from the China confusions and made him Secretary of State to handle new and larger confusions. President Truman before recalling Marshall made a press statement about American policy toward China, released by the White House on December 18 on the anniversary of his statement announcing the Marshall mission. At peak strength in December, 1945, the President remarked, the United States had 113,000 soldiers, sailors, and Marines in China; a year later the number had gone down to 12,000. "It is a matter of deep regret that China has not yet been able to achieve unity by peaceful methods." There followed what cynical observers might have described as platitudes about American policy toward China, but were American purposes: we were ready to help China move toward peace and genuine democratic government, would not interfere in China's internal affairs, wished no involvement in civil strife, would persevere to help the Chinese people, our hopes for China were identical with what the Chinese people so earnestly desired.[13]

Less diplomatic were Marshall's remarks in a statement to the press as he took up the secretaryship of state. "In the first place," he said, "the greatest obstacle to peace has been the complete, almost overwhelming suspicion with which the Chinese Communist Party and the Kuomintang regard each other. . . . They each sought only to take counsel of their own fears." He discerned "a dominant group of

reactionaries" in the Kuomintang vis-à-vis the "dyed-in-the-wool Communists" who did not hesitate at the most drastic measures to gain their end. He pointed out the vicious Communist propaganda, worse than misrepresentations of Nationalist propaganda. "Though I speak as a soldier, I must here also deplore the dominating influence of the military." The salvation of the situation as he saw it "would be the assumption of leadership by the liberals in the Government and in the minority parties, a splendid group of men, but who as yet lack the political power to exercise a controlling influence."[14]

Generalissimo Chiang approved the Marshall report and blamed the Communists for continuing civil war in China.

CHAPTER THREE

THE NEW DEPARTMENT

I N THE mind of President Truman there never was doubt as to who would succeed James F. Byrnes as Secretary of State. Byrnes had given in his resignation in early 1946 because of fear for his health, but after reassurance from his doctors he continued in office until conclusion of the satellite peace treaties in negotiation with the Russians and British and French in Paris. Meanwhile "the Boss," as Truman's intimates playfully described him, had decided on Marshall, and sent word via General Eisenhower, then Army Chief of Staff, who was making a trip through the Far East and met Marshall in China. Almost no one other than Eisenhower and the principals was party to this future appointment. Marshall had chosen Undersecretary of State Dean Acheson as his "rear echelon" during the long negotiations in China, and Acheson knew of Marshall's designation. Acheson's superior, Secretary Byrnes, did not. Until almost the end of Byrnes' tenure Truman held the secretarial cards close to his chest. He seems to have asked Admiral William D. Leahy, who had continued to bear the grand title (bestowed by Roosevelt) of Chief of Staff to the Commander in Chief, for suggestions for the post of Secretary of State, and Leahy recommended Secretary of the Navy James V. Forrestal as first choice and General Marshall as second.[1] Doubtless the admiral was not simply rec-

ommending a Navy man first, but thought Forrestal a more likely choice because the Navy Secretary was younger and, unlike Marshall, had not completed so many grueling years in government service. Truman did not tell Leahy of his own prior choice of Marshall.

Marshall was the Secretary-designate. Characteristically, when the time came the general left China without formal farewell to his staff, and flew back quietly to Washington to take up the new duties.

1

An air at once of confusion and of reassurance followed the White House announcement that Marshall would be the new Secretary. The confusion was not large and disappeared, but many observers who felt certain that Secretary Byrnes had the President's confidence and had grown accustomed to seeing Byrnes in Washington in positions of high authority, and remembered that Byrnes had been a leading contender for the Democratic nomination for the vice presidency in Chicago in the summer of 1944, could not believe that the gay South Carolinian had come to the end of his power. They sensed something wrong. Marshall would be Truman's third Secretary of State, the fourth Secretary within twenty-six months. Was Truman engaging in some repetition of General Ulysses S. Grant's presidency where Secretaries shuttled in and out of the Cabinet with bewildering speed, raised to prominence or dismissed to obscurity for reasons which defied analysis? Perhaps Byrnes

had disagreed with the President. The Secretary's resignation came "with the advice of his physician." Such explanation sounded arranged. The New York *Times* was hollowly reassuring when it told its readers there could be no policy disagreement: "We find the whole incident disconcerting, but we find this particular explanation of it almost incredible."[2]

Whatever the confusion, there was the air of reassurance that accompanied Marshall's appearance anew in the capital. The President heralded him as the greatest living American. The columnist Arthur Krock wrote in the New York *Times* that the Secretary of State designate was "the one veteran of the war and post-war conferences who looms above all the other survivors in talent and general esteem."[3] The *Times* editorial page announced that "General Marshall becomes the first high-ranking military man to hold his new office, but at no time has such an appointment been more appropriate."[4] It noted Marshall's solidness, the feeling he gave of integrity and substance. According to the reporter James Reston, Washington liked the "casualness of Jimmy Byrnes and the brisk salesmanship of Ed Stettinius, but in a reassuring way—perhaps because it sees the combination so seldom—it reserves its greatest confidence for the man of character and experience." Marshall, wrote Reston, was a man like Elihu Root and Stimson.[5]

Under inspiration of the Republican spokesman for foreign policy in the Senate, Arthur H. Vandenberg of Michigan, the Senate unanimously confirmed the general's nomination on January 8, 1947, the same

day President Truman submitted it. Vandenberg had no advance notice of Byrnes' resignation, and the suddenness of his friend's departure bothered him. In remarks on the Senate floor he described Byrnes as a very great American and mentioned the Administration's "sudden and unusual interruption of the State Department's personnel." But he said Marshall would have bipartisan support: "I think it is highly important that the Senate of the United States, continuing to pursue what has been an effective bi-partisan foreign policy, should make it perfectly clear immediately that there is no interruption to this unity by the episode to which I refer."[6]

Marshall took the oath on January 21, in a ceremony at the White House presided over by the Chief Justice of the Supreme Court, Fred M. Vinson, in the presence of the President. After the ceremony the President talked with the new Secretary for a half hour, in company of Admiral Leahy. The old admiral noted that Truman "called to Secretary Marshall's attention the Atlantic Charter as a statement of National Policy."[7]

By this time Marshall already had made a first public pronouncement. There had been talk of drafting one of the leading wartime generals for the Democratic presidential nomination in 1948. The talk meant setting aside the nomination of President Truman. Names had appeared—Eisenhower, MacArthur, Marshall. The Republicans likewise were looking for an available general. Upon arrival in Washington, General Marshall thoughtfully said to reporters at the train: "I never can be considered as a

candidate for political office. . . . I never could be drafted."[8] The declaration was not so brief as that of General William T. Sherman, nor so colorful, but had the look and sound of finality. It was a highly intelligent thing to do. President Truman had not asked for a disclaimer, nor would he have thought of it, but Marshall sensed the political aspect of his reappearance in Washington and with a nice military—and diplomatic—directness set the unpleasant rumors at rest.

He told Truman privately, right after the swearing-in ceremony, that he did not consider the State Department a political office at that time and did not desire and would not accept any political office.[9]

It was well he showed political acumen, for he would need it. The President was in a difficult position and could give only personal support to the new Secretary. In the first postwar years Truman was not a popular President, for seemingly everything he did produced mediocre or poor results. Jokes were going the rounds, such as "To err is Truman," or the query, "What would Truman say if he were alive?" The new President had succeeded a strong and popular Chief Executive, and faced a spiraling inflation, with demand everywhere that he take off price ceilings and let the economy operate freely in "the American way." He received the blame for the postwar adjustments of the American economy. Foreign policy under Secretary Byrnes had not been going well, not because of anything the President or Byrnes had done or failed to do but mainly because, as the pre-

ceding volume in this series has shown, Byrnes had no military force behind him—the nation had disarmed so quickly after the victory of 1945 that the Secretary of State had little to back his diplomacy except the atomic bomb, and to employ the latter weapon diplomatically was difficult in the pacific-minded years 1945-46.

Then there was the Eightieth Congress. The congressional elections of 1946 had been catastrophic for the Democratic Party, the Republicans gaining both Houses: 246 Republicans to 188 Democrats in the House of Representatives, 51 Republicans to 45 Democrats in the Senate. Before the election the House had 243 Democrats and 190 Republicans, the Senate 57 Democrats and 38 Republicans. Here was "the greatest Republican victory in eighteen years."[10] To deal in questions of foreign policy with this Republican Congress would require skilled leadership from the White House and Department of State.

Perhaps bipartisanship could continue under Senator Vandenberg—so Marshall must have hoped. In wartime and the early postwar era there had been the bipartisan approach to policy in the Senate engineered by Vandenberg who had thrown over his prewar isolationism and become one of the front-rank fighters for collective security. Vandenberg was a heavy-set, balding, bespectacled newspaper editor from Grand Rapids, Michigan, who had served in the Senate since 1928 and become a canny practitioner of congressional politics. He had a knack of bringing together diverse individuals and ideas, often blurring or (probably a better word) confusing

the diversity with his windy oratory. After the Senator's untimely death in 1951 his son would write affectionately that he had a special way with words: "He could split an infinitive at twenty paces with consummate ease, and seldom missed an opportunity to do so . . . he believed that they were essential to his style."[11] Vandenberg considered himself a leader of men. The Senator's favorite Biblical character was St. Paul. He hoped sometime to write a life of St. Paul.

Vandenberg wanted to support Marshall, but he shared authority in the Senate with Robert A. Taft of Ohio who would not be easy to get along with. "Senator Taft was an industrious, tireless worker in behalf of measures he favored at the moment. . . . He tried to assert leadership on too many questions to be really effective on the important ones. No matter what issue came up, he always popped into the middle of it. 'The junior senator from Ohio [so Senator Tom Connally once told him in debate] . . . knows less about more subjects than any man I know.'"[12] It would be difficult for Vandenberg to work out with Taft a bipartisan approach to foreign policy. The tentative arrangement seemed easy, whereby Vandenberg as chairman of the Foreign Relations Committee would retain Senate command over foreign policy, and Taft give attention to domestic matters. Still, the new leader of the Senate Republicans (Taft was chairman of the Republican Policy Committee) was an enigmatic figure, staunchly conservative in domestic politics. "Mr. Republican," as he had become known, was beginning to take inter-

est in foreign affairs. Taft later said publicly: "I am charged with moving in on foreign policy; the truth is that foreign policy has moved in on me." It was an uneasy situation. Any excess of Senate Republicanism could wreck the nation's foreign policy.

If the new Secretary of State had fears of what he could accomplish, he did not show them. He presented himself before the American people as a deeply interested and concerned but essentially nonpartisan figure, not above but outside of politics. He refused to attend the Jefferson Day dinner on April 5, a notable Democratic occasion, and the refusal struck some of Truman's White House assistants as a little odd. Refusal it was. "As you know," he wrote former Ambassador Joseph E. Davies who had invited him, "it is my desire to make my tenure of office as Secretary of State as completely bipartisan as possible."[13]

The Secretary acted as if he were going to take decisions for the good of the country. He would face down problems large and small, administrative or policy. He would do his best to solve them, and if solutions did not suit everyone and a clamor arose for his resignation he would get in his automobile and drive down to Dodona Manor in Leesburg, and the President and Congress, Democrats or Republicans or both, could look for a better man.

2

One of Marshall's first acts as Secretary was to give the Department a "new look." He moved its offices into a new, or relatively new, building.

In many ways it was a wrench to move. The Department had been at the corner of Seventeenth and Pennsylvania in the old State, War and Navy Building next to the White House for seventy-two years, since the time of Hamilton Fish and the Grant Administration. Old State, with its slatted swinging doors and cool high corridors, the vaulted rooms with their fireplaces and marble mantels, the spittoons, the grandfather's clock in the office of the Secretary, had seemed inseparable from American foreign relations. No matter if its internal appointments were so rococo that they lent a near-comic aspect to American diplomacy. Marshall's first press conference in the old building was in Room 464, a monstrosity: "It is about 40 feet long, 30 feet across and 40 feet high. It has a gallery that performs no visible function. The walls are paneled in mottled green marble interspersed with fake columns painted the color of liver and gold. In the four corners are heavy bronze winged angels supporting three large round white bulbs arranged like pawnshop balls. And worst of all, it is durable."[14] To oldtimers such haunts were home. They hated leaving the building of Cordell Hull, Stimson, Hughes, Root, Hay, and Fish.

But lack of space had become almost a scandal. In the 1930s and early 1940s the bureaus and divisions spilled out of the old building and employees of the Department niched themselves all over the District of Columbia until in 1945 there were forty-six annexes. The master of the National Grange, A. S. Goss, heard that a new State Department building might go up in a place which would force demo-

lition of the Grange building, and wrote the President about his problem. Truman exploded: ". . . if we expect to carry on a Foreign Policy, and it is forced upon us to carry on a World Foreign Policy now, the arm of the Government, which has to carry out that policy, at least, should have the office space in which to work."[15] The Department received a choice between a new building, put up in the hypothetical future, or a building once planned for the War Department, admittedly too small, out in "Foggy Bottom" at Twenty-first Street and Virginia Avenue S.W.

Under Marshall the Department took the latter choice. The new building had gone up in 1940 as War Department headquarters, and then that department had passed on to more splendid location. New State, as the War Department building eventually became known, had a grand entrance to the east loading into a dark marble cavern. Banks of elevators lifted communicants to several upper stories. Just before the elevators where it would have faced all incoming diplomats, the Department administrative officers to their horror found a most embarrassing mural portraying the arts of war, done for the War Department; decorators hastily covered the mural with a huge curtain (as of the present writing, 1965, the military mural is still there, lurking behind the drapes). The building had 604 offices. The office of the Secretary was a large place at the east end of one of the floors and looked like a general's headquarters. From the outset there was not enough room in the building, and the Department had to make do with temporary buildings and apartment houses—soon

there were some twenty annexes. New State lay in a rundown section of the city, remote from most other government offices, and in some ways was not much better than being in Old State, but at least the building was air-conditioned, an improvement over its predecessor. One should add that New State became a more suitable structure in 1957-61 when the Department appended a vast rabbit warren of offices to the west of its building, long rows of windows and open-glassed staircases and an inner court and modernistic entrances. The new part cost $50,300,-000, its furnishing $1,700,000. The extended building took 11.8 acres. The original building is now little more than a facade for the present structure.

3

While the Department's files, the usual array of desks and chairs and four-drawer file cases, moved in truckloads down the side streets to the new building, Marshall attempted to reorganize the ponderous Department mechanism. State had grown to Gargantuan dimensions. In 1790 under Secretary Thomas Jefferson there were 8 employees; in 1833, 33; in 1870, 52; in 1909, 209; in 1922, 631; 1938, 963; 1943, 2,755; and in 1946, 7,623. This did not include the Foreign Service: in 1924 the Foreign Service had 3,431; by 1934, 3,609; 1939, 4,139; 1943, 5,230; 1946, 11,115. During the war whole new Department divisions appeared, such as the information and intelligence services. There was necessarily a certain confusion. Postwar reorganizations had not done much

to get things going efficiently. A friendly observer outside the Department described the confusion as chaotic; red tape lay everywhere; if a Federal worker made a good decision he was

> likely to be assailed by the heads of other departments for having infringed on their authority. If he makes a bad decision, he is overwhelmed with obloquy from all sides. The easiest and safest thing to do is to make no decisions at all. Keep the problems "under study"; report "progress" from time to time; "consult" with every other agency involved; request more funds occasionally, and when they are not granted point out how the work is being handicapped; defer any decision until "joint action" can be taken, thus simultaneously spreading the responsibility and winning a reputation for careful thinking and cooperation. These are the officeholder's success formulas, known collectively to the citizenry as "red tape." No real improvement in the State Department or any other governmental agency can be expected until measures are taken to cut this red tape.[16]

Probably there was too much reporting, too much paper moving back and forth from the embassies to the Department and vice versa. The Ambassador to Poland in 1947-48, Stanton Griffis, admitted that the State Department was

> enormously complicated, a fantastic network of men, women, and typewriters, who report to Wash-

ington from all parts of the world on the political, economic, labor, and agricultural conditions of the countries in which they serve. The filing cases in Washington are voracious eaters and are fed daily from the great pouches that come in by air from the various embassies; in the meantime the home team, having properly disposed of the information from the field, proceeds to write its own endless reports to go forward to the same ultimate fate in the embassies throughout the world. Hardly anyone, much less an ambassador busy with constant conferences, the ordinary housekeeping of his embassy, and the care and feeding of visiting Americans, can read, let alone understand, the flow of departmental contributions that comes across his desk. Of the tons of reports on every subject that are rushed with great haste and at great cost by airplane, I doubt if fifty per cent serves any useful purpose or contributes anything to the Department's knowledge.[17]

Some of the troubles had nothing to do with the Department but rather with its many competitors in other parts of the government. Important problems of foreign policy had left the jurisdiction of the Department of State, usurped or otherwise acquired by all sorts of agencies. Pearl Harbor had placed not merely military but also quasi-diplomatic matters in the hands of the War and Navy Departments, and as late as 1947 many of those matters were still there—the occupations in Germany, Austria, Korea, and Japan were under military and not State

Department jurisdiction. In 1947 the new Atomic Energy Commission took jurisdiction over an indubitably vital problem in international relations. The Departments of Justice, Commerce, Treasury, Labor, and Agriculture all had direct and important dealings with other peoples and governments. Lines of authority held by these departments and agencies were interwoven but not interlocking.

In annoyance and pique at this situation in and out of the Department of State, Congress was taking potshots, verbal and fiscal, at all this reordered bureaucracy, and Secretary Marshall, doing his level best to reorganize the Department, had to run a serious congressional gauntlet of suggestions for reorganization during his months of office. Typical were the remarks of one Congressman, Fred F. Bushey (Republican, Illinois), who contended that the activities of the cultural and information division of the State Department "must not be confused with a sound program. As carried on today, they are a monstrosity costing the Nation millions of dollars, and serving no constructive purpose for the United States. Conducted by a group of pro-Communist fellow travelers and muddle heads, they fill the ether and tons of paper with a combination of material favorable to the Soviet Union and the Communists, or just plain twaddle."[18] At the time the House of Representatives was debating the Marshall Plan appropriation, Marshall had to go to the Senate Appropriations Subcommittee and ask restoration of funds hacked off the Department budget amounting to millions of dollars. In testimony of March 23, 1948, he requested

over $4,000,000 for Department services, without which he would have to fire 780 employees by June 30, *i.e.*, one of every six members of the Washington staff. Already, he said, in the past fourteen months, he had reduced Department staff including the information program by twenty per cent, more than 1,300 employees. He asked restoration of the $2,672,-615 cut from Foreign Service estimates, otherwise he would have to discharge 500 employees in the field. At that time Congress had sliced nearly nine million dollars from other Department funds.[19] All when the Marshall Plan envisaged expenditure of twelve or thirteen billions!

In reorganization Marshall had help of two successive Undersecretaries: Dean G. Acheson and Robert A. Lovett. Acheson he inherited from Byrnes. Assuming the Secretaryship, Marshall told Acheson to "straighten out the lines of command," much as a commanding general would instruct a chief of staff. Acheson's first task was to route ideas and correspondence from the country desks up through the various committees and offices and bureaus to the Secretary's office, in some system which would avoid choking ideas halfway up the chain of authority. It was a big job, and Undersecretary Acheson enjoyed himself thoroughly in doing judicious firing as he cranked the Department into order. A friend dining one evening with the Undersecretary found Acheson in rarest good humor:

Dean spent a good deal of the time bubbling over with his enthusiasm, rapture almost, about

General Marshall. He had admired him for a long time. But to work with him is such a joy that he can hardly talk about anything else. I am delighted about this, for Jimmy Byrnes' erratic and often thoughtless (as well as sometimes just plain inept) administrative and other ideas had about driven Dean crazy. Marshall has put great responsibility upon Dean. Partly because he trusts him, I have no doubt, partly because Marshall would have been completely sunk if he had done anything else, and partly because Marshall has neither the excess of energy nor the interest in detail that would permit him to get into administration of the department. But it has made a new man of Dean, and this is a good thing for the country right now.[20]

At mid-year, on July 1, 1947, Acheson gave up his Department office because of acute need to recoup his private funds—he was not a rich man, and his government salary had long been insufficient to keep his family going—and his post went to Lovett, an able Wall Street banker who had worked under Stimson as Assistant Secretary of War for Air. Lovett found much left to do. Getting accustomed to his duties in mid-June he told Secretary of the Navy Forrestal that preceding Secretaries of State had made almost no progress toward a rational organization, with the result that while there were many good men in the Department the means for using their abilities were extremely limited.[21] Lovett and Marshall got on so well together, one should add, that when Marshall returned to the Pentagon

as Secretary of Defense in 1950-51 he picked Lovett as Undersecretary of Defense, and Lovett eventually succeeded the general in the top Defense office.

During part of Marshall's tenure there existed a special post of Undersecretary of State for Economic Affairs, held by William L. Clayton. Clayton's position was in addition to what one might call the regular undersecretaryship held first by Acheson and then by Lovett. Acheson later would explain that Clayton, who remained in this undersecretaryship from August 18, 1946 until October 15, 1947, acquired the title because it was necessary to convince Mrs. Clayton that her husband should stay in Washington. During his undersecretaryship there was no statutory definition of who—Clayton on the one hand or Acheson and Lovett on the other—was the senior Undersecretary.[22]

Out of Marshall's reorganization came two new Department units. One was the Executive Secretariat, for central control of communications to and from the Department, particularly to and from the Secretary's office. The Secretariat was to screen all policy papers and cables to avoid wire crossing at home and in the field. Gone were the days when as during the Hull regime an ambassador might receive one directive from Sumner Welles, another from Adolf A. Berle, and a third admonition from his desk man.

Secretary Byrnes had had the idea of asking country desks and policy offices to arrange in paper form the principles of American policy toward all countries of the world, so that the Secretary of State wishing

to find American policy toward Portugal could literally pick up a book and look for the letter "P" and
read what the United States had done and would
do to Portugal. This system of encapsulated policy
was going into operation when Marshall took over.
The new Secretary preferred a Policy Planning Staff,
a small group of eight men with a permanent secretary who would meet around a long table in an office
next to the Secretary of State with a connecting
door between the two offices. As head of the staff
he chose George F. Kennan, then forty-three years
old, a professional Foreign Service officer with experience mainly in Russia but also in prewar Germany. Executive Secretary of the staff was an experienced Department employee, Carlton Savage, a
protégé and intimate friend of former Secretary Cordell Hull.

4

In his first weeks the Secretary retired into the
depths of his private office and "went to school" on
his new tasks. Acheson met Senators and most other
visitors and freed the Secretary's time for thought.
Meanwhile the entire Department was to get to work
and come to conclusions. "Gentlemen, don't fight the
problem; decide it!" was one of Marshall's favorite
pieces of advice.[23] The Secretary preferred to stay
out of committee meetings, and have problems largely
resolved before he examined them. Unlike his predecessors he disliked committee talk and tended to describe it as "hot air." A professional soldier, he believed

in staff work. If he wanted an answer to a question about the Soviet Union he asked the Department division that dealt with the Soviet Union. In briefings on the German question he listened to men from the division charged with responsibility for Germany. He did not resort to his own private experts, least of all his personal expertise. In event of choices of policy he wanted things put briefly and concisely, and he would make the choice with a minimum of fuss. Reports began coming up to him in three sections: Facts, Conclusions, Recommendations. At the bottom of the report would be two small boxes, one marked Yes and the other No. If he initialed a memorandum it was with a strangely identifiable rounded scrawl in which his three initials—G and C and M —all seemed to circle in on each other. If he signed a piece of Department paper it was with similar economy, for his name always appeared "G. C. Marshall."

The Secretary often betrayed his background by referring not to Europe but to the European Theater. He referred to his associates by their last names, "Acheson" and "Kennan." When he spoke over the telephone it was always with a crisp "General Marshall speaking."[24]

Marshall in many ways as Secretary of State did not have to act much differently than as Chief of Staff during the war, for in 1947-48 there was a kind of war in progress against Soviet Russia. In 1949 he gave a speech at the Waldorf in which he said that "I found the problems from the viewpoint of geographical location and of pressure to be almost iden-

tical in many respects with those of the war years. There was the same problem between East and West; the same limitations as to our capability; the same pressures at home and abroad, in regard to various areas, and there was the same necessity for a very steady and determined stand in regard to these various problems."[25] It was in his time that the phrase "cold war" came into currency. Herbert Bayard Swope used it in writing a speech for Bernard Baruch to give in April, 1947, in Columbia, South Carolina. Walter Lippmann picked up the phrase for the title of a book published the same year. Everyone realized that the war ending in 1945 had turned into a political conflict that reflected the European Theater of Operations, the ETO, all over again.

Secretary Marshall's personal routine was not much different from that which he had followed as Chief of Staff during the war, when he lived at Fort Myer and went back and forth to the Pentagon. He arrived at the State Department between 8:00 A.M. and 8:30 A.M. in his chauffeur-driven limousine, from a downtown club. He returned to the club between 5:00 P.M. and 5:30 P.M. Mrs. Marshall usually stayed at Leesburg where the Secretary went when he could.

CHAPTER FOUR

THE MOSCOW CONFERENCE

ONE OF Marshall's biographers, Robert Payne, has remarked that all his life a strange fatality accompanied him, that he always managed to come into authority or be present at crucial moments in American and world history.[1] If his first years in the Army had been uneventful, they led to large power of decision during the staff days with Pershing at Chaumont; if subsequent years in the 1920s and early 1930s passed in humdrum, threatening at one point a total obscurity, he received promotion to brigadier at precisely the right time to emerge on the fateful first day of September, 1939, as Chief of Staff. During the war Marshall's duties brought him to the vital center of the diplomatic-military problems of the Western Allies. His first full postwar year, 1946, he journeyed about China talking to individuals who either were leaving power or coming to power over a nation which numbered several hundred millions of people and was to be the major enigma of the age. In January, 1947, he received appointment as Secretary of State and almost immediately went to Moscow for the turning point of the West's postwar relations with Russia.

In preceding months of dealing with the Russians the chief problem had been to believe that the Soviet Government was as intransigent as it seemed after the wartime cooperation in which the United States

and Britain and latterly France had worked with
Russia to defeat Nazi Germany. In terms of human
and material expense the effort of defeating Germany had been so large that Western diplomats, not
to mention the Western peoples, could hardly believe the Russians would enter the postwar era filled
with malevolence and cunning. When the near-in-
credible occurred it took time before Westerners
could believe it. Secretary Byrnes had labored in that
uncertain period, and if to some people, even to
President Truman, he appeared a little pliant toward
the Russians, the problem of deciding their intent
lay behind his actions. In his Stuttgart speech of September, 1946, Byrnes hinted of a tougher policy.
It remained for his successor to experience the grueling futility of the Moscow Conference.

The new Secretary of State took to Moscow an
acute sense of historical values. Marshall in 1947
had a premonition that he was about to participate
in an historic action. A sense of history had always prevented him from "thinking small," saving
him from the attacks of egotism and the personal
follies which afflicted some of his contemporaries.
In a Washington's birthday address at Princeton before he went to the Moscow Conference he set out
what was almost his philosophy of history. He spoke
in the impromptu manner for which he was justly
famous. "In order to take a full part in the life which
is before you," he told his audience, "I think you
must in effect relive the past so that you may turn
to the present with deep convictions and an understanding of what manner of country this is for which

men for many generations have laid down their lives."
His peroration was splendidly historical:

> Therefore, a deep understanding of history is
> necessary—not merely recent history which con-
> cerns itself with the trivia surrounding conspicu-
> ous men and events, but an understanding of that
> history which records the main currents of the
> past activities of men and which leads to an un-
> derstanding of what has created and what has
> destroyed great civilizations. . . . It has been said
> that one should be interested in the past only as
> a guide to the future. I do not fully concur with
> this. One usually emerges from an eminent under-
> standing of the past, with its lessons and its wis-
> dom, with convictions which put fire in the soul.[2]

1

Almost from the outset the Moscow Conference of
Foreign Ministers (March 10-April 24, 1947) promised nothing but failure, another illustration of the
wide divergence of views separating East and West.
The setting, the physical environment, anyone would
have agreed, was bad. The Russian capital in early
1947 was a depressing place for an international
meeting. General Lucius D. Clay flying in from
Germany found Moscow indescribably dreary, with
winter snow piled everywhere and covered with thick
black soot from soft-coal fires. Life and movement
filled the streets, but Clay saw few happy smiling

faces and then only among the young children.[3] John Foster Dulles, another American delegate, had read in a guidebook that "Moscow is the city of emancipated and joyous labour." He beheld leaking roofs, dirty windows, areaways dumped with garbage. Consumer goods were terribly short—shop windows contained mostly papier-mâché dummies, store shelves held ill-sorted loot from Germany.[4] Another visitor at about this time wrote that

> No words of mine could describe the incredible poverty, filth and degradation of Moscow and its citizenry. In the very heart of the city people live in indescribable slums; countless families live and cook in deserted churches; mud and puddles fill the streets; and a Communistic Vogue or Harper's Bazaar would delight in the completely nondescript clothing which consists largely of padded sacking, ancient and much-darned skirts and trousers and felt boots or—merely rags. The whole atmosphere to me was one of such horror that even Warsaw seemed like "Home, Sweet Home" to return to and its people, tragic as they are, like the Easter crowd on Fifth Avenue as compared with the denizens of Moscow.[5]

Highlighting this dreary setting were some colorful individual negotiators. First of all, Ernest ("Ernie") Bevin, an arresting character. The Prime Minister of Great Britain, Clement Attlee, willingly delegated foreign policy to Foreign Secretary Bevin. In his memoirs Attlee cited a proverb that "If you have a

good dog, don't bark yourself." In Bevin, he added, "I had an exceptionally good dog."[6] Bevin was a new type of negotiator, quite different from his predecessors in the Foreign Office, Anthony Eden and the Earl of Halifax. Short and too fat, he "suffered cruelly from attacks of angina, but continued to eat heartily and drink his whiskey sodas. His gait was the rolling one of a fat man; his clothes gave the impression of being enormous. His best feature was his eyes which, even behind heavy, horn-rimmed spectacles, lit up a face made undistinguishable by an unusually broad and flat nose above full lips."[7] As Marshall would learn, Bevin was no speedy negotiator. He could be clumsy and confused. But he had essential strength of character. He relied on the Foreign Office staff rather than his own judgments. Within Britain he was a first-rank political figure, a leading trade union man, close to the prime minister, and could speak with authority.

The French Foreign Minister, Georges Bidault, was no stimulating type, though at the time he seemed stronger than he turned out to be: he had served in the Resistance. His once-elegant face and figure was giving way to corpulence, a result of too many good banquets and diplomatic cocktails. He could be disorganized in negotiation. He could make scenes, indulging in a little theater to raise the weak international position of his government.

Then there was Molotov, distant cousin of the composer Scriabin, who in revolutionary days long past had taken a new name, "the Hammer": the apparently permanent man in Soviet diplomacy, phlegmatic, in-

flexible, the human ice cube, automatic in smile or scowl, an actor like Bidault but in a different role, the trial of all Western statesmen who met him.

Secretary Marshall arrived in Moscow with an air of hope. His big C-54 plane touched down at the airport on March 9, 1947, in (as Ambassador Walter Bedell Smith recalled) "the frosty wind and clear sunlight of a Russian early spring day." The Ambassador, himself a retired general, looked forward to seeing his old military chief for whom he had a gingerly respect. "I knew that he would say little" at the conference, Smith wrote in his memoirs; Marshall would wait "until he had the situation and all the facts well in hand and . . . make no mistakes. When necessary, he is patience personified, and no one ever takes liberties with him." Marshall seemed in a good mood. He greeted "Beetle" Smith in friendly fashion, and looked disapprovingly at the Ambassador's bowler hat, an ill-fitting headpiece purchased in Paris during a hasty moment.[8]

Moscow's housing shortage gravely affected management of the conference delegation. The Russian Government had tried to give the conference adequate facilities, emptying the Moscow Hotel and several smaller hotels of semipermanent and transient guests, renovating the hotels from cellar to attic, fitting doormen and other attendants in new uniforms, stationing fleets of Zis taxis outside. The Americans set up working quarters at their Embassy, Spaso House. For an office Marshall used a bedroom upstairs, with nearby rooms for an adviser or two. For the rest of the delegation space was at premium. The

delegation was "rather short on clerks and stenographers" but "we had plenty of V.I.P.'s. In fact, we
had so many generals, ambassadors, and consultants
that Ambassador Smith set up improvised desks in
every cubbyhole of his official residence."⁹ Smith established the Embassy's billiard room as the location
of the four senior members of the delegation—General Mark W. Clark who was military governor in
Austria, Ambassador Robert D. Murphy, H. Free-
man Matthews (head of the East European division
of the State Department), and General Clay. In a
small alcove stood desks of the special advisers, Dulles and Benjamin V. Cohen (the latter Counselor of
the Department). Other experts, secretaries, clerks,
stenographers, and the files filled the Embassy ball-
room. The latter was an eerie place; the zealous Embassy security officer closed the windows and pulled
down the shades in apprehension that the Russians
might set up acute hearing devices or long-distance
cameras to record or photograph conversations and
papers.

Security was a major problem, and no one took any
chances. Rumor had it that a member of the British
delegation had discovered six concealed plastic dic-
taphones in the walls of his office. The American delegates received instruction to discuss no matters of
substance in hotel rooms, "although frequently some
American fed up with security restrictions would
shout rather unprintable descriptions of our hosts
in the hope that they would be permanently inscribed
in the record."¹⁰ General Clark took advantage of
the hotel microphones to talk about "some good, faith-

ful Communist official in Austria" who had been "working for us as a spy or a saboteur." Like most Americans, Clark did his serious talking when strolling up and down the streets or walking around the Kremlin walls.[11]

The conference opened on March 10, at the Hall of Aviation Industry, which Ambassador Smith remembered was on the site of the old Czarist restaurant, the Yar, famous as a haunt of the wild and wealthy young prewar nobility.[12]

Secretary Marshall established a routine, about which the rest of his delegation arranged their work as best they could. He lived at Spaso House. He left preparation of policy almost entirely to his staff. Each day at 10:00 A.M. he called his chief advisers to his room for a brief meeting, and seems to have listened to their advice and accepted their statements without much change. He was new to his office, and had much to learn about recent conferences of foreign ministers, not to mention topics for the current conference. After a brief period the Secretary would indicate that his staff meetings were over, and retreat to his room and appear only when it was time to drive to the daily meeting of the foreign ministers. Sessions began at four o'clock in the afternoon and lasted three or four hours. At the end he was usually the first person out of the conference chamber. Unlike his predecessor Byrnes, who had stayed after formal meetings and drank and otherwise communed with colleagues, Marshall made no effort to carry on informally. He returned to Spaso House and disappeared into his quarters. His staff would then as-

semble, after a cafeteria dinner at the Embassy, and take the agenda for the next day and attempt to prepare for the various topics—that is, to prepare positions which they would communicate to the Secretary of State in the briefing session next morning at 10:00 A.M.[13]

Newspaper report had it that in evenings and at odd moments the Secretary of State read books, and that one of his volumes was Harold Nicolson's *Congress of Vienna.*

2

As for issues and their resolution—or lack thereof —gradually things became clear, and likewise the delegates' positions, of which there were usually two, West and East. At conference sessions Marshall sought a proper atmosphere for negotiation by renewing the United States proposal for a forty-year, four-power treaty to insure the world against German aggression. Byrnes had offered such a treaty at Paris in July, 1946, and Molotov had said it was inadequate but did not turn it down. In Moscow the Americans pressed the Russians into a corner, and Molotov rejected the proposed treaty. The Soviets wanted no treaty ties of good will among the former Allies, and believed negotiation over Germany should proceed to specifics.

The latter were economic unification of Germany, Germany's provisional government, the German-Polish boundary, reparations, reduction of Allied occupation forces in Germany, independence of Austria.

The Soviet position in general was that Germany and Austria must be economic and political dependencies of the USSR.[14]

Economic unification of Germany was the largest subject of debate, and the chief detail here was food. By the spring of 1947 Europe had passed through its hardest winter in many years. German agriculture was in saddening shape. Production had fallen to a third of prewar. The United States and Britain were shipping in food at a rate of $700,000,-000 a year. About nine million more Germans were in the Western zones than before the war; despite millions of war deaths there had been increase due to refugees from the Soviet zone and the former German-speaking areas where the victors had expelled the vanquished. Would it be possible to get farm products from the Russian zone? The Russians had no desire to ease gratuitously the West's task of feeding Germans. If (as General Clay once remarked) it was true that the zones gave the Russians the agriculture, the British the industry, and the Americans the scenery, the problem was how to obtain Russian-zone agricultural products without allowing Russians into the Ruhr.

Germany's future government had close connection with economic problems. In the economic near-chaos of the time the Russians could promise to solve everything with an all-German provisional government. To this end they stood ready to employ communist parties in their zone and the Western zones. A provisional government could enforce reparations, and especially allow Russian entree to the Ruhr.

The German boundary with Poland was no novel question and involved mostly an arrangement already carried out by the postwar Polish Government, then firmly under Russian control. At Yalta the Soviets had asked for the Oder-Neisse line, and by Neisse meant the Western Neisse and not its eastern branch. The Yalta Conference had agreed tentatively to the line of the Oder, but delayed settlement of the boundary until a German peace conference. The Poles by 1947 had taken over up to the Oder and Western Neisse. The Russians argued that acceptance of "Polonization" on a temporary basis had been a *de facto* settlement and that any future peace conference over Germany would only ratify the frontier already agreed on. This argument the Americans, British and French refused.

On the issue of reparations the Soviets showed complete disregard for previous views if the earlier declarations stood in the way of what they now wanted. At Potsdam it had appeared as if Soviet reparations, ten billion dollars out of a total Allied bill to Germany of twenty billion, could come best from German capital assets. The Potsdam decision was only confirmation of the looting which the Russians had begun: it was common knowledge that the returning hordes of the Red Army were carrying out of Germany everything portable; long trains of railway cars were en route to the East with every piece of German machinery the Russians could pry loose from factory floors. But this effort to take capital assets (the same thing was happening in Manchuria where the Russians looted Japanese industry)

proved of little advantage, as much equipment found its way onto sidings and became lost and then underwent exposure to the elements which ruined it; foreigners traveling by rail from Berlin to Moscow in the months after the war reported German machinery jamming every railroad yard and siding, deteriorating from rain and snow. So the new Soviet diplomatic position at the Moscow Conference of 1947 became one of taking reparations not from capital assets but from current production. The Soviet conferees flatly denied their Potsdam agreement about capital assets, and asked that all German factories go to work on the Soviet reparations account. No matter that the Western Allies were feeding the Germans, and that this Soviet demand if carried out would put the West in a position of setting up an endless chain of production going one way, West to East. Soviet diplomatic arguments waxed large on the subject of reparations; countless sessions at Moscow went in listening to Russian oratory which ignored the economic situation in Germany.

It is possible that the Russian demand for payment out of current production represented less a desire for goods than a device to set up economic and thereby political control of all Germany. Western negotiators, admitting in principle the justness of the Soviet Union's desire for German reparations, had to keep this possibility in mind.

The Russians tried to reduce Allied occupation forces—not their own, which they estimated required 200,000 men, but those of their new antagonists. They set the combined Anglo-American total at 200,-

000, arguing that the two nations had unified their zones economically and might as well do so militarily. They conceded 50,000 troops to the French Eventually the foreign ministers referred this minor subject to the Allied Control Council in Germany which could do nothing about it.

Last was the independence of Austria, disguised in an argument over what constituted former German assets in that country. By previous agreement those assets were to go to the Soviet Union. The German economy in Austria had been so complex that it was possible to argue that almost any firm employing one workman and a lathe was German-owned. If the Russians obtained enough assets they could dominate Austria as effectively as if a Russian marshal were the Austrian president. At one point the Russians raised the issue of Carinthia; they proposed cession of part of Carinthia to their satellite Yugoslavia: a bargaining point to widen the definition of German assets. Such arguments and the reality behind them helped prevent Austrian independence until 1955.

Six weeks and forty-four sessions passed slowly by, without agreement on virtually any item on the agenda. It became obvious that the Soviets were unwilling to compromise anything, and just tying up the time of the Western delegations. They knew that the foreign ministers of the United States, Britain, and France were important personages; if Molotov were the errand boy of his Kremlin superior, such was not the case with Marshall, Bevin, and Bidault, not to mention their high-level staffs.

General Marshall had become Secretary of State after over six hundred time-consuming, useless conferences in China, and his Army training had taught him how to sit patiently and listen to arguments national and international. Underneath the mask Marshall was a squirmer, a highly impatient man. At Moscow he managed to seem patient.

Not so his Western colleagues. At first Bevin took refuge in humor, and on March 28 at the sixteenth meeting said to Bidault: "Where are we?"

"God knows," said the Frenchman.

Replied Bevin: "I didn't know He was a member of the Council of Foreign Ministers."

On April 7 after nearly a month, Bevin said: "There doesn't appear to be any agreement anywhere." A few minutes later, during a wrangle over procedure, he growled: "I don't care what you take up tomorrow."

Bidault came close to losing his temper. The Russians voted against an economic union between the Saar and France, which deeply hurt Bidault, the more so because the Russians were using the Saar as a trading point to get access to the Ruhr. That night Marshall gave a dinner and the French Foreign Minister sat through it without eating a bite, and when the time came for toasts he proposed, with cutting meaning for Molotov who was present: "To those of us here who love freedom."

Before reaching a seemingly inevitable conclusion about Russian malevolence at Moscow, the Americans went through what one might describe as two major episodes of naiveté. One came when

they decided that the trouble at Moscow was partly the differing versions, East and West, of what constituted democracy. The political scientists and philosophers in the delegation thereupon took over. The delegates had a ponderous discussion in which the senior advisers spent six hours getting up a definition. General Marshall gave it at a conference session, somewhat like a school declamation. The result was a hurried comment by Molotov about "a number of valuable remarks," after which he plunged into another enumeration of "war-mongering capitalist piracy."

The other example of American naiveté occurred at a conference with Stalin. Marshall waited until Bevin and Bidault had made their Kremlin calls, and asked for an interview and hoped that logic might prevail. During the war a wave of Stalin's hand sometimes ended months of argument by deputies, and such demonstrations of good will were in everyone's memory. This time Stalin put on a show of affability. The occasion was impressive. Stalin had a habit of receiving foreign visitors in his paneled conference room next to his private office. He sat quietly at the table, flanked by Molotov and a young interpreter, and puffed long cigarettes or doodled with a blue pencil on the notepaper before him. The meeting took eighty-eight minutes. He listened while Marshall gave a "situation report" on the afflictions of the world and the need for peace. Bohlen translated. The Secretary recited a long list of proposals and communications sent to the Russians and to which the United States had received

no answer. He said such conduct was not merely discourteous but contemptuous. Stalin agreed that this was sloppy government on the part of the Soviet Union, and then asked about the Russian request for a loan from the American Government which, he said, he had sent two years ago without any answer yet from the United States. Bedell Smith interrupted to say the US had answered a year ago, which however represented a year's delay.[15] At last Stalin started to talk in his customary way, the undictator-like gentle manner which impressed foreign observers. He seemed friendly and referred to misunderstandings. "It is wrong," he said, "to give so tragic an interpretation to our present disagreements." They were like a family quarrel. Current differences, he said in what became a famous phrase, were the skirmishes and brushes of reconnaissance forces, and compromise would come after people had exhausted themselves in dispute.

After a final dinner in the Kremlin—no bacchanalian feast such as during years past, but a tasteful, well-appointed banquet—the Moscow Conference came to an ineffectual end.

Marshall left next day for Berlin where he stopped an hour at Tempelhof and instructed General Clay to get together with his British opposite, General Sir Brian Robertson, and strengthen bizonal economic organization to insure self-sufficiency. During the long plane trip home the Secretary reviewed the lessons of Moscow with his senior advisers, and all agreed that the Soviet Union was stalling while Europe disintegrated economically. Upon arrival the Sec-

retary reported pessimistically to President Truman, and reinforced the capital's "black and cynical mood" about the conference.[16] In a radio talk on April 28, he set out affairs with remarkable bluntness: "Agreement was made impossible at Moscow because, in our view, the Soviet Government insisted upon proposals which would have established in Germany a centralized government adapted to the seizure of absolute control."

Moscow was the end of a road, the finish of a grand attempt by American democracy to get along with Russian communism. In the United States such an effort had had its supporters ever since the Bolshevik Revolution of 1917, and had gone tentatively forward when President Roosevelt extended recognition to the Soviet regime after long conversations with Commissar Maxim Litvinov in 1933. The war of 1941-45 galvanized American popular opinion in favor of Russia, and it took the strongest Russian countermeasures in 1945-47 to break that feeling. Now, exactly as the Russians had foolishly antagonized the people of Europe by their occupation excesses, they destroyed their reservoir of good will among Americans. They could have worked with that large wartime sentiment and obtained many results favorable to themselves. It was an odd performance, hardly diplomatic in the precautionary sense of the word, proof that Soviet diplomacy under Stalin often created its own obstacles.

If Americans found the performance almost incredible they still had to deal with the illogicalities of Russian action, and the Moscow Conference had

two fairly quick results. For one, it persuaded Secretary Marshall that he must take economic measures to right Europe's problems. ". . . we faced the choice of quitting Europe altogether or of completing the task of European recovery. We had no intention of quitting."[17] He announced the European Recovery Plan in June, 1947. For another it presaged a new American concern with the connection between diplomacy and military power. Secretary of the Navy (and after mid-1947, of Defense) Forrestal would constantly keep the problem of power in mind. "As to war?" he wrote a friend a year later, "I do not think that follows, unless we do ten or fifteen years of a Ramsay MacDonald-Baldwin-Chamberlain appeasement. A balance is entirely possible, but in my opinion, at least, there is no way of seducing or beguiling our friends into good behaviour. They think in terms of only one thing—power. The day we lack that, will be an unhappy one for us and the world."[18] During the Moscow sessions in 1947 Marshall as a military man was extremely sensitive to his country's military posture, then at nearly its postwar worst. As he told an audience at the Pentagon in November, 1950:

I remember, when I was Secretary of State, I was being pressed constantly, particularly when in Moscow, by radio message after radio message to give the Russians hell . . . When I got back I was getting the same appeal in relation to the Far East and China. At that time, my facilities for giving them hell—and I am a soldier and

know something about the ability to give hell—
was 1-1/3 divisions over the entire United States.
This is quite a proposition when you deal with
somebody with over 260 and you have 1-1/3. We
had nothing in Alaska. We did not have enough
to defend the air strip at Fairbanks . . .[19]

CHAPTER FIVE

TRUMAN DOCTRINE

T HE DOCTRINE announced to Congress by President Truman on March 12, 1947 was the beginning of a self-consciously new course in American foreign relations. "The epoch of isolation and occasional intervention is ended," the New York *Times* remarked. "It is being replaced by an epoch of American responsibility."[1] Ever since the end of the American Revolution, in which contest the United States had allied with monarchical France to wrest independence from Great Britain, there had been a national desire to keep away from the Old World and foreign entanglements everywhere. We occasionally intervened or interfered with European and world concerns, but with distaste and an evident wish to get the business over and pull back to the national, continental, or hemispheric limits. Walter Lippmann has written that during the Second World War when the United States fought virtually singlehanded a great power, Japan, for the first time in the nation's history, the non-European location of the conflict obscured any sense of emergence into the realities of great powerhood. Lippmann believed that "It was not until after that, not until about 1947, that we began to think of ourselves as having a primary interest and responsibility—not only in the Pacific but in Europe as well. I would mark the change in our at-

74

titude towards Europe as beginning with Mr. Bevin's call upon us to intervene in Greece."[2]

General Marshall, then Secretary of State, presided over the beginning of this new era, and deserves a good deal of credit for the change. Marshall was attending the Moscow Conference during the Truman speech to Congress requesting aid for Greece and Turkey, but before his departure he had sat in on Department discussion of the new policy. He approved the President's speech in advance, Undersecretary Acheson having cabled it in entirety to Paris on March 6 for his suggestions. In the Department there had been much support for the new policy, from Acheson and especially the Undersecretary for Economic Affairs, Clayton. Senator Vandenberg, the bipartisan expert, stood behind the new departure. But it was Marshall's responsibility and he accepted it gladly.

1

The immediate reason for the Truman Doctrine was, as mentioned, need to support the troubled regimes in Greece and Turkey when it suddenly became clear that the British Government could not continue to aid those Eastern Mediterranean governments.

Greece was an especially difficult problem for the British to have to drop in American laps, for Britain had protected Greek independence since the war of liberation in the 1820s. During the Second World War the Greeks had come on evil days. There was

the drain of the war against Italy, a conflict maintained victoriously but not easily for a small country.
Then came the massive attack of the Germans, and
a vicious occupation which ended only during the
German retreat from the Balkans in 1944. In a Moscow meeting in October, 1944, Churchill obtained
a British sphere of influence in Greece, a ratio of
influence with Russia of 90/10 (as compared with
50/50 in Yugoslavia and Hungary, 25/75 in Bulgaria,
and 10/90 in Rumania).[3] During the German retreat, danger arose that local Greek communists
would take over, and Churchill assumed personal
responsibility for political interference by the British
Army during what in the first months of liberation
amounted to open warfare against the Greek communists. Under British auspices the Greek Govern-
ment-in-exile, returning to the homeland, managed
to establish itself shakily and tried to create a national army to fight the communist guerrillas. It
was a slow task. Seven changes of government within
two years after liberation did not improve matters;
Athens politicians shuttled in and out of power. The
Greek Government was corrupt as well as ineffective.
Its unpopular monarch George II returned from London in 1946 in the baggage of the British, like Louis
XVIII to France in 1814. The Greek Communist Party
began to raise guerrilla bands in the mountains in the
summer of 1946. Despite the best of efforts, the
British by 1947 had accomplished little in Greece
other than the negative success of keeping the country out of communist hands. If only they could pass
their responsibility to the Americans!

Greece was a mess. Aid from the United Nations Relief and Rehabilitation Administration (UNRRA) would end March 31, 1947. Foreign exchange reserves had disappeared. The prospective deficit of the Greek Government for the year was nearly $300,-000,000, three times the currency in circulation. By February, 1947, a flaming inflation presaged economic collapse.[4]

Turkey's troubles were less exigent but otherwise about the same. Unlike the Greeks, the Turks were not ready to go down the drain, and there was some belief that their well-known determination, evident in refusal nearly thirty years before to accept the treaty dictated for them at the Paris Peace Conference, might take the country through a new time of troubles. But in 1919 the Turks had confronted only a weak if hostile Greek Government and an enfeebled Russia, and in the new postwar era the Russians were pressing the Turks' eastern neighbor Iran and had made ominous pronouncements about obtaining the Turkish straits and a condominium over Istanbul. The Turkish Army was brave but ill-equipped, the country's economy so fragile that a crisis could collapse it.

Turkey was no attractive chestnut to pull from the fire. The Turks had played off the Germans and the Allies during the Second World War, and until the end of hostilities refused to grant large favors to either side. In the middle years of the war, 1941-43, there were times when the Germans had a fairly easy arrangement with the Turks and it appeared as if in return for munitions the Turks might come into the war on the German side. Perhaps it was too

much to have expected better behavior from a country which like Spain desired neutrality above all else. The British understood the need to live and let live better than did the more intense Americans, many of whom felt that Turkey like Spain and Argentina had acted badly during the recent conflict for civilization and could hardly expect any easy time in the postwar era.

For at least two years there had been ever clearer indication that the United States would have to shore up Greece and Turkey. During the Second World War the British preferred the United States to concentrate in Western Europe or in the Pacific and leave the Mediterranean and Middle East as a British sphere, but as early as autumn 1945 the British suggested American assistance in Greece, especially financial help. Not much happened until the end of 1946 when the Greek Government asked a huge reconstruction loan and President Truman sent out the former administrator for the Office of Price Administration, Paul A. Porter, as head of an economic mission with the personal rank of ambassador. Then on February 3, 1947, Ambassador Lincoln MacVeagh cabled from Athens reporting rumors that the British were going to withdraw troops from Greece. A few days later Secretary Marshall brought the President a cable from MacVeagh advising aid. On February 18, 1947 one of the American representatives in Greece, Mark Ethridge, cabled that signs pointed to a communist move to seize the country. On February 20 the American Embassy in London reported the British Treasury opposing further aid to Greece

because of Britain's own precarious financial condition.

The crisis on February 21, 1947 was not therefore unexpected, at least from the British point of view. On that date the Embassy in Washington presented to the Department of State a memorandum drawn in strong terms. The British confidentially admitted their desperate plight with Greece and Turkey. They informed the State Department that after March 31, the end of the British financial year, they could not support the governments in Athens and Ankara. Despite a large loan from the United States in 1946 they were in heavy financial trouble, and could not maintain their old imperial commitments, even smallish ones in Greece and Turkey. In 1947 the raj was ending in India. That same year the London government gave the United Nations the prickly problem of Palestine where Jews and Arabs were fighting a civil war. Greece and Turkey were part of this dismal picture. The United States would have to step in with financial support or those two countries, unable to maintain their armies (the Turkish Army on the frontier against Russia, the Greek Army in action against guerrilla communists in the mountains), would dissolve in chaos.

To the delight of the British, the Americans moved. First came an emergency meeting at the White House. Talking it over with congressional leaders on February 27, Secretary Marshall did not gloss problems. "The choice," he said, "is between acting with energy or losing by default." If Greece broke up in civil war its government would pass to Soviet

control. Such a result would surround Turkey, and force the Turks to give the Soviets the Dardanelles. Russian domination could extend over the entire Middle East to India. It would be difficult to overestimate the effect upon Austria, Italy, and France. Marshall warned that Greece-Turkey was probably the first crisis in a series which might also take Soviet domination to Western Europe.[5]

Despite the difficulties the two Mediterranean countries presented for American succor, despite embarrassment of basing a new, far-reaching change in American foreign relations on domestic situations in Greece and Turkey, President Truman took the advice of his State Department and decided to go ahead. The President was not in a strong political position within his own country, but did he hesitate when he received the State Department's advice? On his desk was the homely motto, "The Buck Stops Here." There was a stubbornness about the man that appeared in crisis. The Cabinet meeting of March 7 was of epochal proportions. Admiral Leahy wrote in his diary that "This is the first Cabinet meeting that I have attended where a definite decision was reached and clearly announced." Leahy opined: "The President's stand in this matter will require courage of a high order. He will be sustained by a sense of righteousness, and he has plenty of courage."[6] Truman told his Cabinet, perhaps with exaggeration, that he faced the greatest decision of any President in the nation's history. He later would compare it with his earlier decision to drop the atomic bomb.[7]

A speech seemed necessary and he decided to make

it. When in conference on February 27 with congressional leaders Senator Vandenberg advised him to take his proposal of Greek-Turkish support to Congress in a ringing declaration of principle and national interest—in a speech which, as Vandenberg put it, would "scare hell out of the country"—the President did just that.

The speech had extremely careful going-over. The first version from the State Department was not at all to Truman's liking, full of background data and statistics about Greece, "and made the whole thing sound like an investment prospectus." The President returned this draft and received another more satisfactory. Even that one had some halfhearted passages, including the key sentence: "I believe that it should be the policy of the United States . . ." Truman took his pencil and scratched out "should" and wrote in "must." "In several other places I did the same thing. I wanted no hedging in this speech. This was America's answer to the surge of expansion of Communist tyranny. It had to be clear and free of hesitation or double talk."[8]

As for the labors down in the Department's oratorical workshop, Will Clayton was the leading architect. Undersecretary Acheson selected lines of argument, phrased parts, and edited. A State Department draftsman, Joseph M. Jones, worked over the speech "in the interest of a homogeneous style."[9] Jones recalled afterward that

I have never worked on an important State document before that went so smoothly. . . . The

character and identity of my original draft was
preserved throughout. The force of the argument
was increased by the editing, rather than the contrary. This I attribute primarily to the fact that
the President had promised to explain this situation frankly to the public and there was no possibility of going back on that promise and thus of
watering down the argument. But entirely aside
from that, I discovered no inclination whatever
on the part of anybody in the Department or the
White House to water it down. It represented gen-
uinely the unanimous opinion of the Department.
. . . Dean Acheson told us at the first conference
on this matter that we should proceed in our work,
and with the President's message to Congress,
without regard to General Marshall's position in
Moscow. The General made this decision himself
and ordered it emphasized to all concerned. . . .
the Government functioned in the crisis: fast,
brave, and clean. It seemed to me as though it
marked our passing into adulthood in the conduct
of foreign affairs.[10]

The President looked suitably grim as he spoke on
the rostrum below the presiding officers of the House
and Senate, before the members, guests, and such of
the public as could obtain tickets. He remarked that
Greece was about to succumb to an armed minority
and that not even the United Nations could save it.
If the Greeks went down there would be "immediate and serious effect" on Turkey, "confusion and

disorder" through the Middle East, discouragement to the people of Europe "struggling against great difficulties" to retain their independence. "Totalitarian regimes," the President asserted, "imposed upon free peoples, by direct or indirect aggression, undermine the foundations of international peace and hence the security of the United States." He came to the heart of what people almost immediately would be describing as the Truman Doctrine: "I believe that it must be the policy of the United States to support free peoples who are resisting attempted subjugation by armed minorities or by outside pressures. I believe that we must assist free peoples to work out their own destinies in their own way." He asked for $400,000,000 to aid Greece and Turkey until June 30, 1948 ($300,000,000 to Greece), and permission to send civil and military personnel to supervise reconstruction and training.

The President spoke in a positive way. He did not mention the Soviet Union.

His address encountered a restrained response in the House Chamber. To be sure, everyone present —as customary on such occasions—arose and applauded and remained standing while the President and Cabinet took leave, but the applause had a bewildered quality and there were no vocal outbursts, no rebel yells.

Probably one should conclude that a demonstration of some proportion, any kind of outburst of enthusiasm, was too much in view of the change in foreign policy presaged by the speech.

2

Public and congressional debate which followed
revealed all the positions one would have predicted
—most of them reluctantly in favor of Greek-Turkish
assistance—but did not amount to overwhelming
popular understanding of what the President had
asked of his country. It was perhaps just as well.
Most Americans later would admit that the Truman
Doctrine was a timely pronouncement, and yet for
the Administration to have made too much of the
change which it initiated would have been to court
defeat. Dean Acheson shrewdly had decided on tactics of the debate. When the Department draftsman,
"Joe" Jones, went to the Undersecretary for advice,
Acheson leaned back from his desk, looked over at
the White House, thought a while, and said slowly,
"If F.D.R. were alive I think I know what he'd do.
He would make a statement of global policy but
confine his request for money right now to Greece
and Turkey."[11] Jones edited the draft accordingly.
Americans learned of a new policy, but in debate
could address their points to two small countries in
the Eastern Mediterranean.

Most opposition to the Truman Doctrine came
from the extreme left and right of the political spec-
trum. The position of the left was easy to predict.
Truman had said the United Nations could not stop
disintegration in Greece, which was correct enough,
but he thereby stirred a feeling that he was bypassing
the United Nations and taking a unilateral act of

the old prewar variety, outmoded since establishment of world government. So said Senators Claude
Pepper of Florida and Glen H. Taylor of Idaho; unilateral acts could only lead to war, as in the past.
A second liberal argument was that the Greek Government was undemocratic, corrupt, and reactionary,
and Turkey not a democracy and had been neutral
during the war. The Truman Administration could
do little but agree, yet could point out that in diplomacy one often had to overlook the character of
regimes in favor of larger issues—in the present case
keeping the people of Greece and Turkey on the
west side of the iron curtain. One also could hope
that the regimes in Athens and Ankara would improve.

Another part of the argument of the political left
came from former Vice President Wallace who in
1947 was editor of the *New Republic* and anticipating the presidential campaign of the next year.
Wallace would run for the presidency on arguments
advanced against the Truman Doctrine, but it is
fair to add that he believed them and advanced
them out of no sense of personal advantage, even if
Senator Vandenberg on the Senate floor described
the ex-Vice President as an "itinerant saboteur." In
a radio address of March 13, 1947, the day after the
presidential speech, Wallace accused Truman of "be-
traying the great tradition of America," acting as
"the best salesman communism ever had," plunging
into a "reckless adventure" that would cause a "century of fear." The new policy was "utterly futile" and
amounted to "a military lend-lease program." It would

require the United States to "police Russia's every border." Wallace wrote to one inquiring correspondent that there was more than a Greek crisis: there was an American crisis. American economic power used for political or military purposes instead of economic rehabilitation would not correct the troubles that led to communism. It was better, he believed, to handle communism by what William James had described as "the replacing power of the higher affection."[12]

The most controversial part of Wallace's opposition was his European trip, taken at the height of congressional debate over the Truman Doctrine. At this time the individual, who would have been President of the United States had it not been for Truman's vice presidential nomination in 1944, went to England and attacked his own government for "ruthless imperialism." At London airport he said that "The over-all purpose of my visit is to discover the forces in England and the western world which believe in the unity of the world, people who look ahead and not behind and who look up and not down." Soon he was speechifying that the United States had committed itself to a war against the Soviet Union; he advised the British to stand aloof from the Americans if they wished to avert war; by opposing the Soviet Union, so ran the argument, the United States was breaking the wartime coalition, setting the stage for an apocalyptic world conflagration.[13]

Anti-Wallace forces in the United States, never cool-tempered about this outspoken American, now boiled over. Hostile reporters noted that when Wal-

lace arrived in London airport he brought along a crate of eggs, not to eat but to be hatched in a British research station. Gerald L. K. Smith telegraphed President Truman that he, apparently, wanted to eat Wallace himself: "Please let Henry Wallace alone. He is my meat." Another American wrote the President: "I think Wallace is the worst trater [sic] the country had for many years." Congressman Frank Boykin telegraphed: "See by the papers that Henry Agard Wallace is going to Europe. Also by his statements he has not read your speech. He is the only person I know of that hasn't. I suggest you have it printed in the Russian language." The House of Representatives of the State of Texas resolved, 102 to 7, to repudiate and denounce the activities of Wallace. A notable Whereas read: "One Henry A. Wallace, an outcast from all political parties of American origin, is now in foreign lands criticizing and denouncing the President of the United States and condemning the foreign policies of this Government," and another read that "The said Wallace is a political 'Maverick' and is without authority to speak for the American people." Truman thanked the speaker of the House, W. O. Reed, in a letter of April 19: "I read the Resolution with a great deal of satisfaction." A certain Quimby Melton in a telegram of April 12 beseeched the President to "Take the hide off him, and read him out of the Party." To Melton the President wrote in reply: "I appreciated very much your good telegram of the twelfth in regard to Henry Wallace and I am certainly glad to have your viewpoint on his antics

in Europe." The President almost came to grief in one letter to a sympathizer, Louis E. Starr, in which he wrote rather harmlessly that "There is not very much that can be done about Henry's wild statements and if I take notice of them it only gives him more publicity." Starr gave the substance of the above comment to Robert S. Allen of the North American Newspaper Alliance who wrote a long column embroidering on it. Starr wrote the President cheekily denying that he, Starr, had let out the letter.[14]

Wallace had some support. One nice lady, Mrs. C. L. Beitzell of Upland, California, told the President that she hoped he would not agree with the overbearing Congressmen who wanted him to persecute Henry Wallace for speechmaking in Europe. Wallace, Mrs. Beitzell explained, had gone on a crusade.[15]

All in all the erstwhile Secretary of Agriculture, Vice President, and Secretary of Commerce put on an extraordinary performance. Admiral Leahy from his vantage point in the White House was nonplussed. Such talk in Europe, he wrote in his diary, was "convincing evidence of mental unbalance that will, in my opinion, permanently remove him from political participation in American affairs. . . . A realization that he might have been President at the present time is appalling."[16] At the time Wallace's attacks stirred political fear, for it was impossible to know that after the election of 1948 Wallace's star would set and he later would even take back his criticisms of the American Government.

The political far right shared Wallace's hatred of aid to Greece and Turkey, if for different reasons. They had no love of the Soviet Union, that archfoe of capitalism, but took their stand on traditional and fiscal reasons. From the archives of tradition they trundled out the Farewell Address and Monroe Doctrine and other such documents and exhibited them in support of what undoubtedly had been American foreign policy for many, many years. If they chose to ignore the qualified phrases of President Washington—that the nation could safely trust to temporary alliances for extraordinary emergencies—they were in the main line of tradition. They used financial arguments, pointing to the huge national debt and the untold millions that would go into foreign welfare if the Greek-Turkish precedent spread round the world. "Communism is a bugaboo, but we are asked to send our money to another sink hole—Greece," so went one epistle to the President. "Kindly explain this in a concrete and logical analysis the next time you go on the air."[17]

Old Bernard Baruch, adviser to Presidents, a Democrat but a conservative one, threatened to get off the reservation during debate over the Truman Doctrine, largely because the President had the temerity to recommend Greek-Turkish aid to the country without consulting Baruch. The President's advisers had a time bringing Baruch around. Truman, rather humorously, flatly refused to court the old man. The President's counsel, Clark Clifford, told David E. Lilienthal, who put the remark in his diary, that the President said: "I'm just *not* going to do it. I'm

not going to spend hours and hours on that old goat, come what may. If you take his advice, then you have him on your hands for hours and hours, and it is *his* policy. I'm just not going to do it." The President said there was a decision to make and it was going to be made. Secretary Forrestal gave a dinner for Baruch, and Secretary of War Robert P. Patterson and Secretary of Commerce Averell Harriman were there; beforehand Forrestal called up Lewis Strauss, who attended, and said the purpose of the meeting was "to grease the old boy." About this time Lilienthal was moving carefully with Baruch for another reason, and noted that "They really work at it, too. Everyone does. Everyone, apparently, but the President, who says he just won't."[18] As mentioned, Baruch eventually came around.

There was the question of China, implicit and sometimes explicit in the Greek-Turkish problem. Admiral Leahy, a political conservative although intimate adviser to the Truman Administration, could not understand Marshall's China views: "I am unable to understand General Marshall's apparent willingness to become involved in saving the Greek and Turkish Governments in view of his present attitude toward the Government of China. The two situations seem to be identical and it appears to me that a stable non-Soviet Government in China is of much more importance to America than the Mediterranean States, and with the use of Chinese manpower its accomplishment would be much less costly in American lives and treasure."[19] When Truman consulted congressional leaders in the Cabinet Room

on March 10, shortly before his speech to the joint session, Senator Vandenberg remarked that China was more important than Greece, and that the China situation had been badly handled.[20] These private explanations were accompanied by public statements from such conservative Republicans as Representative Walter H. Judd of Minnesota, a former medical missionary in China. Judd brought the Chinese into the Greek-Turkish argument in a manner awkward to refute: "If it is a wise policy to urge . . . the government of China to unite with organized Communist minorities there, why is it a wise policy to assist the Greek government to fight against the same sort of armed Communist minorities in Greece?"[21] In response Undersecretary Acheson hedged, replying that circumstances in Greece and in China were entirely different. It was of course impossible to aid China on any modest scale such as for Greece and Turkey. China was forty-five times as large as Greece, its population eighty-five times. Judd may not have been prepared to advocate the billions of dollars involved necessarily in his argument, but his argument was at least ingenious.

3

Fortunately the Administration had good support in Congress, from both middle-of-the-road Democrats and middle-of-the-road Republicans. From the rich prairies of Kansas, Alfred M. Landon, unsuccessful Republican presidential candidate in 1936, backed the Truman Doctrine. In the *Rocky Mountain News,*

Landon came out loud and clear: "There is an absolute vacuum existing in the world. Until a United Nations organization or an association of European nations is formed, capable of handling international difficulties, someone has to move in and occupy that —let us hope—temporarily vacant spot. If we prize the right and privilege of Western civilization we have to take that step."[22] There also was some shrewd calculation by the Republican leadership in the House. According to Speaker Joseph W. Martin:

For a great many Republicans the incentive to help the Allies was keener in the 1940s than it had been in the 1930s because, among other things, of the rise of the Soviet Union and the spread of Communism. To us the Communist menace looked more alarming than had the Hitler menace, dangerous though the latter was. In addition to military power, there was the threat of subversion in Communism that had not been present in Hitlerism, and Republicans were quick to sense that in militant, imperialistic Communism the United States faced a deadly enemy. Also the problem of dealing with Russia was less complicated politically than the problem of dealing with Germany had been because, whereas there were few voters of Red Russian descent in the United States, there were at the time of the pre-Pearl Harbor debates something like 15,000,000 voters of German descent. Then there was another very subtle factor after the war. This was that by taking the liberal, the progressive, one might even say (in view of

Republican traditions) the radical line in foreign policy, we were in a stronger position to champion conservativism at home. Somehow it provided for us a political equilibrium that probably could not have existed if we had pursued the conservative course in both fields.[23]

The Senate gave bipartisan support. Tom Connally, who had been chairman of the Foreign Relations Committee before the Eightieth Congress, angrily attacked the idea that the United Nations should take on the job in Greece and Turkey. As he wrote in his memoirs, the UN was not able to handle such a problem and the result would have been only a buckpassing arrangement, just a dodging and trimming and flimflamming around.[24] Vandenberg, new chairman of the Committee, went into action. The day after the presidential speech Vandenberg invited all members of the Senate to send him questions on the issues, and received more than four hundred. He consolidated them into 111 items and sent them to the State Department. On March 28 the Department made a reply, immediately printed for use of Congress.[25] The Senator also undertook to meet the argument that the proposed aid by-passed the UN. He had been unhappy about failure to consult or otherwise bring in the UN, the organization which he regarded as "our first reliance and our prime concern." "The Administration made a colossal blunder in ignoring the U.N.," he had written in a penciled note at the time.[26] He recast the aid bill's preamble to include fulsome reference to the world

organization, maneuvered into the bill a proviso that the Security Council or General Assembly might terminate the American program whenever it found it desirable, and provided that in such case the United States would waive its veto in the Security Council. And in his Senate speech of April 8, Vandenberg produced the sort of oratory, the primerlike logic, which had brought him to his position of senatorial eminence:

Let us be totally plain about it [the aid bill]. It is a plan to forestall aggression which, once rolling, could snowball into global danger of vast design. It is a plan for peace. It is a plan to sterilize the seeds of war. We do not escape war by running away from it. . . . We avoid war by facing facts. This plan faces facts.

And again:

Mr. President [of the Senate], what would you think if you were a citizen of Athens? Where would you be forced to turn in your hopeless extremity? What would you think if you were a citizen of any other of the weary, war-worn nations who are wondering this afternoon whether the torch still burns in the upraised hand of liberty; whether it is hopeless to struggle on toward democratic freedom? And what would you think, Mr. President, if you were the Politburo in Moscow's Kremlin?[27]

With such remarks the Truman Doctrine could not die in Congress. On April 22 the bill for Greece and Turkey passed the Senate by vote of 67 to 23. Of those in favor, 35 were Republicans and 32 Democrats; against were 16 Republicans and 7 Democrats. The bipartisan majority "was the largest ever given in the Senate to any major controversial measure in the whole field of American foreign policy since the outbreak of the war in Europe." In the House on May 8 the vote was 287 to 107—127 Republicans and 160 Democrats for, 93 Republicans and 13 Democrats against, plus one American Labor.[28]

President Truman planned to sign the bill at a White House ceremony on Monday, May 19, but illness of his mother prevented it. He signed the bill in Kansas City on May 22.

A presidential press release followed which was not as good as it could have been. At the time of signature the President doubtless had turned his attention to his ailing mother, who was shortly to expire. The release accompanying the Truman Doctrine said a few good things about the new measure and attempted in brief compass to allay some of the criticisms still heard of Greek-Turkish aid. But before going to his mother's bedside in Missouri, perhaps, the President had written a peroration to the release which for some inexplicable reason he did not use. In the Truman manuscripts at Independence, in the President's hand, is the following comment: "We are guardians of a great faith. We believe that freedom offers the best chance of peace and prosperity

for all, and our desire for peace cannot be separated from our belief in liberty. We hope that in the years ahead more and more nations will come to know the advantages of freedom and liberty. It is to this end that we have enacted the law I have now signed."[29]

What of Secretary of State Marshall—what did he contribute to the Truman Doctrine? Marshall did not figure large in its arrangement, but the doctrine had his complete approval. It fitted well with his concurrent stand at Moscow and, after return home, with his sponsorship of the Marshall Plan.

It is a long story, impossible to relate in detail here, how the Truman Doctrine did save Greece from communism and ensure Turkey's security in alliance with the West. The Greek story was the more dramatic. When word of the doctrine arrived on the scene the government was in a state of uneasiness, for the communist guerrilla movement was growing rapidly. The communists had an easy tactic in Greece, raising dissatisfaction and hopes among the terribly poor peasantry, enrolling young men in the armed bands who otherwise would have been nothing but village loafers or delinquents—the stagnant economy hardly permitted them any occupation until the communists created one. The communists knew what they wanted. As for government politicians in Athens, they were unsure what they wanted. The national army, distrusting politicians, unwilling to fight fellow Greeks, took a languid view of the whole state of affairs. The politicians became alarmed, and there was talk of deals. As William H. McNeill has written, they saw no recourse: "Communist lands were

very near; Britain was embarrassed by financial difficulties; the United States was far away."[30] Everything was set, right on the edge of the abyss, until
President Truman announced American help. To head
the mission to Greece he made the nonpartisan appointment of Dwight P. Griswold, former Republican governor of Nebraska, despite the muffled
screams of Nebraska Democrats.[31] Assistance turned
almost at once to military help, and soon a mission
under General James A. Van Fleet was giving the
Greek Army technical instruction, including complete reequipment. What had been weakness in
equipment compared to the communist guerrillas became crushing superiority. The defection of Yugoslavia from the communist camp closed the borders
to the west, with Yugoslav territory no longer a privi-
leged sanctuary, to use a later phrase. The Greek
Army closed the border to the north. Lacking support from abroad the communists surrendered, or
abandoned their foreign allegiance and returned to
at least silent support of the regime in Athens.

Parenthetically one should say that the Russians
foolishly ensured the Truman Doctrine's success in
Greece by provoking Tito to defect in the summer of
1948. If they had played along with him, putting up
with his intransigence until they could secure a communist victory in Greece via the Yugoslav bases, they
afterward could have indulged their ideological and,
behind it, their power struggle with Tito. Western students measuring Soviet diplomacy under Stalin have
begun to see how on many occasions the Russian dictator miscalculated.

Assistance to the Turks continued from 1947 onward, much of it military. Turkey organized a strong force, despite the weakness of Turkish economy. The economy stayed sick, and perhaps necessarily so as the country had few natural resources. The Turkish Government became a staunch ally of the West, hospitable to American air bases and missile installations on Turkish soil and, maybe even more important, emplacement of giant radar screens which swept large areas of Russia and monitored Soviet plane and missile flights. In the developing East-West conflict after 1947 Turkey was a helpful ally, easily worth the price of protection extended under the Truman Doctrine.

CHAPTER SIX

MARSHALL PLAN: ORIGIN

D URING Marshall's administration of the Department the largest single act of statesmanship, aside from the declaration of principle in the Truman Doctrine, was the European recovery plan which took his name. The plan proved phenomenally successful. It came at the right moment economically and psychologically. It was the major act needed to stop the postwar disintegration apparent to everyone in the spring of 1947. Without the plan Europe probably—we can be almost certain of this—would have gone down to the politics of communism.

The Secretary could not accept complete responsibility for the plan; he had some help. Marshall had measured the Russian tactics of evasion and delay during the forty-four sessions at Moscow and upon return was in a mood of crisis, sensing that the Russians were trying to help Europe sink. At first he seems to have thought he was without much support. "Nobody will believe me," he kept repeating to colleagues and callers. But he soon was reckoning with a galvanized State Department, full of ideas and hope. At long last the Department got off dead center, and ideas were coming up through the administrative layers of command. Acheson's staff work, as Marshall called it, was proving of value. The Marshall Plan, announced at the Harvard Commencement in

June, 1947, was part the inspiration of the Secretary of State, part that of his enthusiastic Department staff in Washington.

It is another matter, difficult to set out here, how in later years the economy of Western Europe moved ahead. The Russians allowed the North Koreans to begin a war in 1950 and thereby gave Europe's economy the Korean War boom which lasted well into 1954. By that time the Continent's economy was making a breakthrough to the consumption habits of the United States in the 1920s. This breakthrough permitted Europe to enter the 1960s with a productive apparatus of a kind never seen on the Continent before.

1

There was a far different scene in 1947. Great Britain was the most dramatic case of economic sickness: in the winter of 1946-47 a succession of the worst blizzards in many years had descended on the British Isles, interspersed with bitter, unrelenting periods of cold; weather blocked roads and railways, froze rivers, held ships in port, isolated hundreds of communities, closed coal pits, killed winter wheat; a coal shortage became so acute that London went on four to five hours of electricity daily. The British were in pitiful shape, and suppliants of the United States where there were major coal stocks and the ships to transport them. How odd today—in the mid-1960s—seems the message that Prime Minister Attlee sent President Truman in February, 1947:

My colleagues and I have learned with warm appreciation of your offer to do all in your power to help in relieving our coal shortage and in particular to support measures for diverting to this country United States coal now en route to Europe. I need not say how grateful we are for your readiness to assist in the difficult times through which we are passing. But the need for coal in Europe is no less pressing and we could not ask that cargoes should be diverted from Europe to the United Kingdom.[1]

By spring, with relief at last from the bad weather, the British faced a financial crisis. The United States had propped the British through the war with large appropriations of lend-lease, and there had been the postwar loan in 1946 of $3,750,000,000. All to no avail. By spring of 1947 the loan was beginning to run out. The loan bore a proviso that the British Government had to ensure free convertibility of sterling to dollars by no later than July 15, 1947, and this requirement threatened what funds were left. By the end of July, 1947—at the moment Marshall Plan discussions were going on in Paris—the British were in dire currency straits, warning the Americans they could not hang on. They rescinded free sterling convertibility on August 20; July drawings on the loan had totalled $700,000,000.[2]

On the Continent matters were equally bad. In France a severe drought had killed most of the 1946 wheat crop; the cold then destroyed an estimated 3,200,000 to 3,800,000 acres of winter wheat and the

French would have to import wheat at about a hundred dollars a ton. There was currency trouble too, farmers refusing to send in supplies to the cities. In the chilled urban areas, with food prices climbing, people were reaching a point where they might accept any government that would feed them and keep them warm. Communists were in cabinet posts. It appeared as if that spring the Communist Party, organized and waiting two years for a takeover, might succeed. The minister of defense was a communist. The communists left the government only in May, 1947, during a cabinet reshuffle which momentarily went against them. They intended to return, and during discussion of Marshall's proposed plan in the early summer of 1947 their return seemed imminent.[3]

Italy had the same troubles.

Germany offered an abysmal economic picture, though the Western zones seemed safe because of the armies of occupation. German industrial production in early 1947 was only 27 per cent of prewar. Reporting to Americans in late 1947, former President Herbert Hoover said Germany's food supplies had sunk to a level not known in the Western world for a hundred years. Hoover wanted ten million tons of American potatoes sent to Germany because there were so many that farmers were using them for fertilizer. The Germans had no funds, and the Department of Agriculture claimed the potatoes inedible, being of a low grade. Germany in 1936 had produced 85 per cent of its food; now it produced 25 per cent. Population in the West zones was nine million more than in 1939. Part of the trouble of German produc-

tion was manpower, because more than three million prisoners remained in Russia.

All Eastern Europe, occupied and unoccupied, was in difficulty. With UNRRA ending on March 31, Poland, Hungary, Greece, Italy, Austria and Yugoslavia would have to get foreign exchange as best they could. They had little to export, either industrial or agricultural, and there was no bullion to send out— currencies were inflating.

Everything pointed in the same direction. In a famous phrase Churchill declared in May, 1947, that Europe was "a rubble-heap, a charnel house, a breeding-ground of pestilence and hate." A later writer would remark how "Like a whale left gasping on the sand, Europe lay rotting in the sun."[4]

What to do for the "dollar gap," the distance between what Europe could earn in dollars and needed to buy with dollars? The United States was the single large, healthy industrial complex in the Western world, and production needed to get Europe going would have to come from the United States without hope of immediate and perhaps later payment. Hanson Baldwin wrote in the New York *Times* on March 2, 1947 that "The United States is the key to the destiny of tomorrow; we alone may be able to avert the decline of Western civilization, and a reversion to nihilism and the Dark Ages."

2

It is difficult to say who first thought up the Marshall Plan. The best conclusion the historian can

reach is that European conditions were so obvious
that the plan had many authors, in and out of the Department of State. Americans are by nature planners,
dedicated to organized effort first set down in a speech
or on paper or both. There was a lot of talk over
the winter of 1946-47 that the United States needed
to plan its foreign largesse, that care and feeding of
the world needed definition and proportion. Walter
Lippmann later recalled writing a series of columns
setting forth the need of a plan for European reconstruction. The Council on Foreign Relations devoted
its entire winter program to the topic.[5] The economist Walt Whitman Rostow concluded that the unity
of Germany could not occur without the unity of
Europe, and unity of Europe would be elusive unless approached crabwise through technical cooperation in economic matters, rather than bluntly in diplomatic negotiation. James Reston of the New York
Times and Dean Acheson talked it over. Acheson
may have alluded to plans under consideration;
through Reston's column in the New York *Times*
the head of the Policy Planning Staff, George Kennan, could have heard that the Department had
plans, and since Kennan was head of planning it
would not do to let somone else plan: Reston to
Acheson to Reston in the *Times* could have galvanized Kennan. It is, surely, impossible to know
who was responsible; a large idea took shape at an
obvious moment.

The Department's reaction to Europe's need came
slowly at first, and then with a rush. The Administration proposed to Congress an emergency appropria-

tion of $350,000,000 for Austria, Greece, Italy, Hungary, Poland, and China, which the President signed on May 31, 1947, underlining the importance of long-term planning for the Continent instead of a dole or, to use the phrase current in Congress, "Operation Rathole." By the time of appropriation Hungary had come under full communist domination, and Poland reportedly had no need of further relief; nothing went to either country under the Act of May 31. Undersecretary Acheson on May 8, 1947, meanwhile made a speech at Cleveland, Mississippi—perhaps the prologue to the Marshall Plan—before a group of people interested in foreign affairs and known as the Delta Council.[6]

As yet there was no formal diplomatic *démarche*. Instead Acheson spoke on the campus of the Delta State Teachers College, to the Delta Council. The Council's custom was to hold a single meeting a year, an all-day affair built around a barbecue. Senator Eastland told a State Department man that the Council was "one of the most influential organizations in the world," for it "largely controls the policies of the states in the Mississippi alluvial area."[7] Perhaps that was why Acheson decided to speak there. In fact, President Truman had promised to speak, but asked Acheson to fill the engagement. Standing before the cotton farmers and small-town businessmen, in informal fashion with his coat off, after everyone had eaten picnic lunches outside the auditorium, the Undersecretary spoke of European realities. During the year 1947, he said, the United States would export goods and services totaling $16,000,000,000, a figure

representing one month's work for each man and woman in the country and one month's output from every farm, factory and mine. In return the world could supply us with goods and services of only half that amount, leaving a deficit of $8,000,000,000. That year, 1947, Congress had authorized about $5,000,-000,000 in loans and grants, and the rest would come from private investment, remittances by American citizens abroad, gold shipments by foreign countries. "But what of next year, and the year after that? Continued political instability and 'acts of God' are retarding recovery to a greater degree than had been anticipated." This speech prepared the way for Marshall's famous address at Harvard. "Its reception," Acheson said later,

was interesting, but not unexpected. The local audience was most receptive, and a few papers in the South printed parts of it and commented upon it. But for a week or ten days it was received with rather monumental indifference and silence in most of the papers. It came back to the American press via the British and European. *The* (London) *Times* printed it almost in full, the Continental press published considerable parts of it. It became the subject of lively comment abroad. As these papers and dispatches came back here, the columnists began to look at this speech which was creating so much interest in Europe and so little in the United States, and gradually, two or three weeks after it was made, it began to be talked about.[8]

At this point Undersecretary Clayton got busy. Clayton had a habit of writing pithy memoranda about whatever he was studying. Such complex subjects as the economy of Europe did not daunt this distinguished student and practitioner of economics: his business experience, mostly as head of Anderson, Clayton and Company, the world's largest cotton merchant firm, had accustomed him to big market calculations. In early 1947 Clayton had been sending memoranda to the Department on the distressing European scene and the need for American-led solutions.[9] He left Europe by plane for the United States on May 19, and while in flight made some notes which, in form of a memorandum, were to bear the date of May 27 but which he communicated to the Department before then. In the memorandum, full of short paragraphs, he guessed the need of American support of Europe for three years to the tune of six or seven billions a year. He showed Europe's current annual balance-of-payments deficit standing at five billions, not including the smaller countries. Only until the end of 1947 could England and France meet their deficits out of reserves of gold and dollars. Italy could not go that long. Bernard Baruch had proposed a commission to study the Continent's needs; Clayton said such study was not necessary, as facts were obvious. He wished to send over coal, food, cotton, tobacco, including shipping services etc. He would base the three-year grant on a European plan which the principal European nations headed by England, France, and Italy should work out. He had in mind a European economic fed-

eration on the order of Benelux. Above all he did not want another UNRRA: the United States "must run this show."[10]

Meanwhile Kennan and the Policy Planning Staff had drawn up a memorandum dated May 23. Harry B. Price in an official history of what became the Economic Cooperation Administration has urged the importance of the Kennan paper.[11] Kennan recalled to Price that shortly after Clayton's return Secretary Marshall had outlined the general European problem and asked the Policy Planning Staff for a plan, so the Department might take the initiative instead of waiting for Congress "to beat me over the head." Marshall asked Kennan for an outline and, in closing, proffered the laconic advice: "Avoid trivia." According to Kennan, the Staff put together a proposal. Kennan's "Policy with Respect to American Aid to Western Europe," the first paper produced on any subject by the Policy Planning Staff, was an interesting composition. It considered kinds of problems: short-term, breaking obvious bottlenecks in Western Europe's economy; and long-term support of a program drawn by the European governments. Kennan's Staff wished the dispatch of instructions to certain European missions to get views of local people in the governments, and secret discussions with the British. It asked immediate measures to straighten out public opinion on some implications of the President's message on Greece and Turkey, a demonstration that the Truman Doctrine was not simply against communism, no blank check to countries in trouble with the communists, that it was for

aid only in cases where prospective results would bear a satisfactory relation to the expense of American resources and effort.[12]

3

There followed the Harvard University speech of June 5, 1947. Things as mentioned were humming in the Department, and a speech was in the works. The indefatigable Department speechwriter, Joe Jones, had produced an address for the Secretary of State to deliver at the University of Wisconsin on May 25, and the Secretary had told him he would like to "hit the same line" as Acheson at the Delta May 8 affair. Jones on May 20 sent a copy of the completed speech (Marshall turned down the Wisconsin talk) to Acheson. A day or two later Acheson told Jones he had taken Jones' draft personally to Marshall and urged him to give it. Acheson had discussed the draft also and praised it at his, Acheson's, May 21 staff meeting.[13] Then Senator Brien McMahon on May 28 talked with Acheson during a lunch session in the office of the Secretary of the Senate, Leslie L. Biffle, and said he would vote against any credits or grants to Europe if confronted with a *fait accompli*—sudden announcement of a new policy by the Administration similar to the Truman Doctrine. He thought that Marshall should begin talks with Senator Vandenberg and there then should be some considerable speechmaking, especially a speech by Marshall, not laying down any solution but stating the problem and showing it was not ideological but

material. According to McMahon, solutions could come after full discussion within the government and on the Hill. The Department then advised that the Secretary should make a speech. Use of Harvard's commencement to announce the new venture in American foreign relations was a last-minute decision, as Marshall had turned down an invitation to appear there; at his direction the Department asked for re-extension of the invitation. The Department Counselor, "Chip" Bohlen (by this time Ben Cohen had resigned), hurriedly drafted a speech, using the papers by Clayton and Kennan. The address had no newspaper build-up, no hints to the press that the Secretary would deliver an important pronouncement. The idea was to create surprise in Europe and afterward work up opinion in this country. Undersecretary Acheson did advise three British correspondents in the United States that the Secretary was going to deliver a speech of major proportions and they should telephone the full text to London as soon as the Department released it; Acheson advised them to get it into the hands of Foreign Secretary Bevin.[14]

The Harvard occasion was not altogether impressive, to individuals not in the know. It was the first regular commencement since before the war. President James B. Conant led the parade through the Yard and the Cambridge streets to Memorial Hall, that Victorian monument to Harvard's Civil War dead. Then followed awarding of honorary degrees and granting of the regular sheepskins. Marshall received a degree with suitable citation: "An American to whom freedom owes an enduring debt of gratitude, a soldier and statesman whose ability and character

brook only one comparison in the history of this nation." As was Harvard custom, in the afternoon the graduates and alumni and friends gathered under the elms and listened to speeches by various individuals, among them the Secretary of State. Marshall did not wear his military uniform, not academic costume. He stood there in his business suit, a tall and graying figure, and went through his speech in his dull, offhand way. He spoke in a soft and almost inaudible voice, with his marked Southern accent, gazing doggedly at the notes before him, playing with his spectacles, never looking at the audience.

The speech read much better than it sounded. The Secretary called on Europe to pull itself together, with only assistance—not direction—from the United States. He had determined that there would not be another lend-lease in which Europeans would bring their shopping lists to the United States and the American Government trim demands down to some reasonable amount, never sure that countries with the most overblown requirements came out best after the reduction. Marshall's demand was European leadership. "It would be neither fitting nor efficacious for this government to undertake to draw up unilaterally a program designed to place Europe on its feet economically. This is the business of Europeans. The initiative, I think, must come from Europe. The role of this country should consist of friendly aid in the drafting of a European program and of later support of such a program so far as it may be practical for us to do so. The program should be a joint one, agreed to by a number, if not all, European nations."

CHAPTER SEVEN

MARSHALL PLAN: FULFILLMENT

1

How would the Europeans react? The British Government showed immense enthusiasm at the prospect of American aid under a plan, even if the Americans seemed uncertain of details. When after Marshall's speech the Permanent Undersecretary of State for Foreign Affairs, Sir William Strang, came to Ernie Bevin with the suggestion that the Washington Embassy ask for explanation of the speech, Bevin almost literally jumped into action. "Bill," said he, "we know what he *said*. If you ask questions, you'll get answers you don't want. Our problem is what *we do*, not what *he meant*."[1] Bevin arranged a meeting in Paris of the European foreign ministers —Britain, France, and Russia. He announced his intention to the Americans, saying he was going to Paris for preliminary talks with Premier Paul Ramadier and Foreign Minister Bidault, and would be glad to carry any message. The British Ambassador in Washington, Lord Inverchapel, bringing these tidings to Secretary Marshall, expressed hope that Will Clayton would come to London soon and not delay because of Bevin's proposed foreign ministers session in Paris. Meanwhile Bevin told a member of

112

the American Embassy in London that the United States was in the same position in 1947 where Britain had been at the end of the Napoleonic Wars. In 1815, he said, Britain held about thirty per cent of the world's wealth. The United States after the Second World War held about fifty per cent. Britain for eighteen years after Waterloo, Bevin ruminated, had practically given away her exports, but the result had been stability and a century of peace.

The French were apprehensive of Bevin's fast footwork, and showed both their usual postwar sensitivity to France's European prestige and a certain fear for the opinions of French communists. Bidault told the American Ambassador in Paris, Jefferson Caffery, that he was not too happy about Bevin coming over, as it looked as if Bevin were trying to steal the show after the new American *démarche.* Caffery thought privately that Bidault wanted to steal the show but Bevin had beat him by a day or two. Ramadier remarked that France and the other West European countries were heading for economic and financial disaster and would get there during the latter part of 1948 unless someone headed off Europe's troubles. The communists had been demonstrating high glee at the prospect of chaos, and their tactics of obstruction greatly bothered him.

As soon as Bevin arrived the question arose of Soviet cooperation. Both Bevin and Bidault told Caffery, separately, that they hoped the Soviets would refuse to cooperate, and in any event they would go ahead full steam. A momentary embarrassment occurred when Bevin and Bidault were deep in their

cooperative planning stage, preparing for the Soviets:
the French minister of information inadvertently
gave out an announcement that they were planning,
before they had opportunity to communicate with
the Russians, and the ministry then had to deny that
the two foreign ministers were planning.

Shortly after this initial Anglo-French diplomacy
in Paris, Will Clayton and Ambassador Lewis Douglas held some sessions with members of the British
Cabinet in London. Chancellor of the Exchequer
Hugh Dalton did not take kindly to Clayton and
behind the civilities of the sessions Dalton wrote in
his diary a critical analysis of the American Undersecretary:

> There have been many foreigners in London
> lately. Will Clayton—doctrinaire Willie of impos-
> ing Texan stature but indecisive and slightly nerv
> ous manner—and Ambassador Lew Douglas, for
> whom I have an increasing affection and respect,
> have spent quite a lot of hours with Attlee, Bevin,
> Cripps and myself. It is surprising how many hours
> one can spend with people and yet reach no sharply
> outlined conclusions. Clayton has no plan, but we
> have tried to help him both by giving him large
> quantities of statistics on our, and other people's
> dollar shortages, and by impressing on him that
> we are something more than just a bit of Europe.
> Now he goes on to Geneva, Paris and Rome . . .[2]

Whatever the personal appraisals, the sessions with
the Americans were sad affairs, at least in their airing

of Britain's fiscal position. At the first meeting on June 24, 1947, Dalton protested to Clayton that American wholesale prices were up by forty per cent, reducing the value of the British loan by a billion dollars. Bevin said the United Kingdom wished to be a partner in the proposed European plan but if it could not get in a position of financial strength so it could carry on an active partnership then its relation to the United States would be somewhat similar to that between the USSR and Yugoslavia. Clayton said he could not see how the UK could find itself in a Yugoslav position, and that not all the financial difficulties of Britain had come because of the US price rise—implying that the British had not maintained the best of fiscal policies. Bevin said that somehow they had to break the "circle". He needed some assurance of a continuity of supplies from the United States in 1947-48—perhaps 1949—which he called two desperate years ahead.

A second meeting in the Prime Minister's office, held on June 25, proved equally gloomy. It was an hour-and-a-half session with Attlee, Bevin, Dalton, Sir Stafford Cripps and a few advisers. Bevin saw great hope in an American plan; if Europe received economic assistance, Russia might not be able to hold the satellites. But the Foreign Secretary feared that nothing might be done. He asked for a UK-US financial partnership and said a six-to-eight-week supply of food for Europe would assure 1,800 calories until the year 1949. Dalton elaborated the serious position of British resources: use of the American loan had increased rapidly in the last six months;

the British would use up the loan by the end of 1947. Price increases had taken more of it than the government had anticipated, and there had been demands for dollars by Canada and Argentina. Replenishment of stocks in Britain had been part of the first six months of drain in 1947, and charges to the loan had included some nonrecurring items such as purchase of ships. In the next six months the convertibility of sterling (postponement of which Dalton said he was not suggesting) and the policy of nondiscrimination in imports—nondiscrimination was also a requirement of the American loan—would counterbalance these charges. Bevin commented that the convertibility and nondiscrimination obligations had come three years too soon. At this second session Clayton and Ambassador Douglas sought to raise British sights to Europe, outside of their own problems which were so considerable. The Americans made clear that United States plans contemplated no piecemeal assistance and that only an inclusive program for Europe would have any chance in Congress. Individually, the problems of Italy seemed the most acute, but Italy had to await an attack on the whole European crisis. Clayton and Douglas asked the British how they considered themselves in a different position from other European countries. Dalton said that one difference was that the UK was helping Germany. There followed general agreement that wartime destruction in Europe combined with moral or psychological disintegration were important factors in European production and also that, without expressing views as to the rights or wrongs of the problem, the

nationalization, socialization, and breakup of land holdings or other economic structures had retarded recovery.

Caring for the Germans was no easy task, and its details constantly entered the London discussions. An Anglo-American agreement concluded by former Secretary of State Byrnes, for an eighteen-month period from January, 1947, contemplated UK-US assistance to Germany costing altogether $860,000,000, of which the UK share was $460,000,000; Hugh Dalton said in the session of June 25 that the original estimate of the dollar drain on the UK was $200,000,-000, which would have to come out of the American loan to Britain. Price changes in America had raised the dollar drain to $275,000,000. A further general increase in costs for Germany to provide additional calories had added $150,000,000 to the Anglo-American bill—$75,000,000 for the UK—which made the present rate of drain on the UK for Germany alone, for the period January 1, 1947, to July 1, 1948, some $350,000,000. Dalton thought this "pretty poor." There was great need, so he wrote in his diary, to "stop spending our dollars on these bloody Germans."[3]

The third London meeting, June 26, turned attention to expected Russian difficulties at the forthcoming Anglo-French-Russian conversations in Paris. Clayton said he thought there would have to be radical change in the Russian position on European recovery and other matters before the American people would approve financial assistance to Russia. Clayton thought the Russians might not need

short-term assistance with the "three f's"—food, fuel, and fiber—for they had these, but might require long-term credits. Dalton said the Russians, not members of the International Bank, could not borrow, but could join the Bank if they wished. An aide interjected that this course seemed unlikely because as a member of the Bank the USSR would have to reveal its gold holdings. Dalton closed the session by reverting to the note that the timetable for the US loan to the UK was so erroneous, that Britain could take on convertibility only with great trouble.

The meeting of the three foreign ministers now opened in Paris, on June 27. The United States, not present, had exact recounting of the conversations. Molotov at the outset proposed to ask the US for further information, and then ran into the Franco-British opinion that the three nations should draft a plan. Bidault offered a compromise, asking clarification on the extent of US willingness to help with a proposal. Jefferson Caffery obtained the notion from what he heard of the meetings that the French, in event of Soviet tactics of delay or obstruction, would let Bevin get out in front and carry the ball. Fortunately Anglo-French unity held. It proved fairly easy for Bidault and Bevin to stay together in their proposals as the meeting turned into a considerable trial for Foreign Minister Molotov: Bidault told Caffery that Molotov's "hungry satellites are smacking their lips in expectation of getting some of your money. He is obviously embarrassed."[4]

The Russians may have tried, but if so without success, to stir trouble for the French Government

by encouraging the communists. Bevin told Caffery that the 140 technical advisers and assistants, so-called, whom Molotov brought along for the conference had little if anything to do with the discussion. He believed these Russians were all agents, brought along in view of the Communist National Congress then in session at Strasbourg, all in hope of getting communists back into cabinet positions in the government.

The Paris conference quickly came to an end. Bevin took the French proposal and reduced it to a single page, taking out the extra words, and sent this page to Bidault and Molotov on the morning of July 1. That afternoon the Russian Foreign Minister reiterated arguments of previous days—no infringement on sovereignty of European states, each should establish its needs and submit total dollar costs to the United States. Bidault strongly supported Bevin. One of Molotov's aides brought in a partly decoded telegram from Moscow repeating the old arguments. Bevin said to Molotov that the Russians wanted a blank check from the Americans, and what would happen if he, Bevin, went to Moscow and asked for a blank check from the Russians? The meeting of July 1 adjourned on this note. The final meeting, held next day, brought a clean break. Bevin presided. Molotov repeated his arguments, and finished by saying that any joint Anglo-French action without Russia might have very grave consequences. Bidault said the French would go with the British. Bevin said that he, like Bidault, proposed to carry on.

The following day, July 3, the British and French

Governments invited all European states to meet in Paris and draw up a proposal for the American Government.

Despite the break at Paris the Russians still were welcome to attend. Secretary Marshall had never excluded Russia from his offer. There had been Department discussion of Russian participation, with advisers taking positions pro and con, but Marshall decided to give the Soviets a chance. In reply to the Secretary's questions Kennan had advised, "Play it straight." The Soviet Union and its satellites were great producers of food and raw materials that Western Europe needed and it was sensible to encourage East-West trade. The Secretary could confront the Russians with their own Marxist maxim, "From each according to his ability, to each according to his need." There would have to be sharing of information on economic and financial conditions about which the Russians traditionally had been secretive. If they changed their spots and came in, so much the better. Marshall privately described his offer as including "everything up to the Urals" and he meant it.[5] He said "if Europe was to be divided he was not going to be the person to divide it, therefore U.S.S.R. should be let in on the plan."[6]

This great opportunity Stalinist diplomacy threw away. If they had participated in the plan the Russians could have made congressional approval of Marshall Plan outlays difficult if not impossible; Congress was in a suspicious mood, unlikely to approve billions of dollars for Russia and the satellites. Or if by some minor miracle the plan with Russian par-

ticipation passed Congress, the Soviets could have ruined economic planning for Europe by sabotaging it—delaying, evading, all the devices of which they were masters. Staying out of the plan, they ensured its success.

Unfortunately for the apparent unity of the Eastern block they did not stay out of the Marshall Plan quickly enough—a confusion of signals between Moscow and the satellites led to an open Russian veto of participation by the Czechoslovak and Polish governments. Those two regimes gave tentative indication of desire to join the plan. They took pains to say that, although they wished to send delegates to the organizing meeting in Paris which was to open on July 12, final acceptance depended on the scope of the plan. Then came the belated advice from Moscow. The Polish Government backed water immediately. Foreign Minister Modzelewski had some trouble informing Ambassador Griffis that his country was not sending a representative to Paris, talked continuously and refused to look Griffis in the face. Modzelewski had told Griffis a few days before that the Poles would go to Paris. But the Czechoslovak Government got into the worst trouble. President Eduard Benes told an American diplomat on July 9 that he did not anticipate a Soviet veto on Czechoslovak membership in the plan, but that in event of a veto a showdown would occur in the Prague government, forcing a choice between East and West. That very afternoon a telephone message arrived in the Czechoslovak capital from the delegation, including Prime Minister Klement Gottwald, which

had gone to Moscow for consultation. The message, of course, told of a Soviet veto. The Russians had said the Americans were trying to buy up Europe, that Czechoslovak membership in the Marshall Plan would be an act of hostility against the USSR. Stalin advised the Prague regime to withdraw its acceptance and justify this action by pointing to the fact that nonparticipation of the other Slav nations and the other East European states had created a new situation. The Czechoslovaks had had two interviews, first Gottwald alone with Stalin, then a reception of the entire delegation by Stalin and Molotov. The second session was fairly relaxed, although the Russians made their points clearly and categorically. The first meeting *à deux*, Gottwald and Stalin, was the business meeting, and not so pleasant: Gottwald had returned to his hotel almost scared, and said he had never seen Stalin so angry.

Lacking Russian and satellite attendance, representatives of the sixteen nations met in Paris on July 12: Austria, Belgium, Denmark, France, Greece, Iceland, Ireland, Italy, Luxembourg, the Netherlands, Norway, Portugal, Sweden, Switzerland,[7] Turkey, and the United Kingdom. Under chairmanship of Sir Oliver Franks the Europeans set up an interim Committee of European Economic Cooperation (CEEC), drew up a report, and presented it to the United States on September 22.

The Russians meanwhile organized a meeting at Warsaw where the satellites received from Moscow their own bogus economic plan, known as the Molotov Plan. The Russians announced a revived Comin-

tern, the Communist Information Bureau ("Cominform"), on July 6, 1947.

2

For Americans some months of investigation and public and congressional debate remained before Congress passed the necessary legislation for the Marshall Plan.

In the United States one of the first initiatives came from Senator Vandenberg, who on June 13, 1947, suggested that the American Government take stock of Europe's requirements, simultaneous with investigation by the European nations. He proposed that the President appoint a bipartisan advisory council composed of "our ablest and most experienced citizenship" to produce the "facts and recommendations and judgments." He sent word to the White House that he would not cooperate on the Marshall Plan until the President had done this.[8] Truman on June 22 announced creation of two committees, and directed the newly established Council of Economic Advisers to develop a complementary analysis. The work went on through the summer. Reports, studies, and findings of the American committees, chaired by Secretary of the Interior Julius A. Krug, Secretary of Commerce Harriman, and the chairman of the Council of Economic Advisers, Edwin G. Nourse, when placed side by side overflowed a five-foot shelf.

By autumn it was clear that investigation and debate would last into the spring of 1948. Something would have to be done to tide the European nations

through the winter—some sort of interim aid. In early September, 1947, Secretary Marshall cabled President Truman, then in Brazil attending an inter-American meeting, that Europe's economy was deteriorating rapidly, that the more important countries, notably Italy, France, England, possibly some of the others, would be in a dangerous position before the end of the year. He asked support for an approach to Congress for short-term aid. Truman on November 17, 1947, addressed a joint session of the Senate and House at a special session of Congress convened that day, and asked interim funds for Europe. The President told Admiral Leahy privately that the address probably would hurt his Administration and Party, but he was right and could not fail to act.[9] The Administration bill for interim aid ran into intense opposition, so much so that Senator Vandenberg began to fear the worst. In a letter to his wife of November 18 he wrote: "If the resistance which is showing up to the short-range European relief bill . . . is any criterion, our friend Marshall is certainly going to have a helluva time down here on the Hill when he gets around to his long-range plan. It is going to be next to impossible to keep any sort of unpartisan climate in respect to anything. Politics is heavy in the air."[10] The interim aid bill passed the special session in December, $522,000,000 for winter relief in France, Italy, and Austria.

The President gave the Marshall Plan proposal to Congress in a message of December 19, 1947, and for the most part—and contrary to Vandenberg's premonition—the public reception was everything he

could have wished, except for the New York *Daily Mirror* which pronounced economic aid to Europe the "greatest fool's gamble ever proposed with a straight face to an intelligent Nation." The New York *Times* said Truman's message was "among the historic papers of the United States," and the other major papers echoed this appraisal: "a distillation of the greatest effort toward international economic planning that has ever been undertaken" (*Herald Tribune*); "most challenging proposal ever presented to a democracy in peacetime" (Minneapolis *Star-Tribune*); "great and bold conception" (Baltimore *Sun*); "Operation Survival for our free world" (Washington *Post*).[11]

The opposition did what it could to the big bill, but lacked the aggressiveness and bumptiousness of old—perhaps sensing that the American public was overwhelmingly in favor. Henry Wallace, preparing to fight Truman in the 1948 presidential campaign, thundered against the Marshall Plan, describing it as the Martial Plan, a highly unfortunate confrontation of Soviet Russia. Truman's mail filled up with commentary against Wallace. "Almost every kid that ever owned a toy balloon wasn't satisfied until he blew more air into it than it was originally intended to or could hold," commented one friendly observer. James R. Wallace wrote: "It was an act of God and not the human choice of the undersigned that he is a second cousin of Henry Agard Wallace." One man informed the President: "Have just heard that Henry A. intends to change his name to Wallaceoff." By March, 1948, the President himself was feeling ferocious on

the Wallace issue; in an address to the Society of the Friendly Sons of St. Patrick he looked up from his prepared speech and said: "I do not want and I will not accept the political support of Henry Wallace and his Communists."[12] It looked as if Wallace, for one, was not going to be effective against the Marshall Plan.

Other individuals such as Ohio's Robert Taft spoke of "global New Dealism." Taft had not opposed the Truman Doctrine, being then in uneasy alliance with Senator Vandenberg. The Marshall Plan required a much larger financial outlay, and debate running over several months offered larger opportunity for opposition. Taft also was beginning to seek the 1948 presidential nomination of his party. In a private letter Vandenberg observed that "Evidently I am to have some degree of trouble with Bob Taft. So be it! The world is full of tragedy; but there is no tragedy greater than that we have to have a presidential election next year in the U.S.A. That must be what's biting Robert . . ."[13] In the predominantly Republican Eightieth Congress "Mr. Republican" unlimbered his big guns and did his best to bombard the Secretary of State's measure. Eventually he voted for it.

Total figures for the Marshall Plan were arrived at after intricate calculation. The European nations at first had asked for $29,000,000,000 spread over four years. The total came down to $22,400,000,000, and then dropped to between $15,100,000,000 and $17,800,000,000. The Administration asked for an initial fifteen-month appropriation of $6,800,000,000.

Financial opposition arose, and ex-President Hoover opposed the Administration figure, suggesting ex-

penditure of $3,000,000,000 in a period of fifteen months; the former President called for "more safeguards." Former Vice President Wallace proposed a larger, longer-range program administered by the United Nations. When the Administration bill came before the Senate, Taft moved to cut $1,300,000,000 off the authorization. This latter effort to "hack off" a billion, as Vandenberg put it, met defeat in a roll call vote, 56 to 31.

Like the soldier he was, the Secretary stood his ground against all comers. Some observers felt Marshall was a little offhand and almost imperious with the Foreign Relations Committee when he made a formal appearance on January 8, 1948. The reporter James Reston, watching the aging general on the stand, observed that Marshall looked good after the first year as Secretary. "He was clear. He was calm. He was patient and courteous. And yet he acted like a man who was determined to get substantially the Marshall Plan he wanted or, as is already rumored in the capital, retire at last to Leesburg."[14]

In testimony before the committee the Secretary would not budge. He said there could be no separate organization for the plan, apart from the Department of State; everything had to be done under control of the President and Department. The Secretary read his prepared statement in dull fashion. As was his wont he came to life in extempore talk. But he was firm. Reston noticed that when interrupted once he went on unruffled. When interrupted twice in the same passage, by Senator Alexander Wiley of Wisconsin, he stopped the Senator with a

look and proceeded. "At no time did he abandon the 'Yes, sir, No, sir,' of his military speech, but always there was that direct look and manner that kept the hearing on the basis of absolute equality."[15]

Arguments in favor of the plan were really irrefutable. The appeal to American good will was undeniable. With considerable subtlety the Administration in late 1947 organized the Committee for the Marshall Plan to aid European Recovery, under chairmanship of Henry L. Stimson, and made a prodigious effort to get down to the grass roots, reaching leaders and groups at that level, stimulating local organizations to push recalcitrant members of Congress. Secretary Marshall enlisted foreign policy associations, church groups, women's clubs, labor unions, chambers of commerce, the innumerable groups of the knife and fork circuit—Rotary, Kiwanis, Lions.[16]

In speeches and addresses during summer and autumn and early winter of 1947-48, prior to enactment of the recovery plan on April 3, 1948, Marshall seldom failed to strike a popular chord. "Historical records clearly show," he said in July, 1947, "that no people have ever acted more generously and more unselfishly than the American people in tendering assistance to alleviate distress and suffering. The history of past decades records numerous examples of readiness to lend a helping hand in situations where there could not possibly have been other compensation than the satisfaction that comes from assisting those in need." And in October, 1947: "We are proceeding in a determined campaign which has for

its purpose world stability, a condition necessary to world peace. It is a difficult business. It requires infinite patience and a constant effort to understand the other fellow's point of view . . . Above all things, a regard for the American tradition is required, the typical American readiness to assist those in need . . ." November, 1947: "Whether we like it or not, we find ourselves, our Nation, in a world position of vast responsibility. We can act for our own good by acting for the world's good." January, 1948: "Dollars will not save the world—but the world today cannot be saved without dollars."[17]

He insisted that Europe help itself: "There has been constant reference to a Marshall plan. The reference to me personally was unfortunate, but the reference to a plan was definitely misleading. There was no plan. There was a suggestion. Now we are in the process of drafting a plan as a proposal to the Congress of the United States. That is the situation at the moment."[18]

A demand for support to China out of Marshall Plan funds became difficult to resist, and the Secretary reluctantly allowed $275,000,000 to China for technical aid and $125,000,000 for military aid during the period ending June 30, 1949. These funds were a foolish addition to the recovery plan, for China was going downhill and Nationalist leaders were hoarding dollars in anticipation of taking them to Formosa or leaving them in the United States; in the summer of 1948 Ambassador John Leighton Stuart saw Nanking fall to the Communists because

Nationalist leaders would not appropriate about $15,000,000 of arrears in pay for soldiers defending the capital.[19]

Arguments foreign or domestic failed to fluster the Secretary of State; Marshall kept his composure, unruffled, calm. In the Washington Cathedral on March 11, 1948, he told a meeting of the Federal Council of Churches that

> The world is in the midst of a great crisis inflamed by propaganda, misunderstanding, anger, and fear. At no time has it been so important for cool judgment, for an appeal to one's self for a proper sense of justice, for a realization of conditions—material, political, and spiritual—in other parts of the world. Virtually everything we do in connection with our foreign relations is misunderstood by some abroad. Our most generous motives are suspected, our good intentions are condemned, and we on our side are apt to grow passionate or fearful—overzealous in our passions or failing in action because of our fears. . . . In the midst of this clamor of propaganda in vigorous and sometimes reckless statements, I personally, in my responsibility as Secretary of State, have tried to keep a level head.[20]

The Russians helped the Marshall Plan through Congress by communizing Czechoslovakia on February 25, 1948. This act, followed on March 10 by the accidental or suicidal or forced leap of Czechoslovakia's Foreign Minister Jan Masaryk from a window

of the Foreign Ministry in Prague, shocked governments of the West, especially the United States. Americans long had taken interest in Czechoslovakia, many of them having come to the New World from that country; during the First World War the exiled leader—and father of Jan—Thomas Masaryk had concluded an agreement with the Slovaks at Pittsburgh, the Pittsburgh Declaration, believed by many to be the political foundation for the country. When Czechoslovakia passed to the communists in 1948 there was anguished outcry in America. In response to a question in his press conference of March 10, Marshall said:

I think you correctly described the situation in your question—that there are great fears as to the developments. There are also very strong feelings regarding these developments and a considerable passion of view on the part of a great many in this country. The situation is very, very serious. It is regrettable that passions are aroused to the degree which has occurred. It is tragic to have things happen such as just occurred in Czechoslovakia, particularly what has happened to some of the officials, as in the affair today of the death of Jan Masaryk, all of which indicates very plainly what is going on. It is a reign of terror in Czechoslovakia and not an ordinary due process of government by the people.[21]

The Marshall Plan passed the Senate (March 13) and House (March 31) with large bipartisan ma-

jorities, 69 to 17 and 329 to 74. As already mentioned, President Truman signed the Economic Cooperation Act on April 3.

In June, 1948, one should add, the House of Representatives suddenly threatened to sink the plan before it started, for at instigation of Congressman John Taber the House cut the appropriation by $2,160,000,-000. Here was what the Russians had been predicting to governments of Western Europe. American ambassadors cabled their distress. Vandenberg was furious. Eventually the House arrived at a compromise, obligations for Marshall Plan aid for the fifteen months from April 3, 1948 through fiscal 1949 (ending June 30, 1949) amounting to $5,850,100,000.

The mechanics of organization and disbursement remained, and after an abortive effort to appoint Dean Acheson, the President named the head of the Studebaker Corporation, Paul G. Hoffman, to take charge of the American side of arrangements, the Economic Cooperation Administration (ECA), an independent agency under presidential control.[22] His Special Representative in Europe was Harriman who had been organizing the plan ever since Marshall's Harvard speech. Hoffman and Harriman set up a large corps of assistants in Washington and abroad. On March 15, 1948, the interim Committee of European Economic Cooperation (CEEC) representing sixteen countries and the zones of Western Germany gathered in Paris to form the Organization for European Economic Cooperation (OEEC).[23] To OEEC the ECA (and its successor at the end of 1951, the Mutual Security Administration) between April 3,

1948 and June 30, 1952 gave $13,348,800,000. Three nations took over half this sum: the United Kingdom obtained $3,189,800,000; France $2,713,600,000; Italy (including Trieste) $1,508,800,000. West Germany received $1,390,600,000. The Netherlands received $982,100,000 under the Marshall Plan. Other states tapered off with lesser sums, down to Iceland with $29,300,000.[24]

The program ended on June 30, 1952, as Marshall insisted it should. In a private meeting at the State Department in 1949 after he had left the secretaryship he said that "it ought to be terminated in 1952. Part of the reason why they imply it cannot be terminated then comes from the opponents of the present appropriations, and part comes from the foreign fellows who naturally would like to see it prolonged beyond 1952, but you have got to stop somewhere."[25] By its end the plan had turned from an economic to a military arrangement. Prior to June, 1950, there had been stipulation that no Marshall Plan aid should go into military supplies. This did not prohibit European nations from shifting budget appropriations, and American administrators had hoped the plan would ease pressure to cut military appropriations. Early in 1951 with the Korean War at a crucial stage the United States informed the Europeans that aid under the plan would have to go for defense. By 1952 eighty per cent of aid was in weapons, the other twenty per cent in defense support.

Contrary to some feeling expressed at the plan's inauguration, it did not disrupt the American

economy. Far from bankrupting the country, it stimulated production and probably braked a fall in demand for American food and industrial products, for the initially large postwar domestic demand had slowed down. The money involved in the plan, $13,-348,800,000, was a stupendous sum. But inquiry into the peculiar statistics of American consumption showed a domestic liquor bill of more than thirteen billions, an athletic bill of far more than thirteen billions, a tobacco bill of more. The economy had plenty of slack. It is true that the Marshall Plan added large budget deficits to the national debt—moving beyond $250,000,000,000 by 1952. The Korean War added far more. Americans could congratulate themselves that because of the Marshall Plan they did not have to spend even more in an enormous war in Europe.

CHAPTER EIGHT

BERLIN

1

BERLIN WAS the biggest problem during Marshall's months at the Department of State. It was impossible for the general to have gone through two years as Secretary without trouble over Berlin's uneasy postwar status, but this problem came to sheer crisis during his era. At the end of the war the city lay toppled over, so to speak—a gigantic shambles. In the words of a later American sector commandant it was "the world's biggest heap of rubble."[1] Some 3,200,000 dazed people scrambled about the ruins of Germany's capital in 1945 wondering what to do with themselves. What could the Western Allies do for them with the city deep in the Russian zone of Germany? And so much else was at stake here, otherwise the Western Allies might have given the heap of rubble to the Soviets, evacuating key people of their sectors; that would have been that. The city was a symbol of the division of Germany. Its continued independence, at least the independence of the British, French, and American sectors, gave evidence of the will power of the Western nations on the whole German question and even more: if Berlin went completely to the Russians, all Germany could follow, and such a procession of calami-

ties might collapse Western Europe and perhaps, even probably, bring down the British and wreck the world position of the United States.

At the outset in 1945 the victorious Anglo-Americans had no clear idea of what to do with Berlin nor for that matter Germany. Until near the end of the war President Roosevelt had avoided planning and once wrote Secretary of State Hull that "I dislike making detailed plans for a country which we do not yet occupy."[2] War's end had seen the division of Germany and similar division of Berlin. The French obtained a zone in the western part of the country carved out of the zones of Britain and the United States, and in Berlin out of the British sector. Otherwise the Allies had no German policy. It was said that the British attitude toward Germany was dominated by fear, the French by national honor, the American by desire to go home. There was vague talk of internationalization of the Ruhr. The governing Joint Chiefs of Staff paper which was the skeleton of the American occupation, JCS 1067, showed a mixture of humanity and hardness toward the former enemy, with some traces of the Morgenthau Plan for the pastoralization of Germany. The Western Allies believed the Germans guilty of aggression. Nazi Party membership of course appeared as collaboration with the Hitler regime, not forced enrollment to obtain or hold a livelihood. Even nonparty Germans seemed guilty of something—"collective guilt." The Western Allies felt that Germany after 1945 needed the "de" treatment: demilitarization, decentralization, denazification, general decontamination.

Russian policy showed no such negative aims. Upon entering Berlin the Russians put up the clever poster about "Hitlers come and go, but the German people goes on." The Soviets refused to blame the average German burgher or peasant or his wife or children for the excesses of Adolf Hitler, despite agreement with the doctrine of unconditional surrender set out at Casablanca in 1943 and all that doctrine implied for the collective guilt of the German people. The Russians proved unable or unwilling to control their soldiery before, during, and immediately after the victory, and the wanton behavior of individual Russians in all Eastern Europe, occupied German areas not least, stamped itself in the memory of Germans and East Europeans for a generation, despite the kind poster about the German people. Still, the principle of a community of interest between the Russian people and German people, forgotten in practice, appeared in propaganda at the moment of Russian liberation of Germany and was the foundation of Russian policy in succeeding months and years.

Russian tactics initially confused the Western powers, who innocently thought a joint occupation would take care of everything. The West believed that the Allied Control Council and the Berlin Kommandatura, each with four-power representation, could govern Germany and Berlin. The Soviets proved uncooperative. They refused to allow food from their rich agricultural zone to go to the Western zones, and willingly watched the Western Allies import, via the Byrnes Agreement of the US and Britain, several hundred million dollars worth of food for the Ger-

mans. All the while they spoke enthusiastically of German unity, with proper (overwhelming) representation of suitably democratic (communist) elements. The German central government could administer conquered Germans for benefit of the Soviet Union. The Western Allies were not keen on complete German unity, wishing at the most a loose central government. They wanted to emphasize the old nineteenth-century provincial elements in the country, and avoid centralization which could again produce a major war machine. This was particularly the view of the French who, having been excluded from the Big Three meeting at Potsdam in 1945, did not feel bound by the Potsdam agreements.

The Americans at last lost patience, after failure of the Moscow Conference in April, 1947.

The meeting of the foreign ministers at London (November 25-December 15, 1947) offered distressing confirmation of Russian intransigence. General Clay at London found that when he reported to Secretary Marshall on November 23 everyone was using the same briefing papers prepared for Moscow months before. Partly by chance and part by design the American delegation at London was the same as at Moscow, with exception of Ben Cohen who no longer was in the Department. A new figure, Ambassador Douglas, had taken over the London Embassy. Marshall's staff met each morning with the Secretary and examined the preceding day's discussion of the foreign ministers. Marshall listened to his staff, and after these situation reports made his decisions and set out his moves for the forthcoming

session. The London Conference had seventeen sessions, a fortunate number compared to the forty-four at Moscow. It took two sessions to settle agenda, and then the old East-West argument began, with Molotov refusing settlements and making accusations.

Marshall had his fill of Molotov at Moscow, and at London gave the Russian Foreign Minister little chance to maneuver. At the second session Molotov compared the Soviet position, which he said would lead to a democratic peace, to positions of other countries desiring imperialistic peace. Marshall with all the coldness of which he was a master remarked that Molotov was too intelligent to believe such nonsense. The Secretary refused to "rehash" old charges about Western failure to carry out the Yalta and Potsdam agreements. Molotov charged that the United States had been giving money to the Austrian Government to enslave the Austrian people, which presented Marshall a chance to compare our assistance in Austria with that of the Soviets, which he said only caused trouble. Molotov proved adamant on the German issue, refusing to abandon the Russian claim for huge reparations, refusing to place the resources of East Germany in a pool with those of West Germany—he said Russia could not do that until the Germans had met the reparations bill.

Before long Marshall tired of these statements. He noticed that his colleagues Bidault and Bevin were even more annoyed but chary about calling for adjournment. Bevin, usually a man of no small resolution, appeared reluctant to stand up to Molotov.

When it became evident that the Russian Foreign Minister was stalling the sessions at London, the three Western foreign ministers agreed that at the beginning of the next session Marshall would blast Molotov, after which Bevin would ask for adjournment. "The General fired the blast, but Bevin made no motion. So, after some confusion, the General had to make it." When Marshall asked for adjournment he said with dignity: "When we meet again, I hope that it will be in an atmosphere more conducive to the settlement of our differences."

Incidentally, Marshall's successor at the Department, Acheson, has remarked that ever after the London meeting Marshall disliked Bevin, thinking the Foreign Secretary had let him down. Acheson believes the general made up his mind too quickly. According to Acheson, Bevin was slow-moving, "no split-second operator," easily confused. To a soldier like Marshall, trained to precision, the confusion seemed deliberate.[3]

London set no time or place for the next meeting, and so the Council of Foreign Ministers, the device which the Western Allies at Potsdam hoped would prove the organizing body for European and world peace after the Second World War, fell into suspended animation. Its next meeting occurred in May, 1949, a meeting the Russians asked for, attended by Marshall's successor Acheson.

It was after the 1947 London Conference that the United States and Britain took steps toward economic and political unity in their zones of Germany. In early 1948 the two Western powers began to start

solving the German problem, inviting France and the Benelux countries to a special conference in London. Conversation began on February 23 in India House, a building which the British Government had taken over after Indian independence. General Clay noted that the room for plenary sessions was dominated by great gilt portraits of early British governors and soldiers who had gained India for the empire. "I could not but wonder at their comments if the paintings had come to life and had witnessed British representatives arguing for a progressive relinquishment of their authority and the early establishment of popular government in Germany."[4] Talks lasted until June, with recess during much of March and April. The agreements of June 2 became known as the London Recommendations: coordination of economic policies in the three Western zones; West Germany to have full participation in the Marshall Plan; an international authority including the six London powers and also the Germans to govern the Ruhr. There was a proviso that German state authorities should draft a constitution for a Federal Republic. This latter clause led straight to trouble over Berlin.

2

The Russians watched the London talks with care, and one could almost see the screws tighten on Berlin as the Western powers moved toward German unity.

As the powers knew, Berlin was open to pressure.

About 2,250,000 Germans lived in the city's three West sectors. There were no more than 20,000 Allied military, civilians, and dependents, and Allied military forces were insignificant compared to the two or three dozen divisions the Russians could have summoned to the city within days if not hours after outbreak of trouble. As the commandant of the American sector, Colonel Frank L. Howley, put it in a later book, the two battalions of American troops would have gone down before the Russians "before you could say, 'Politburo!' "[5] Berlin utterly depended on food from the Western zones. The Russians in 1945 had refused to allow their occupied provinces of Saxony and Thuringia to provision the city as in presurrender times.

Allied routes into the city were a problem of special delicacy. When Secretary Hull had gone to Moscow for a Foreign Ministers Conference in October, 1943, one result of that meeting had been a European Advisory Commission with headquarters in London. Its task was to study and recommend ways to meet problems of victory in Germany. By September, 1944, the EAC had set out the three zones which the Allies should occupy. Curiously, the major American concern at this time was not access to Berlin across the Russian zone but rather which nation, United States or Britain, would receive the more valuable northwestern zone containing the Ruhr, and whether the United States would have free lines of communication across whatever area of Germany became the British zone.[6] The Yalta Conference confirmed the general decision for zones and set up the Allied Con-

trol Council. The Allies occupied their zones on June 5, 1945. President Truman in a message to Marshal Stalin on June 14, 1945, had specified the right of free Western access to the city of Berlin. Stalin gave assurance two days later that he would take all necessary measures. American troops in occupation of parts of the Soviet zone in Saxony and Thuringia had withdrawn.

At this time General Clay, who was Eisenhower's deputy to work out arrangements with the Russians for occupying Berlin, made no attempt to put the right of free access in a written agreement. Clay believed that to set out routes in writing would have implied limitation on American rights in a city under shared control of four powers. Previously Ambassador John G. Winant, US representative on the EAC, told James Riddleberger: "I will not demand an access agreement in writing and so offend our Russian allies."[7] Nonetheless, and fortunately for the Western Allies, there was a specific route for air travel to and from Berlin, and this agreement was in writing. On November 30, 1945, the Allied Control Council in Berlin approved a paper providing three corridors of communication between Berlin and West Germany, and flights through these three corridors could proceed without notice. The powers including Russia established a four-power Berlin Air Safety Center in February, 1946. This Center continued to operate through the Berlin blockade of 1948-49, with Russian members coming daily to their offices as if everything were normal.

Meanwhile the Western Allies discovered a con-

siderable political vigor among Germans in their city sectors. It was a piece of luck that the air routes were in writing, and also that prior to the blockade the Allies had, so to speak, made their peace with the people of their sectors and obtained political support against the Russians. It would have been useless to have air access to the city only to find the people of Berlin against the West or else—the danger in 1945 and early 1946—politically indifferent.

The West made understandable but foolish mistakes in the first months of occupation as British, French, and Americans sought to get along with the Russians. Perhaps the most unfortunate mistake was the West's initial attitude of indifference. Berliners in mid-1945 had looked forward to Western troops in the city, anticipating protection against the wild looting and raping by Russian troops in the first days of victory. They found the Western soldiers coldly neutral. If Berliners complained because of some Russian brutality they were apt to learn that Germans had it coming after the Nazi regime. The first few months of occupation saw the city politically stunned. The Russians went rapidly ahead, setting up their men in key positions in city government and infiltrating the police.

But by summer and autumn of 1946 they were getting serious German opposition supported by fed-up Western troops. The Russians tried to take control through a postwar coalition party, the Socialist Unity Party (SED). Old-line Socialist Party members asked support of Western sector commanders and the latter supported the old Social Democratic Party

(SPD). The climax of this maneuvering came in a city election on October 20, 1946, when of some 2,300,000 Germans in Berlin entitled to vote there was a turnout of 92 per cent and a massive vote in favor of the Social Democrats (SPD) and against the Russian puppet party (SED).

Russian authorities resorted increasingly to hostility and force against the Berliners and their Western sponsors. They spread rumors that Western troops would withdraw and inspired the West's commanders to deny the rumors which gave rise to new rumors. One American general said maladroitly that in case of dire emergency the Army could supply its personnel by air but that responsibility for feeding the civil population rested on the Russians.[8] At the beginning of 1948 Russian coal deliveries to the Western sectors stopped, an ominous signal. On January 24, 1948, the Russians detached civil coaches from Allied military trains. Early in March, US Commandant Howley reported to General Clay that he was concerned that the Soviets intended to: first, destroy the elected Berlin government; second, break up the Berlin four-power Kommandatura; third, take steps to drive the Western powers out of Berlin.[9] On March 20 the Russian military governor walked out of the Allied Control Council. Arrests of Americans entering the Soviet sector became frequent, 93 detained in the first half of 1948; in many cases the Russians held Americans for hours under humiliating conditions in cells with German criminals and occasionally made them clean the floors and walls.

The atmosphere had clouded in the Allied Control

Council where General Clay found Russian statements longer and Western replies shorter. In March, 1948, "I felt instinctively that a definite change in the attitude of the Russians in Berlin had occurred and that something was about to happen. From Sokolovsky down there was a new attitude, faintly contemptuous, slightly arrogant, and certainly assured."[10] At this time—precisely on March 5, 1948—Clay cabled the director of Army intelligence: "For many months, based on logical analysis, I have felt and held that war was unlikely for at least ten years. Within the last few weeks, I have felt a subtle change in Soviet attitude which I cannot define but now gives me a feeling that it may come with dramatic suddenness."[11] This was the time when the United States confronted sending troops to Palestine because of threatened disorder when the British gave up the mandate in mid-May, and Secretary Forrestal had to admit that the American Government could not send more than a division anywhere without partial mobilization.[12]

Clay had no troops for a showdown. If he allowed women and children of Army personnel to leave Berlin it would wreck the morale of Germans who had to stay. Something was going to happen and he sensed it might be war. At the end of March he decided to send a train with a few armed guards through the Soviet zone, hoping to avoid the increasingly irritating measures of Russian surveillance. The Russians sidetracked the train, which had to return ignominiously a few days later. In what became a famous teleconference with the Department of the

Army on April 10, 1948, Clay continued to press for action: "We have lost Czechoslovakia. Norway is threatened. We retreat from Berlin. When Berlin falls, western Germany will be next. If we mean . . . to hold Europe against Communism, we must not budge. . . . I believe the future of democracy requires us to stay. . . . This is not heroic pose because there will be nothing heroic in having to take humiliation without retaliation."[13]

The crisis soon was upon him. Early in June the London Recommendations appeared, to the delight of people of West Germany, to the disgust of the Russians. (Berliners were unhappy for the Recommendations did not include the city in the proposed West German Government.) At the same time the Western powers decided on a long overdue currency reform and announced that on June 18 Germans in their zones—not in Berlin—must exchange Reichsmarks, ten for one, for newly printed Deutsche marks. A hasty negotiation followed in Berlin where the Allies wished to introduce their currency but maintain it side by side with the old currency. The Russians decided upon a Soviet-zone currency reform at a ratio of ten to one, and announced that their currency would be the sole money in Berlin. Currency control meant economic and probably political control. On June 23 the West announced introduction of the new Deutsche mark of the West zones, marked B for Berlin, into the Western sectors of Berlin. Next day, June 24, by chance the anniversary of Germany's attack on Russia seven years before, the Russians began a land blockade of

Berlin's West sectors occupied by the French, British and Americans.

It was a move also well-timed in reference to American domestic politics. June 24 was the day the Republican National Convention then in session in Philadelphia nominated Governor Thomas E. Dewey of New York as Republican candidate for President of the United States. Odds at the time of course were heavily against reelection of President Truman.

3

At the very outset of the blockade General Clay wanted to send an armored convoy to Berlin. The Joint Chiefs of Staff considered the proposal and apparently it went to the President. Meanwhile Clay on June 25, on his own, without asking Washington, ordered an airlift, using planes available in Europe. Next day, June 26, President Truman consented to this decision already taken.

To try an airlift took considerable nerve. Plenty of expert opinion said that such a measure would not supply Allied troops, civil personnel, and the Germans. Before the blockade the West had shipped in 6,000 tons of coal a day—how could a bulky, dirty, combustible item come into Berlin by air? The Western powers had coal stocks in the city good for 45 days. Food stocks would last 36. The United States had over 100 C-47 planes with 2½-ton cargo capacity. British resources were limited; the French had just a few planes. The Joint Chiefs of Staff desired eighteen

months to prepare for a Russian challenge in the city.[14] General Hoyt S. Vandenberg of the US Air Force told President Truman that to supply the Germans in Berlin would weaken our ability to wage strategic war. General Clay had no confidence in the airlift. When announcing the experiment to the editor of the *Neue Zeitung* in Berlin he said as he snapped his fingers: "I wouldn't give you that for our chances."[15]

The American Government went ahead. Secretary Marshall asserted the United States right to be in Berlin: in a statement to the press on June 30, 1948, he said that "We are in Berlin as a result of agreements between the Governments on the areas of occupation in Germany, and we intend to stay." In a note of July 6 to the Soviet Ambassador he announced "the right of free access to Berlin. This right has long been confirmed by usage. . . . In order that there should be no misunderstanding whatsoever on this point, the United States Government categorically asserts that it is in occupation of its sector in Berlin with free access thereto as a matter of established right deriving from the defeat and surrender of Germany and confirmed by formal agreements among the principal Allies. It further declares that it will not be induced by threats, pressures or other actions to abandon these rights. It is hoped that the Soviet Government entertains no doubts whatsoever on this point."[16]

A diary note by President Truman, made about this time, shows how this message to the Russians well represented the Administration's views:

Have quite a day. See some politicos. A meeting with General Marshall and Jim Forrestal on Berlin and the Russian situation. Marshall states the facts and the condition with which we are faced. I made the decision ten days ago to *stay in Berlin*. Jim wants to hedge. . . . I insist we will stay in Berlin—come what may. Royall, Draper and Jim Forrestal come in later. I have to listen to a rehash of what I know already and reiterate my "Stay in Berlin" decision. I do not pass the buck, nor do I alibi out of any decision I make.[17]

Coincident with these public and private declarations the Americans brought planes into Germany to break the blockade, and—*mirabile dictu*—proved masters of the "logistics" of such an operation. General Clay was an engineer and had cleared the harbor of Cherbourg. A methodical, crusty officer, he was the man for the new job. He imported Major General William H. Tunner who had supervised the fabled wartime hump ferry from India into China. Planes came from Alaska, Panama, Hawaii, Japan, the Middle East, continental United States. As soon as possible Clay replaced the C-47s with C-54s, the latter with capacity of ten tons, four times that of C-47s. He surveyed the airports in Berlin, the major field being Tempelhof in the American sector, with Gatow in the British sector; he decided on a large landing strip at Tegel in the French sector. Remembering experiences in China in 1943 he employed 20,000 German workers to do construction largely by hand, working round the clock. Rock-crushing

machinery came by air, cut apart by an "acetylene expert" and welded back together after arrival. Clay's engineers said they could ready Tegel in March, Clay insisted on December, which deadline they met.

As for flying coal, that enterprise at first appeared impossible, but ingenuity won out. Clay called General Curtis E. LeMay in Frankfurt and asked, "Have you any planes there that can carry coal?"

"Carry what?" said LeMay.

"Coal," repeated Clay.

"We must have a bad phone connection," said LeMay. "It sounds as if you are asking if we have planes for carrying coal."

"Yes, that's what I said—coal."

Rallying LeMay said stoutly: "The Air Force can deliver anything!"[18]

The coal arrived in sacks wetted down prior to shipment to avoid fire, packed in duffel bags of which there was an excess supply of several million. When the bags wore out Clay arranged for hemp bags and finally strong waterproofed paper bags.

The airlift had only one bad time when it looked as if the operation might not succeed: November and December when half the days were overcast, weather so bad that planes could not land. There was an acute shortage of coal, but when the weather lifted in early January everything worked out.

Clay and his assistants calculated that 4,500 tons of coal, food, and other supplies a day would be minimum for the city. By October, 1948, the average

was close to 5,000. Over the winter, with exception of November-December, the airlift (dubbed by American airmen the "LeMay Coal & Food Co.") pushed up delivery until in one 24-hour period, April 15-16, 1949, Allied planes in 1,398 flights landed a record 12,941 tons. That day planes came in every 61.8 seconds. Altogether the airlift, lasting 321 days from June 24, 1948, until May 12, 1949, delivered 1,592,787 tons, over half a ton apiece for each of the 2,250,000 Berliners in the Western zones. It was a magnificent show. Americans named it Operation Vittles. The ration of the average Berliner rose during the blockade, though one should add that people in the city received only twenty-five pounds of coal with which to keep warm and lived in the latitude of Labrador. Everyone could see planes coming over almost any minute, day and night. "The roar of the airplanes became the recurring motif of the resistance and the pulsation of the life in the besieged city."[19] The thunder of the huge four-motored C-54s underlined, in Soviet as well as Allied parts of the city, the power and generosity and purpose of the West. In a burst of imagination an American flyer undertook Operation Little Vittles, parachuting bags of candy for small Berliners, and soon all Allied flyers were in on the special benevolence.

By spring of 1949 it looked as if the airlift could go on forever. The United States had set up a training ground in Montana where pilots received four-engine flight training with air corridor and approach paths and navigation aids exactly like those in Ger-

many. Americans established the latest radar techniques on Berlin fields, with landings possible under almost unbelievable weather conditions. Safety was remarkably good; the blockade cost the lives of 42 Allied airmen and 24 other individuals but it was a small price in the human currency of the twentieth century. Monetary cost of the operation proved cheap, $137,498,000 to $350,000,000, estimates varying on whether one included the cost of maintaining the military forces involved. As battles go in our time, it was cheaply won.[20]

The political battle went on until the end of the blockade and would last for many, many years thereafter. During the blockade the city administration of Berlin split in two. When communist rowdies made the work of the city Magistrat impossible in the Soviet-occupied sector the democratic parties migrated to a Town Hall in the American sector. An old-line socialist, once a communist, Ernst Reuter, became mayor of West Berlin. The city's morale hardened, and a new Free University of Berlin confronted the communist Humboldt University in the East. Newspapers under Western supervision received permission to print diplomatic documents concerning the Russo-German Pact of 1939—compromising material from the captured German archives which the Western Allies published in their own countries at this time. On March 20, 1949, the three Western city commandants made West marks the only legal tender in West Berlin.

If for the most part the Berlin confrontation brought

a long monotony of tension and strain there were a few lighter moments. Colonel—now Brigadier General—Howley, the attractive and irrepressible American commander in the city, has recounted the Russian difficulty constructing a war memorial at Pankow during the blockade. The Soviets had contracted to a West German builder for a large statue of Lenin, and the German thoughtfully sent over all the material except Lenin's head which he kept as security until he should receive payment for his work in the more valuable West marks. The Russians wanted to pay in East marks and appealed to Howley.

"But we must have the head!" wailed General Kotikov. "How can we unveil the monument next week without it?"

"Too bad," was Howley's reply.

The Russians paid in West marks.[21]

At the outset of the blockade the Americans caught Marshal Sokolovsky's car in a speed trap on an autobahn, and the marshal—whose bodyguard had jumped out to face the Americans with guns—cooled his heels for an hour, with an American gun in the pit of his stomach, until an officer came along and identified him. And there were two other episodes involving Sokolovsky. One related to his house where Howley discovered the heating arrangements were via a gas main which ran through the American sector. Howley turned off the gas. Sokolovsky had to move. The marshal's assistants then foolishly put his furniture in a van and tried to truck it surreptitiously through the American sector, and Howley captured the furniture.

4

Gradually the blockade came to a diplomatically arranged end. Diplomacy had begun months before in the summer and autumn of 1948 when the Americans, British, and French negotiated through their Moscow embassies.[22] The Western powers on July 6, 1948, had sent almost identic notes to the Soviet ambassadors in their own capitals; eight days later the Soviet ambassadors delivered notes in return; then the Western envoys in Moscow sought an interview with Stalin. The first meeting at 9:00 P.M. on August 2 found the Soviet dictator saying that "After all, we are still Allies." Discussion ran on for about two hours when Stalin looked at Ambassador Bedell Smith and asked, smiling, after lighting a cigarette, "Would you like to settle the matter tonight?" It seemed like agreement: the Russians would introduce their zonal currency into all of Berlin, in return for which they would not object to the Allies' carrying out the London Recommendations for a West German government. But Molotov in subsequent days and weeks began to put conditions on the bargain and reduced it to nothing.

A second meeting with Stalin on August 23 began auspiciously: "Gentlemen, I have a new plan," said the mustachioed ruler of Russia. Ambassador Smith said the Western representatives too had a new plan. "Good," rejoined Stalin, "we can compare them." The arrangement again was to introduce Soviet-zone currency in all of Berlin; the Allied Control Council

was to work out details. Technical discussion took place in Berlin during the week of August 31-September 7, but nothing came of it and there was indication that Marshal Sokolovsky had instructions to do nothing.

Ambassador Smith was not surprised, for he felt that both Stalin and Molotov were sure the attempt to break the blockade would fail and had decided to wait for winter and win by Allied default. The Soviets were making the Berlin currency the chief issue but Smith knew better. The issue was West German government: "We all realized this in Moscow, and during our discussions with Stalin and Molotov, I felt quite sure that we could have produced an agreement in fifteen minutes at any time by an offer to abandon the London decisions."[23]

No diplomatic break occurred until after the new year when General Marshall had resigned as Secretary of State and Acheson succeeded him. Toward the end of January, 1949, the European manager of the International News Service, J. Kingsbury Smith, submitted a series of questions to Stalin which the latter answered on January 31. One of Stalin's answers was curious, for he remarked that there would be no obstacle to lifting traffic restrictions in Berlin provided the three Western powers and the Russians lifted them at the same time. No mention of currency, hitherto the nominal Russian reason for the blockade. On February 15, Ambassador Philip C. Jessup in the United Nations asked the Soviet UN representative, Jacob A. Malik, if Stalin's omission of the currency issue was intentional. Malik said he

would inquire. A month later Malik told Jessup the omission was "not accidental." He said the currency issue could be discussed if there were a meeting of the Council of Foreign Ministers to review the entire German problem. Jessup asked if the Soviets contemplated a meeting while the blockade was in progress, Malik said he would refer back to his government, and on March 21 he answered that if there were a meeting of the foreign ministers it would be possible to set a date for lifting the blockade in advance of the meeting. On May 5, 1948, a joint statement in the four capitals—Washington, London, Paris, and Moscow—announced the blockade would go off on May 12.[24]

Just to be sure, the Allies kept the airlift through the summer, stocking Berlin with coal and food in event of a Russian change of mind.

The Soviets had tired of the air demonstration over the city. The meeting of the Council of Foreign Ministers was a face-saving device, for the sessions which began in Paris on May 23 settled nothing.

The blockade's failure had settled something—the Russians failed both to take over the Western sectors of the city and to delay a West German government.[25] The Western sectors of Berlin established their own administration. And on September 1, 1948, well before the airlift was a third over, a Parliamentary Council opened in Bonn, with 65 members named by the *Land* parliaments according to the strength of political parties represented in them. The Council adopted a new West German constitution on May 8, 1949, the fourth anniversary of V-E Day.

Admittedly everything was not settled as well as perhaps it might have been. General Howley was unsure of at least one result and recently has commented: "Yet having won the Battle of the Blockade should not the Western powers have demanded a return of all Berlin to four-power control under a single elected government? Instead a *status quo* agreement at Paris permitted the Soviets and their East Berlin communist government to hold East Berlin, a control which is now dramatized by a wall."[26]

In considering the Berlin airlift another nagging question also stands out. At the beginning of the blockade would it have been possible to have run through an armed convoy from Helmstedt in the US zone and force the Russians to back down, saving the enormous trouble of supplying the city by air, at the same time asserting the right of the Western powers to land access? This possibility had serious discussion at the time, in public print as well as among high United States officials. It came back to prominence fifteen years after the crisis when Ambassador Robert D. Murphy published his remarkable memoir, *Diplomat among Warriors*. Murphy related the debate among American officials, asserting that President Truman was willing to force the issue but had no support among members of the American military establishment including Secretary Marshall who was vigorously against it. Murphy and General Clay felt strongly on the subject, and even in long restrospect Murphy believed he had made a mistake by not resigning when the Administration ignored his advice to punch a convoy through from Helmstedt.

I suffered anguish over this decision of our government not to challenge the Russians when they blockaded Berlin, and I still deeply regret that I was associated with an action which caused Soviet leaders to downgrade United States determination and capability and led, I believe, to the subsequent Communist provocation in Korea. . . . When the year-long blockade finally was lifted, the American press and public hailed the outcome as a great victory for the Western powers. But I was unable to accept that pleasing interpretation. The success of the Airlift provided a heady sense of triumph, but the Washington policy-makers actually had limited themselves to an experiment which merely proved that it was possible to keep alive a great modern city by the use of air transport alone. Few observers seemed to realize that our decision to depend exclusively upon the Airlift was a surrender of our hard-won rights in Berlin, a surrender which has plagued us ever since.[27]

In his memoir Murphy remarked that during the crisis no American official mentioned the atomic bomb which the Russians then did not have.

Even so, it does seem that Murphy's proposed course would have been risky and indeed carried grave danger. Ever since 1945 and invention of atomic weapons there has been acute danger in going to the brink of war. This is not to deny the occasional need of brinkmanship but any diplomat skirting the edge should do so advisedly. At least some people would argue that only in the gravest of crises

should there be "a punch-through at Helmstedt" and that any diplomatic or pseudo-diplomatic arrangement such as an airlift is far preferable. Stalin by testimony of his successor Khrushchev was a narrowminded despot and in his last years may have been, from psychic or physical reasons or both, verging on insanity. Would it have been smart (diplomatic, one might say) to confront such a man in a showdown at Helmstedt, at a time when the United States had no land armies comparable to the hordes of the Soviet Union, when all that Russian soldiers needed to get to the Channel was shoes, when atomic bombs on Russia would not have delayed the occupation of Europe and might have presented a situation where the United States would have to atom-bomb the Russian forces in Europe? How much better to have sent the planes soaring over Berlin with food and coal, displaying in more modest fashion the physical and idealistic power of the West.

CHAPTER NINE

LATIN AMERICA

1

IT IS A truism to say that Latin America has long
been a special concern of the United States—that
the largest and most powerful of the American republics has found itself deeply involved in Western
Hemisphere affairs. At the turn of the present century, and as late as the 1920s (Mexico, Nicaragua),
the United States concerned itself /closely with Latin
American affairs. In the 1930s the Second World War
approached and Washington statesmen helped arrange and took large part in several important conferences, notably at Montevideo (1933) and Rio de
Janeiro (1936), intended to insulate the American
republics from the coming conflict. During the war
most of Latin America declared war against Germany
and Japan. Brazil and Mexico sent military contingents abroad, and the Cuban navy cooperated
against German submarines in the Gulf of Mexico.
The United States made a lend-lease effort to re-
arm all the Latin American nations with exception
of Panama and Argentina (the latter government
did not declare war until March 24, 1945); lend-
lease amounted to $491,456,432.64. At the end of the
war there was feeling in Washington that it might
be possible both to send down surplus Army stocks

and simultaneously increase by treaty the wartime cooperation so evident in such Latin American pledges as the Act of Chapultepec of March 6, 1945. The Act, American participation in which was by executive agreement, had gone beyond the Act of Havana of July, 1940, asserting that aggression against one American state was aggression against all and that until victory each nation would repel any aggression according to its own choice of means. The Act of Chapultepec proposed a permanent treaty after the war.

Problems confronting Secretary Marshall in Latin America arose out of need to follow up the Act of 1945, the desire of Latin American nations for American arms, and perhaps most important the feeling of Latin American statesmen and peoples that the republics south of the Rio Grande needed large economic assistance from the United States. It seemed difficult to argue against this latter feeling in the same period, 1947-48, when Europe was getting billions from the Marshall Plan. The Latins wanted a plan too. Was the United States Treasury running out of dollar bills (as US officials hinted broadly)? Nonsense, for everyone knew those *norteamericanos* had plenty of dollar bills. In case of need they could just "print some more, as we do." American officials could have pointed out that Latin America had only begun to run out of funds, and had plenty on hand as of very recent times; the Latin nations had enjoyed a golden wartime opportunity, booming trade in manufactures and agricultural produce, and accumulated huge dollar and sterling balances. During

this war boom Latin American statesmen thoughtfully made spectacular promises of postwar welfare and industrial plans. But instead of sticking to some of the more earthly plans and tightening up on imports if need be, their governments at the end of the war announced virtually that every man was a king and entitled to the best of all worlds: the postwar era witnessed a freewheeling effort, so long as the money lasted, to carry forward the ambitious plans and at the same time import shiny new American cars and refrigerators and deep-freezes and all those other sure symbols of American degeneracy. Hard-currency balances tumbled. Then there was a little Latin misfortune in this postwar business: inflation in the United States and England cut the value of the balances. By 1947 the Latin Americans were in a bad mood, rather angry, sure of another Yankee conspiracy to take off their life blood for the benefit of Wall Street and American life blood. Secretary Marshall faced the fair-sized order of telling his expectant Latin colleagues that he could offer no Marshall Plan for their part of the world and, at the same time, asking for a security pact. Meanwhile Congress foolishly delayed enacting legislation which would permit the State Department to negotiate contracts to dispose of surplus military hardware. No arms, no money, only a security pact.

Everything was complicated by the behavior of the government of Argentina. This distinctly "have" nation of Latin America had profited enormously from the war, when it continued its record as a "bad neighbor" by failing to take a stand against Nazi

Germany until the very last moment and then turned against the Axis only to obtain an invitation to the San Francisco Conference of the United Nations, a move President Truman characterized as an effort "to get in on the gravy train."[1] From the end of the war the Argentinians because of their great exports of beef began to profit from the peace. They might have assisted their less fortunate neighbors of the Hemisphere. They gave away little or nothing and frightened their nearest neighbors by talking about some sort of commonwealth of the River Platte which, the neighbors believed, meant Argentinian imperialism. The United States found Argentinian statesmen difficult. The Argentinians perhaps hoped to hide their own hemispheric delinquencies by attacking the United States.

The United States had taken a strong stand against Colonel Juan D. Perón, whose domination of the Argentine Government toward the end of the war ensured a refuge for statesmen, pseudostatesmen, and assorted criminal types who found Europe inconvenient. All kinds of fascist and Nazi sympathizers —including, as it turned out, the late Adolf Eichmann—hurried to Argentina. Ambassador Spruille Braden spoke openly throughout the Argentine in criticism of Argentinian policies. Braden in late 1945 went back to Washington as Assistant Secretary of State for Latin American Affairs and under his inspiration the State Department published a "blue book" detailing the fascist-Nazi nature of the Argentine Government while Perón was running for election as President in 1946. It asserted that Argentina,

with which the United States still maintained diplomatic relations, was virtually unworthy of belonging to the Pan American Union. Perón won handily, partly on a claim of American "intervention." President Truman, under fire because of the Braden affair, began to hear from constituents such as one Lyman W. Sherwood, who wrote in a letter of September 17, 1946:

I have the honor to remind you of the occurrence with Spruille Braden when he publicly interfered in the politics of Argentina with the result that he naturally elected the man he wished to defeat. Any precinct captain in Missouri or anywhere else knows that the greatest blessing a candidate can have is an attempt from someone outside the district, particularly an unpopular or suspected person from outside the district, to come out against him. Any amateur, any beginning politician, knows it. Yet Braden committed this colossal blunder. . . . Why not fire him?[2]

Argentine-United States relations became complicated in the extreme, and this all closely concerned the proposed hemispheric security pact championed by the United States. In Buenos Aires the new American Ambassador, George Messersmith, a brilliant career Foreign Service officer, was recommending acceptance of Perón. As one of his Embassy assistants told him, "Our policy has been developed by, or under the control of, officers of the Government who do not understand the basic motivating forces of

the Argentine temperament. Thus, due weight has not been given to the isolationism engendered by Argentina's geographic position, nor to the Argentine arrogance which, seeing itself as the largest frog in the only visible puddle, assumes its pre-eminence with respect to all the puddles beyond the horizon." It was an open secret in Washington and Buenos Aires that Messersmith and Braden were at daggers drawn over policy toward Argentina. Letters between them passed via the diplomatic pouch addressed to "Dear George" and "Dear Spruille," but it was a strained correspondence. President Truman found Braden annoying, for when Messersmith saw Truman early in 1947 the President "used some very strong language with regard to Braden. I merely observed that the whole matter was bigger than any individual and that I did think that Braden had done enough harm." When Marshall became Secretary of State all observers expected that one of the antagonists would go. On two occasions Messersmith called on Admiral Leahy in the White House and poured out his troubles with Braden, and hoped for better things under Marshall. Messersmith saw Marshall in January, 1947, but the Secretary refused to discuss Argentina until after the Moscow Conference of Foreign Ministers. Messersmith returned to Buenos Aires as Ambassador; Braden stayed on as Assistant Secretary.[3]

President Truman announced on June 3, 1947 that the United States was ready to consult the other republics of America, including Argentina, preparatory to drawing up a mutual defense pact. Within two days the President accepted the resignations of both

Braden and Messersmith. Everything seemed in readiness for the new pact. The inter-American conference
was scheduled to meet in Brazil.[4]

2

The Inter-American Conference for the Maintenance of Continental Peace and Security opened at
the Quitandinha Hotel in Brazil's summer capital of
Petropolis on August 15, 1947, and proved an interesting affair if only because of its physical arrangements. The Quitandinha! The youthful Miss Margaret
Truman, on hand for the conference, later wrote
of the hotel that "It is so fabulous that no description
could be adequate and I will forgo the effort."[5] One
of the American delegates, Representative Sol Bloom
of New York, wise denizen of one of the world's
largest cities, did not find the hotel so fabulous.
Acquainted with hotel keeping and the peculiar
chicaneries of large international conferences, he
quickly decided the Quitandinha conference was a
racket. First thing that caught his eye was the time
of year for the conference, August, the Brazilian
winter, no time to go to Quitandinha, for that vast
country boardinghouse usually filled up in the Brazilian summer—December, January, February. Bloom
decided the hotel management had fallen on evil
days; the reputedly nine-million-dollar hotel had
opened in 1943 as a roulette palace, but a reform
wave had swept Brazil and the hotel threatened to
go under; he suspected some devilish arrangement
between the hotel and government to trap the inter-

national conference for perhaps a total of two to three million dollars in outrageous charges. Sure enough, charges were steep, indeed alpine, perhaps himalayan. Lunch was a minimum three dollars, whether eaten or not. Bar bills bordered on the catastrophic: when Bloom used his own whisky for a small party he received a bar bill of fifty-seven dollars, seventeen of it for soda and potato chips and the other forty for his own whisky. Goodnaturedly he recalled the quip of his late friend Diamond Jim Brady that it was fun to be a sucker if one could afford it.[6]

As for diplomatic business of the conference, some slight difficulty appeared over the agenda but the United States won out. The Latin American republics wanted a Marshall Plan for the Western Hemisphere. In an address to the conference on August 20, Marshall discouraged talk of economic questions, calling attention to heavy burdens of the United States in Europe and the Far East. He hinted that Latin Americans might help the rest of the world rather than ask help. He promised to discuss economic questions on some other occasion, maybe a special conference later in 1948. There was some fear over a show of bad temper by the Cubans, angry because the United States had attached to the latest sugar act (a domestic piece of legislation, of course) a clause positing a decrease in a country's sugar quota if that country discriminated against American private business interests. Prior to the Rio Conference, Marshall had written a diplomatic letter to President Truman stating that it was incorrect to interpret this section of the sugar act as an unfriendly move against

foreign powers and the Cuban Government managed to contain any bad humor at Rio.

The United States attained almost everything it wished. The Rio Pact went farther than the Act of Chapultepec. It stipulated that in case of a dangerous "fact or situation" short of armed attack the parties would meet in special consultation and decide what to do. And under the new treaty there would be not merely a right—as in Chapultepec—but an obligation to assist an American state if attacked. The new instrument retained the permissive character that marks most of the Western Hemispheric treaty structure. If one surveys the terms of later general security treaties, of which the Rio Pact was the prototype (North Atlantic Treaty, Southeast Asia Treaty, adherence to obligations of the Central Treaty Organization of the Middle East), Rio was not altogether impressive. The big question at Rio was *how* to reach decision for action. The Argentine Government stipulated for unanimity, the usual practice in the inter-American system; but such procedure was no foundation for a collective security treaty, for any nation could veto action, reminiscent of the *liberum veto* of prepartition Poland and more recently of the Russian veto in the UN Security Council. Most participants at Rio favored decisions by two-thirds majority vote. The United States and the larger Latin American states except Argentina favored this arrangement, save that the decision should not bind the minority, perhaps themselves. By the time the conference opened the United States had measured the possibilities and found a

formula which would obtain almost everything momentarily possible. This was to agree to the two-thirds vote "with the sole exception that no state shall be required to furnish armed forces without its consent." Such a form of words would please Latin American countries and guarantee passage by the United States Senate and anyway it was difficult to imagine a military action against a non-American or a large American country without United States participation.

The chief virtue of the Rio Pact was that its machinery could operate outside the Russian veto in the UN Security Council, in accord with a latitudinarian interpretation of the UN Charter's Article 51 which had set out that "Nothing in the present Charter shall impair the inherent right of individual or collective self-defense . . ." At San Francisco in 1945, Senator Vandenberg, present at Rio in 1947, had insisted upon Article 51 largely because it would permit a security pact with the republics of Latin America. Vandenberg at San Francisco had waxed wordily eloquent over Article 51 and his thoughts on that occasion approximated his flying spirit at the Quitandinha Hotel:

we have found a sound, practical formula for putting regional organizations into effective gear with the global institution. . . . In my view, we have infinitely strengthened the world organization by thus enlisting . . . the dynamic resources of these regional affinities . . . We weld these regional king-links into the global chain.

One of these king-links is particularly dear to the hearts of twenty-one Republics in this Western Hemisphere. It is a precious inheritance with fifty years of benign history behind it. . . . We in the Americas are deeply proud of it. We in the Americas are profoundly attached to it. . . . We here [in Article 51] recognize the inherent right of self-defense—whether singly or collectively—which permits any sovereign state among us or any qualified regional group of States, to ward off attack pending action by the parent body [the United Nations].[7]

Some individuals in the United States, anticipating the Truman Administration's use of Article 51 for a European security pact, made a large outcry in 1947 against this "betrayal" of the UN by their own country. One can only conclude that it was fortunate for the North Atlantic Treaty of 1949 that the Administration could set a precedent for favorable interpretation of Article 51 with the less politically sensitive Rio Treaty.

The Inter-American Treaty of Reciprocal Assistance was signed at Rio de Janeiro on September 2, 1947, with considerable fanfare. President Truman paid a visit to Brazil to address the conference's closing session.

Incidentally, it is curious to recall that during this South American visit Truman came dangerously close to plunging down a mountainside in an automobile. His death would have made Joe Martin, Speaker of the House, the new President. Martin in his memoirs

remarks that he probably would have appointed Herbert Hoover as Secretary of State.[8]

The treaty floated through the Senate, championed by Senator Vandenberg who for the occasion brought out some of his most florid oratory, his best mixed metaphors. His speech was a grammarian's nightmare. He said we had "reknit the effective solidarity" of the Hemisphere; we had "sealed" a New World peace pact "which possesses teeth." He called the pact a "milestone of incalculable importance upon the highroad to a happier and safer world." He gazed on "the finest flower that has yet stemmed from the peace hopes planted in the United Nations Charter at the Golden Gate." He overwhelmed even the considerable sentiments of his fellow Senators. The vote was 72 to 1.

The pact went into effect a year later upon ratification by the requisite number of signatories. Eventually all twenty-one republics adhered.

3

The conference at the Quitandinha was a special session. During Marshall's secretaryship also occurred a regular meeting of the republics, the Ninth International Conference of American States, at Bogotá in 1948. The meeting was announced for January, but postponed until March 30 so the Colombian Government might clean up the capital city to receive its guests with dignity and éclat.

There was not much advance indication that this conclave would bring dramatic violence, and Sec-

retary Marshall had so many things on his mind in early 1948 that he must have thought about Bogotá only on fleeting occasions anyway. Sessions of the forthcoming conference were scheduled at the time when the first Marshall Plan appropriation was coming before Congress. The communist coup in Czechoslovakia occurred in February, with violence terribly disquieting to Western statesmen, clear sign of Russian intent to have all Eastern Europe by hook or crook. In those early months of 1948 unrest increased in Berlin, and General Clay in March began to have premonitions of disaster and sent his warning in teleconference with the Department of the Army.

There were some signs of trouble for Bogotá. The State Department press officer, Lincoln White, later declared that the Central Intelligence Agency had warned that a communist plot was afoot, but the Secretary had cast off the advice with salty remarks, refusing to be intimidated.[9] From Bogotá, Ambassador Willard L. Beaulac, a long-time career Foreign Service officer, was sending cables about increasing local unrest and a disquieting drift toward violence.[10] Beaulac had noted the fragile wartime economic growth in Colombia, appearance of the "shirtless ones" in the city, an irresponsible newspaper press, vindictive political parties, too trusting reliance of authorities on Colombia's tradition of democratic rule. During preparation for the conference he circulated about the city and sensed easily the difference between the magnificence of the preparation and the capital's troubled society, economy, and politics.

The government kept its eye on the ideal of inter-

American affairs rather than real substance of domestic affairs, and went ahead with the festive decorations. Next to the airport it put up twenty-one huge flagpoles carrying banners of the sovereign states of the Hemisphere. An interesting group of sculptured naked maidens surrounded each pole at its base. A new multilaned highway bordered by freshly planted trees and shrubs and decorated with precolonial stone figures led into the city. The finest houses were readied for the leading delegates. The capital generally was scrubbed and painted. Simon Bolívar's country house, the Quinta de Bolívar, was restored as nearly as possible to its original condition, and his town house, the Palacio de San Carlos, repaired and refurnished complete with a stately bar.

Such was the atmosphere, or part of it, in which the distinguished guests arrived. Secretary Marshall's plane, a US Air Force DC-4, landed at Bogotá airport on March 29, with no sign of unfriendliness as Marshall walked through a large crowd at the airport, closely followed by Ambassador Harriman and other members of the American delegation. There were even some cheers.

At the first plenary session of the conference on March 31 an immense throng gathered in the Plaza Bolívar facing the Capitol to watch the delegates appear, and polite applause greeted them as they came up in shiny new limousines furnished by the Colombian Government. Meanwhile a small group of men walked along the edge of the plaza toward the Capitol, stopping on occasion to let a conference car go by. As the men approached the Capi-

tol the crowd recognized the leader as General Marshall, Secretary of State of the United States. Ambassador Beaulac, still nervous, noted that an "excited hum arose from the multitude, followed by a mighty cheer."[11]

Marshall addressed the conference at its second plenary session on April 1. "Allow me," he said, "to talk to you frankly regarding the tremendous problems the United States is facing. . . . my people find themselves today faced with the urgent necessity of meeting staggering and inescapable responsibilities—humanitarian, political, financial, and military—all over the world, in Western Europe, in Germany and Austria, in Greece and Turkey, in the Middle East, in China, Japan, and Korea. Meeting these unprecedented responsibilities has demanded tremendous drafts on our resources and imposed burdensome taxes on our people." A Marshall Plan for Latin America was impossible. If Europe were saved, then the economies of all countries including the American republics would be safe.[12]

In subsequent days Marshall usually walked between the American delegation offices and the Capitol, each occasion by a different route. People on the streets recognized him almost instantly and he exchanged courteous greetings with everyone. He liked to see the little children and joked with them in English, sometimes adding snatches of Spanish remembered from Army service forty-six years before in the Philippine Islands. On one occasion he stood in line at a postal substation in a local five- and ten-cent store, waiting to buy some souvenir postage

stamps. The Bogotá press commented enthusiastically on the Secretary's ways.

Then came trouble, when on April 9 the leader of the opposition Liberal Party in the Colombian Senate, a rabble-rouser named Jorge Eliécer Gaitán, was assassinated in broad daylight on one of Bogotá's downtown streets.

To the present time no one knows who did this, and all one can say is that such an act could only have profited the cause of world communism—Gaitán's party would not have killed its leader, and the government party had nothing to gain from such procedure in the middle of a decorous Conference of American States. Unfortunately a mob fell on the assassin, a local drifter and onetime occupant of an insane asylum, and beat him to death before he could explain his inspiration.

No sooner was Gaitán dead than a riot erupted as if prearranged. Leaders of the mob which quickly filled the center of the city seemingly had instruction to break into two kinds of stores, hardwares and liquor establishments, and the shirtless ones availed themselves of dangerous refreshment and pieces of lead pipe and other weapons. From that point onward small groups of men hurried to government offices, equipped with gasoline and tree-spraying apparatus —it was difficult to set buildings on fire in the Colombian capital because they were made of stone, brick, stucco, and tile. There was clear evidence of planning in the equipment of the fire parties. Some persons observed that leaders of the gasoline groups had typewritten lists of buildings to put to the torch.

Soon billowing smoke wrapped buildings in the center of the city, including churches and the city residence of Bolívar. Mobs besieged the presidential palace and the President of Colombia barely got out with his life. The first days of rioting the Colombian Army was nowhere to be seen. The riot occurred at the precise time the Army had dismissed recruits of the previous year and taken on a new and raw group of men; at peak strength after training the Army numbered about 10,000 men scattered over much of the country; at the time of the riot only 600 troops were available in the environs of the capital; so here was another sign, if needed, that the assassination of Gaitán occurred at an extraordinarily embarrassing moment.

The Americans in their Embassy like members of the other foreign delegations stood in danger. Flames entered the Embassy's ground floor, threatening the offices which began on the third story, and there was worry that a paint store on a corner of the building would go up, burning everything to the ground. Rumor had it that leading members of the delegations including Secretary Marshall were to be assassinated. Lieutenant General Matthew B. Ridgway, on hand for what he thought would be a diplomatic conference ("If I ever am called upon to attend a peace conference in that region again, I think I shall carry a revolver . . ."), manned Embassy defenses.[13] In terms of the size of his defense force and its equipment, the scene must have taken him back in memory to early days in the Army. Cots were set up, meals served, equipment counted and ar-

ranged, maps distributed, General Marshall informed of the state of defenses. This preparation was no useless bit of bravado; anything could have happened. Nearly a thousand people lost their lives in the *Bogotázo* or (as Ridgway entitled a chapter in his memoir) "Bogotá in riot time."

Colombian Army contingents at last came on the scene and demonstrators and looters disappeared into the countryside. The wrecked city returned to normal ways and the Ninth International Conference of American States regained its composure in a boys' school near the American Embassy residence. Secretary Marshall arranged for the US Air Force to fly in food for the conference delegates. He imperturbably attended sessions in the new quarters and listened to the reviving inter-American oratory. On April 10 he made a statement that "This situation must not be judged on a local basis, however tragic the immediate results to the Colombian people. . . . It is the same definite pattern as occurrences which provoked strikes in France and Italy, and that is endeavoring to prejudice the situation in Italy, where elections will be held on April 18. . . . this is a world affair—not merely Colombian or Latin American."[14] After the principal agreements were reached, Marshall on April 23 arose unexpectedly from his seat at the sessions, thanked the Colombian Government and conference for courtesies shown the American delegation, and left. He went quickly to the airport and took off for Washington.

The Bogotá Conference (March 30-May 2, 1948) apart from its flaring violence was not memorable

for great legislative results although there was a modest harvest of inter-American resolves and suggestions. The Pact of Bogotá, an extremely intricate treaty on pacific settlement of disputes, was so complicated that seven signatories hastily appended reservations. There never were enough ratifications to bring it into force. The major accomplishment was to rename the institution of inter-American unity the Organization of American States so as to permit inclusion—the effort was unsuccessful—of Canada among Hemisphere republics. According to the new hemispheric Charter, the Inter-American Conference was the "supreme organ" and would meet every five years. The Meeting of Consultation of Ministers of Foreign Affairs, an *ad hoc* assemblage, was to consider "problems of urgent nature." The Council of the OAS formed the executive branch and handled routine in Washington. In crisis it could operate for the foreign ministers. The Pan American Union became the OAS Secretariat.

Such was the end of an odd conference, which in its violence had indicated to the Government of the United States that the erstwhile ally in Eurasia would stop at nothing anywhere to embarrass its new antagonist. It was depressing to realize that even the Western Hemisphere, so long a preserve of United States influence, a backwater of world politics, was not immune from the communist virus. Rioting in Bogotá had cost the communists—and one must surely lay the disorders at their door—little in money or effort. They simply imported enthusiastic supporters from other parts of the Hemisphere, including a

young man from Cuba, Fidel Castro, amalgamated the talents of these footloose individuals with those of local communist sympathizers, and set everyone to work.[15] If trouble could stir so easily in one city, how simple would be manipulation of Latin American politics in other places and on other occasions! It was a depressing fact, and Secretary Marshall en route back to Washington and confrontation of larger troubles in Europe, not to mention the collapsing Nationalist regime in China, must have felt that problems of managing several wartime Theaters of Operations during 1941-45 were much less exigent than being Secretary of State of the world's most powerful democracy in supposedly peaceful postwar years.

CHAPTER TEN

ISRAEL

1

ISRAELI independence was the major Middle Eastern diplomatic issue of the time; of that there can be little doubt. It is not difficult to surmise the motives of the Truman Administration in supporting that independence. There was the large sentimental attraction of a Jewish state after the near-2,000 years of the Diaspora and in particular after the terrible physical obliteration of European Jewry in the Nazi terror. And as everyone knew, the City of New York and generally Eastern seaboard of the United States contained a large Jewish population, and Israeli independence held domestic political importance during the close presidential election of 1948. Unfortunately, when the President in May, 1948, recognized the State of Israel he had not thought out the consequences very carefully, the effect of recognition on diplomacy in the Middle East and elsewhere. "The President's announcement made with inadequate consideration," so Admiral Leahy wrote in his diary on the fateful day, May 14, "leaves many questions unanswered."[1]

One has to go back to the end of the war in Europe when there was an agitation for increasing Jewish immigration to Palestine, then a British-mandated ter-

ritory. In a White Paper of 1939 the British Government had fixed a total of 75,000 Jewish immigrants into Palestine within a five-year period, after which there were to be no more without Arab consent. At war's end about 100,000 refugee Jews were in Europe, and Truman believed they should have the chance to go to Palestine, even though such a disposition of the refugees would be troublesome because of Arab dislike for Jewish immigration. Truman knew he had a problem on his hands, and by October, 1945, was writing privately that "The Jewish and Arab situation in the Near East is a most difficult one and has caused us more difficulty than most any other problem in the European Theater."[2]

The Palestine question now began to pass through a series of investigations, maneuverings, and crises which led to Israeli independence. After pressing the immigration issue with the British, the President received from London a proposal for a commission of inquiry of twelve representative citizens, six American and six British, to take a new and unbiased approach—it was the eighteenth committee of inquiry. The President did not regard the joint group as a stalling device. He wrote to Senator Robert F. Wagner of New York that "I believe that the appointment of the Commission will serve a useful purpose, although I do not intend to decrease my efforts to get some additional Jews into Palestine in the meantime."[3] Unfortunately the commission was a group of innocents —so one of its American members, former Undersecretary of State William Phillips, described its ignorance. Its members went out to the Middle East and

in April, 1946, recommended admission of 100,000 more immigrants but said also that relations of Jews and Arabs in Palestine had become so strained that any attempt to establish independence or statehood for Palestinian Jews would bring civil strife. It recommended continuation of the British mandate and an eventual UN trusteeship. Unsatisfied with the report, President Truman announced the committee's recommendation of 100,000 immigrants and gave the impression the committee favored the Jews.[4] In summer of 1946 the President established a Cabinet committee on Palestine, with deputies to go to London and work out some solution. The so-called Grady Committee, named after its deputy chairman Henry F. Grady, a San Francisco businessman with State Department experience, produced a detailed plan in July, 1946, providing for Arab and Jewish autonomous communities in Palestine under a strong central government which would retain control of Jerusalem, Bethlehem, and Palestine's southernmost section, the Negev. The plan agreed on 100,000 immigrants but advised Arab approval, an impossible condition.

The Jewish Agency for Palestine, official spokesman for the Zionists, with offices in London and Washington, about this time began to conduct devious maneuvers apparently involving someone on the White House staff whom Eliahu Epstein (later Elath), the Agency's Washington representative, denominated in correspondence as "our friend." The year 1946 was full of activity for Agency representatives, official and unofficial. When the Grady Committee recommended two autonomous communities

under a central government, and thus by Agency interpretation "failed," Truman was willing to drop
the whole Palestine business until, apparently (according to a revealing letter by Epstein), Rabbi
Stephen S. Wise talked to him.[5] According to Epstein a factor in changing the President's mind
other than Wise's intervention was the activity of
Republican candidates in the forthcoming elections,
especially in New York. Truman on Yom Kippur,
October 4, 1946, released a White House statement
favoring 100,000 Jewish immigrants to Palestine, a
result of good work by "our friend" who—Epstein
wrote—showed great determination and courage in
attempting to overcome all kinds of tangible and in-
tangible difficulties so as to accomplish the matter at
hand. "Our friend" consulted Epstein frequently in
the critical days preceding the Yom Kippur statement. Epstein had wished the statement addressed
to Chaim Weizmann, head of the Jewish Agency, so
as to raise the Agency's prestige and thereby its
bargaining power with the British Government. This
idea his friend declared had been turned down because of "internal politics." But by the 1946 elections
matters had begun to go the Agency's way. Epstein
remarked how, some years before, candidates for
the House and Senate had to remind many Jews of
the existence of Palestine in order to win their votes.
The Agency representative had an interview with
the British Ambassador, Lord Inverchapel, in itself
a sign of change. The British, Epstein said, were
mobilizing their "stooges" in the United States to criticize and minimize the President's Yom Kippur state-

ment, and James Reston had just published a vicious article in the New York *Times*.

The year 1946 was indeed a year of action. Secretary of the Treasury John W. Snyder was getting letters attempting to connect the British loan with the Palestine problem. One critic thought Snyder should stop payment on the loan. Snyder "urged that we think of the broad economic foreign policy of the United States and not be influenced by issues that should be settled separately."[6]

Meanwhile the British were having to deal with barbaric Jewish violence. The President did speak out plainly against terrorism in Palestine, and in an appeal of June 5, 1947, enjoined Americans not to violate the laws of that mandate. Secretary Marshall inspired this latter document: he had sent over a draft to the President with the following memorandum: "It is realized that the issuance of such an appeal might be unwelcome to certain groups in this country who are actively engaged in facilitating immigration into Palestine in violation of the laws of that country and in encouraging the activities of terrorists."[7] The Jewish welfare organizations were fitting out ships in the United States, such as the *Frederick C. Johnson* at Norfolk, to transport refugees from Europe to Palestine. Undersecretary of State Lovett called the Treasury Department about this matter. The State Department on August 7 wrote the Internal Revenue Bureau about tax exemption of funds paid these organizations—charitable organizations which were combatting the mandate policies of a friendly power. The Bureau replied on September

17 that the matter was under study. The Treasury looked into the business of tax exemption and of Coast Guard inspection.[8] It was difficult to do much.

At last in the year 1947, the time of decision for Greece and Turkey and for India, the British decided to give up the Jewish-Arab responsibility, and on April 2 they handed the Palestine question to the United Nations. The UN voted a special committee on Palestine (UNSCOP) in which none of the great powers received representation. A majority of this committee recommended ending the mandate and creation of two separate states, Jewish and Arab, tied in economic union, with Jerusalem under direct UN trusteeship. The Jews were mildly favorable, the Arabs hostile; the Truman Administration supported the partition plan, so did the Soviet Union. The General Assembly on November 29, 1947, voted 33 to 13, with ten abstentions, to partition Palestine. The British announced they would relinquish the mandate on May 15, 1948.

2

The problem essentially became one of enforcing the United Nations decision, and it was here that the UN decision, fair though it probably was, played into the hands of the Zionists. The United States in 1947-48 was in no position to enforce partition. As Secretary Forrestal wrote in his diary, the government could not have sent abroad more than a division of troops, about 15,000 men, without partial mobilization.[9] Quite possibly the enforcement of the UN

partition plan might take 160,000 soldiers (the help-less British had deployed nearly 60,000 in Palestine). Nor could any other government, or combination of governments, send troops. The issue passed by default to Zionists and Arabs fighting it out in Palestine, with victory within the grasp of the well-armed, well-led proponents of a fully independent state of Israel.

For a while this result was not at all clear. The prospect for a completely independent Jewish state in Palestine clouded over. After the vote for partition the Truman Administration, sensing trouble ahead, took a cautious position. Truman tried to calm down former Secretary of the Treasury Henry Morgenthau in a letter of December 2, 1947:

> I appreciated very much your telegram of November twenty-ninth but I wish you would caution all your friends who are interested in the welfare of the Jews in Palestine that now is the time for restraint and caution and an approach to the situation in the future that will allow a peaceful settlement. The vote in the United Nations is only the beginning and the Jews must now display tolerance and consideration for the other people in Palestine with whom they will necessarily have to be neighbors.[10]

In some respects the spring of 1948, the very threshold of independence, proved the worst time for supporters of a Jewish nation. A major crisis occurred because of the enormous Zionist pressure converging on the White House to get the Truman Administra-

tion to go along with the UN plan of partition, once it became apparent that such a plan without enforcement meant an independent state of Israel. The Zionists pushed too hard. Pressure was so heavy and much of it so crude that it infuriated Truman, who refused to see any Zionists whatsoever. His secretaries referred all inquiries to the United Nations. The future president of Israel, Chaim Weizmann, wanted to see Truman. The President said "no." The national executive vice-president of B'nai B'rith, Maurice Bisgyer, and the president of the organization, Frank Goldman, then put Truman's old haberdashery partner Eddie Jacobson up to calling at the White House. There was nearly a row. "In all the years of our friendship," Jacobson remembered, "he never talked to me in this manner." Jacobson argued tenaciously. Truman abruptly turned around in the presidential swivel chair and started looking out the window. "All of a sudden he swiveled around again, faced his desk, and looked me straight in the eyes and said the most endearing words I ever heard: 'You win, you baldheaded . . . I will see him.'" Unnerved, Jacobson fled to the Hotel Statler and downed two double bourbons, before talking to Bisgyer and Goldman who were awaiting him.[11] During a meeting on March 18 the President assured Weizmann that he, Truman, would go forward with the UN partition plan.

Then the State Department proposed a most unsuitable change in United States policy. The day after Weizmann's visit to the White House, namely on March 19, the American representative on the Security

Council, Senator Warren Austin, announced a new United States proposition for Palestine: a temporary tripartite trusteeship by Great Britain, France, and the United States. This move greatly disturbed Truman, who called in his adviser Clark Clifford to find out what had happened, for it looked as if he had broken faith with Weizmann.[12] Clifford discovered that the State Department some time before had elaborated a procedure whereby if partition according to the UN formula began to appear difficult the United States delegate would propose a tripartite trusteeship. Marshall in a memorandum had approved this tactic. Clifford (and Truman) believed, however, that the State Department contained a good many officers who were anti-Israel and some who were anti-Semitic, and that these men had used the opportunity to present the Truman Administration with a *fait accompli*. Truman told Admiral Leahy that the new policy had come without his permission or knowledge. Leahy added in his diary: "Some of the President's staff have privately expressed an opinion that the fault results from a faulty organization of the Department or an inflated growth of the Secretary of State."[13] The President telephoned Marshall, who was in San Francisco, and the Secretary gave out a statement which tried to stop the uproar caused by Austin's speech, but it was difficult to do much about it.

Weizmann, resident in the Waldorf-Astoria in New York, took ill at this time, although his health was to improve surprisingly after May 14. He wrote the President without result, as witness a letter of April

9 in which he said that "The choice for our people, Mr. President, is between Statehood and extermination. History and providence have placed this issue in your hands, and I am confident that you will yet decide it in the spirit of the moral law." Unfortunately history and providence put his letter in the hands of Truman's private secretary Miss Rose A. Conway. The letter went to the file, with notation by "RAC" of "Not ans'd."[14]

But by the middle of May, 1948, everything came to a crisis and went the way of the Jewish Agency. Recalling the embarrassment of March, Truman now wished to move ahead and recognize Israel as soon as the new state came into existence. Weizmann was urging him to do so. The President talked to Marshall who opposed the idea. A small conference assembled at Blair House on May 12, including Marshall, Lovett, Clifford, and the President. Truman stated the question of recognition. Marshall said it was inadvisable. Clifford argued for recognition. According to Jonathan Daniels' account, Marshall's face flushed. "Mr. President," he said, "this is not a matter to be determined on the basis of politics. Unless politics were involved, Mr. Clifford would not even be at this conference. This is a serious matter of foreign policy determination and the question of politics and political opinion does not enter into it." Recalling this confrontation, Clifford added: "He said it all in a righteous God-damned Baptist tone." Truman that day closed the matter by remarking that "I think we must follow the position General Marshall has advocated."[15]

The matter did not stay closed. Marshall and Lovett seem to have backed down and agreed upon recognition if the State Department could have a few days to consult the British and French. Clifford got the President to insist on immediate recognition.

Eliahu Epstein cabled Moshe Shertok (later Sharett, who became Foreign Minister of Israel) on May 14 and gave the details as he knew them.[16] Clark Clifford that day had telephoned Washington adherents of the Jewish cause that the State Department at noon had agreed to immediate recognition in event it received a prompt request for it. After consultation with Ben Cohen, former Counselor of the Department, a letter was drafted and send to the President and Secretary of State. Clifford demanded a pledge of secrecy, so that Epstein could not consult widely. During the day Loy Henderson of the State Department telephoned to ascertain the boundaries of the new state; Epstein or his colleagues advised that the boundaries were in accord with the UN resolution.

Whereupon when Israel announced national independence at midnight Palestine time, May 15, 1948, and it was 6:00 P.M. May 14, Washington time, the United States recognized Israel *de facto* at eleven minutes after six o'clock. Recognition was on the basis apparently of Epstein's letter from the local office of the Jewish Agency, not from any request from the provisional Israeli Government in former British-mandated Palestine.

Truman in his memoirs recalled his wrath at the Department. He interposed some acid comments about

anti-Semitic people in the State Department: "The Department of State's specialists on the Near East were, almost without exception, unfriendly to the idea of a Jewish state." He had made up his mind, he said, to have no more nonsense from the "striped-pants boys."[17]

3

Some weeks after recognition of Israel there was a distinct offhandedness in the way the President appointed a Special Representative to Israel (this title held until the United States in 1949 granted Israel *de jure* recognition, after which it became possible to nominate an Ambassador). Truman met with his aides on June 22, 1948, and decided to offer the appointment to the outspokenly pro-Israel James G. McDonald, former chairman of the Foreign Policy Association centered in New York City. Secretary Marshall was resting in a Washington hospital. Clark Clifford called McDonald that very afternoon and proposed the post. The President's counsel afterward got in touch with the State Department. Undersecretary Lovett told Forrestal in some pique that "he was called at 4:20 yesterday afternoon [June 22] by Clark Clifford, who said the President had asked him to call up Lovett, and, through him, to name James G. McDonald as Minister *de facto* to the Israel state." Lovett protested McDonald's bias and raised other arguments, and "Clifford said he did not know anything about that but that the President had told him he did not want any discussion

of the matter but to have action followed at once in the form of an announcement that afternoon by the State Department."[18]

Somehow, in subsequent weeks the word got through to McDonald that he was *persona non grata* to the State Department. In *My Mission in Israel* published a few years later he could not hide his own distaste for the Department. Secretary Marshall was nice enough when McDonald presented himself at the Department, but after telling McDonald not to fall into the common practice of sending long dispatches when in most cases brief ones would suffice, he got down to the subject of McDonald's appointment and "told me frankly that he had opposed it, not because he objected to me as a person . . . but because he disliked strongly having such an appointment announced before he could be given an opportunity for consultation or comment." The other people at the Department gave McDonald, the presidential appointee, a chilly welcome. The envoy analyzed his annoyance: "I had been three years in the Graduate School at Harvard and a fourth year abroad on a Harvard Fellowship, but since I had not come up through the Service, I did not wear the old school tie. Probably these disabilities weighed against me and partially explain the Department's failure to be as frank with me as with one of their own."[19]

It was an odd appointment, after a distinctly undiplomatic diplomacy leading to recognition of the Israeli state. McDonald was a deplorable choice, as his book so well reveals, a man who knew that he had

come in at the top, via the White House, and did not object to flaunting this state of affairs.

At risk of saying too much about McDonald one should relate the new envoy's experience in London, en route to his assignment, when he visited Foreign Secretary Bevin. The latter had been furious at Truman for all the maneuvers over Israeli independence, and not the least of Bevin's experiences had been the cat-calling and booing when he was in New York for a conference during the years of agitation for independence. Bevin had been so angry about American policy that he had spoken in Parliament. One can imagine his thoughts when he learned that the first American envoy was coming to pay his respects. When McDonald walked in, the Foreign Secretary put on a better scene than usual. He growled, glowered, talked about President Truman, pounded the table, at times almost shouted, charged that the Jews were ungrateful for what Britain had done for them in Palestine, that they had shot British police and soldiers, hanged sergeants,[20] now were alienating British opinion by their attitude toward Arab refugees. Ambassador Douglas, accompanying McDonald, "put in a remark about the general situation, and Bevin replied in effect that what with the Berlin crisis, and economic troubles, it was just too bad that he and his colleagues had to be bothered with Palestine. There was nothing more to be said. With Bevin muttering civilities, we took our leave."

After the Bevin interview McDonald got quietly angry with the discomfited Ambassador Douglas. The latter gave the impression of being pleased that Mc-

Donald had not argued with the Foreign Secretary. As the two men left Bevin's office Douglas remarked that Bevin was perhaps "slightly unsympathetic" to the Jews. McDonald looked at him but remained silent. McDonald's book later compared Bevin to Hitler and Mussolini. As for Douglas, he remarked testily: "Above all, I think, he wanted the Palestine issue played down, hoping that in return our Government would receive support on some other more 'important' issue."[21]

One must add a last postscript to the present chapter's account of the United States and Israel, that once President Truman decided to recognize Israel there was no longer any doubt of his interest and enthusiasm for the new state. His old friend Jacobson kept up a correspondence with Weizmann which shows the presidential humor about Israel. Jacobson on August 6 wrote of a very long visit with Truman the day before, during which Jacobson asked for a loan to Israel. Truman authorized him to tell Weizmann that he would get action in the very near future. In fact, the President said he would call in "Mr. Marshall" and go to work on it immediately. Jacobson wrote again to Weizmann in November, recalling the hectic months that had passed, and his numerous trips to Washington completely off the record during which Truman always listened to him. Despite the British Foreign Office and the American State Department, he said, the cause had triumphed. Truman, he said, had repeatedly told him not to worry—that there should be no worries—about Israel.[22]

As months passed the President, now basking in

Zionist approval, began to feel very good about Israel, and after the 1948 election he drew some interesting parallels between his recent problems and those of his friend Weizmann. He wrote to Weizmann on the first anniversary of the UN partition resolution. "As I read your letter," went the presidential reply, "I was struck by the common experience you and I have recently shared. We had both been abandoned by the so-called realistic experts to our supposedly forlorn causes. Yet we both kept pressing for what we were sure was right—and we were both proven to be right."[23]

4

Was Israel a political football of the Truman Administration? The record of presidential purpose—not that of the Secretary of State and his assistants, which was anti-Israel—is not altogether clear. Circumstances point to a political decision. There is outright testimony in Forrestal's diary. Forrestal sprinkled his diary notes with remarks about how the American Government gave Palestine to the Jews "for squalid political purposes."[24] In the months before the United States recognized Israel, Forrestal did his best to warn political leaders of the dimensions of the Israel problem. After recognition he wrote the military correspondent of the New York *Times*, Hanson Baldwin, that he had several firm beliefs about the Middle East:

First, as one of the most important segments of our foreign policy this should be dealt with on a bipartisan-nonpartisan basis and not on a vote appeal basis;

Second, there was a very serious question whether, in either peace or war, our economy could function without access to the oil reserves there located;

Third, anybody who permitted this strategic heartland to be dominated by unfriendly political forces would be rendering a vast disservice to the United States and its future.

To these I later added the general observation that anything which drove a wedge between Great Britain and ourselves at this juncture might have the most tragic implications and consequences.[25]

These sensible views he found impossible to advance in the politically charged atmosphere of the time.

There were many indications of the intimate connection between Israel and American politics. Senator J. Howard McGrath, chairman of the Democratic National Committee, told Forrestal that support of the Jewish position was highly advantageous for what was going to be a tough presidential contest in 1948. There was testimony of Truman in a meeting with several State Department envoys to the Middle East late in 1946: at that meeting the President listened courteously to a twenty-minute discourse in favor of the Arabs and said, "I'm sorry, gentlemen,

but I have to answer to hundreds of thousands who are anxious for the success of Zionism; I do not have hundreds of thousands of Arabs among my constituents."[26] Great pressure was exerted on Truman to champion the Jews against the Arabs, so much so that, as he wrote in his memoirs, "I do not think I ever had as much pressure and propaganda aimed at the White House as I had in this instance."[27] Undersecretary Lovett told Forrestal the same thing, that the pressure from American Jewry was almost unbearable. The President received at the White House in the years 1947-48, at the height of the Palestine agitation, 48,600 telegrams, 790,575 cards, and 81,200 pieces of other mail. For unsolicited mail it was a record. Forty per cent of mail on Palestine in 1947 came from New York State, and 48 per cent in 1948.[28]

There remains the countertestimony of John M. Redding, publicity director of the Democratic National Committee in 1948. "We have the Zionist Jews in the office every day," Redding told Truman, "and the pressure is building up a terrific head of steam." According to Redding, the President replied, "It's no use putting pressure on the [Democratic National] committee. The Palestine issue will be handled here. And there'll be no politics involved." Redding's book has numerous remarks about the President's resolution on this score.[29]

It may be that the final act of Truman, if favorable to the Jews in Israel, came only after pressure and political advantage coincided with principle, only after the President decided that a Jewish state was

the right and proper result in the Middle East. Truman's makeup had a dogged persistence, evident on many occasions during his presidency. He was not easily moved in large matters. On his desk was a quotation from Mark Twain in the author's own hand: "Always do right. This will gratify some people and astonish the rest."[30] Truman felt keenly that foreign relations were no place for political maneuver, and it is difficult to believe that he championed a solution for the Middle East that was for his personal advantage alone; he must have believed it to the advantage of his country.[31]

Another explanation of the President's conviction that he had handled "the Palestine issue" outside of politics is that when he considered his nonpolitical actions, as he described them, he was thinking not so much of recognition as of a later problem. At the height of the presidential campaign Secretary Marshall, then in Paris, announced himself in favor of the Bernadotte Plan, the formula for Palestine peace advanced by the Swedish diplomat and UN mediator. The plan was for a division of Palestine in a way which the Jews disliked—the Negev would go to the Arabs, and the Jews would receive Western Galilee. The Jews wanted both, despite the UN partition plan which proposed that they should receive only the Negev. They had, of course, occupied both areas. Truman was on his famous whistlestop trip when word of Marshall's statement came to him in Oklahoma City. His advisers wanted him to speak out against the Secretary of State's position. Truman, out of his deep loyalty to Marshall, perhaps also from desire to

keep the Palestine issue out of politics, demurred. Later he talked to Marshall, who said that he, Marshall, had wanted to make both sides in Palestine see that the UN boundaries suggested in the resolution of November, 1947, were not fixed and permanent. Truman decided, again, to say nothing. Then Governor Dewey came out with a strong statement accusing Truman of welshing on Israel's boundaries. Truman answered with a general comment in a speech at Madison Square Garden. That was that.[32] In retrospect the President probably thought he had kept Palestine out of politics because of his restraint in this business of the Bernadotte Plan.

In extenuation of Truman's decision on Israel, whatever the reasoning behind it, one must say that creation of Israel in 1948 came before the great East-West struggle, the cold war, had reached its starkest confrontations. It occurred in the year of the beginning of the Berlin blockade, two years before the Korean War. The United States was just becoming alert to the power-political possibilities of the cold war and found itself not yet able to calculate the risks of Israeli independence.

It was not possible at the time to see that Israeli independence would unsettle the entire Middle East and raise political problems of an explosive nature in this crossroads of three continents. With independence an Israeli-Arab war began which went on inconclusively for a year and ended in an uneasy armistice. Weaknesses of the Arabs, apparent in the war, brought revolution in Egypt in 1952. A caravan of Middle Eastern calamities, beginning in the mid-

1950s with appearance in the area of Russian arms, purchased by Egypt, led to nationalization of the Suez Canal in 1956 and gravely embarrassed the North Atlantic Treaty Organization: Suez produced a spectacle in the United Nations, of the United States and Russia siding against Britain and France. The Suez crisis left a heritage of distrust between the United States and Britain and France that lasted for years. Among the Arabs its confusions begat the Lebanon crisis of 1958 when a division of American troops landed in the East Mediterranean after murderous revolts in Lebanon and Iraq and the near breakup of the Western alliance structure in the Middle East, the Baghdad Pact. These events are fit subject for discussion in later volumes of this Series. In large part they stemmed from dissensions incident to creation of the State of Israel in 1948. Americans, troubled with disorder all over the globe, could take little comfort in the intensely burning antagonism of the Arabs for Israel. Nearly a million Arab refugees would sit sullenly in their tents and hovels ringed about Israel, mulling the iniquities of their displacement. The United States, they rightly concluded, had sponsored this malignant and malevolent (they believed) foreign state on their ancestral soil. In their myopic righteousness they easily regarded the Jews as their prime enemies. Anyone else who gave the Arab nations help, such as the Russians in the mid-1950s, could become their friends.

CHAPTER ELEVEN

CHINA

FROM THE Middle East, and Latin America, one turns to another concern of American foreign policy during Marshall's secretaryship—China (for problems of Japan and other Asian countries, see volume XVI of the present Series). To chronicle American diplomacy toward China in 1947 and 1948 involves a statement roughly of the disintegration in China during those two years and then some commentary on several moves by or toward the United States in hope of changing policy. The latter remained much as Marshall stated it upon return from China to become Secretary of State.

1

Disintegration ran on to virtual collapse of the Nationalist government at the end of the year 1948, and involved everything—finances, army, administration. One writer describing the financial debacle remarked: "The Chinese dollar fell to depths never before explored by a currency; its descent was as interminable and profound as that of the bad angels."[1] A special fiasco in Chinese fiscal history was the gold yuan, instituted in August, 1948, at an exchange rate of four to the US dollar; people of moderate means responded nobly and the government collected $200,-

000,000 from this source; Americans in China co-operated with their public and private resources; whereupon within weeks the paper called gold yuan plunged wildly after the old Chinese dollar (3,000,000 of the latter were worth, in August, 25 cents US). The gold yuan by May, 1949, had gotten down to 2,500,000 for 25 cents US. "If you wish to make a revolution," Lenin once said, "debauch the currency."

The army's efficiency dropped with the Chinese dollar and the so-called gold yuan. The American military chief on the scene, Major General David G. Barr, reported on November 16, 1948 that "no battle has been lost since my arrival due to lack of ammunition or equipment. Their military debacles in my opinion can all be attributed to the world's worst leadership and many other morale destroying factors that lead to a complete loss of will to fight."[2] Civil leadership, what was left of it, began to look sideways toward Formosa, now Taiwan, as a haven from the Communist storm.

As an earlier chapter has shown, the Marshall Plan promised some assistance to China—$275,000,-000 for technical aid during the period ending June 30, 1949, and $125,000,000 in military aid. The military aid did not begin to arrive until the end of 1948, by which time it was too late.

Because of pressures in Congress and from other sources accusing the Administration of pursuing a negative policy in China, probably also to quiet some criticism of his own role in China and to see what an avowedly pro-Chiang officer might do, Marshall in

the summer of 1947 sent Lieutenant General Albert C. Wedemeyer on a special mission to investigate the gathering chaos. Old Admiral Leahy in the White House, rather a reactionary at times, was delighted: "This is a complete reversal of attitude by General Marshall who is thoroughly informed as to Wedemeyer's sympathy with Chiang . . . When he arrives prospects for the survival of the recognized Central Government of China will be much better."[3] Instead, the general's report when finished on September 19, 1947, was unusable, and Marshall suppressed it (it appeared in part in the *China White Paper* in 1949).

The Wedemeyer mission was an interesting episode if only because it showed the frustrations of a true friend of China who went after Chinese reform with the zeal of an American go-getter. Wedemeyer had replaced General Joseph W. Stilwell in the China Theater in 1944, and during two years of careful cooperation with Generalissimo Chiang Kaishek his relations were good and he achieved a considerable Chinese-American cooperation, albeit without major military results because of the dearth of supplies and the approaching end of the war and then the initial confusions of the peace. He had been touted as a replacement for Hurley as American Ambassador, in the months when Hurley was seeking unsuccessfully to resign and before Hurley's blowup in November, 1945. At that time General Marshall, on the verge of retirement, had given the young man some advice: "Do not get mixed up with the State Department unless you are interested in that kind of

work. I think you should remain in the Army."[4] Then
in the spring of 1946, with Marshall himself virtually
in the State Department, the wartime Chief of Staff
asked Wedemeyer to become Ambassador and Wedemeyer consented. But because of Chinese Communist objection Marshall took Leighton Stuart. This
change led to a colloquy between a serious Wedemeyer and a probably inwardly grinning Undersecretary Acheson who had sent for Wedemeyer and
showed him a cable from Marshall that news of the
prospective appointment had leaked with embarrassing results.

"I am sorry about this, Wedemeyer," said Acheson.

"Well," Wedemeyer replied, "I'm not sorry at all
about it. There are two factors that I don't like about
it. One, I don't think that the Communists should
determine who should be appointed by our Government in positions of responsibility, and two, I
bought a trousseau, as it were, an ambassadorial
trousseau to the tune of about eight or nine hundred
dollars."

Acheson disregarded the first remark and said,
"The State Department will take care of the clothes."

Wedemeyer sent the clothes to the Department
"along with the bill," he told an investigating committee some years afterward, "and the State Department did pay the bill and the clothes were sent back
to me and they are in mothballs."[5]

Sans trousseau Wedemeyer went to China in 1947
and surveyed affairs and drew up a report calling for
increased military advice from the United States to

an extent that would have involved maybe 10,000 men, and vastly increased finances for the Nationalist government, but no large-scale participation of American troops in the civil war. To be sure, the United States Government had no troops to spare in the autumn of 1947 and could not even police Palestine, let alone China. But the sticking point of the report was a suggested "guardianship" of Manchuria by five powers including the Soviet Union, or else a UN trusteeship, an idea Wedemeyer had advanced first and to no avail at the end of the war. Wedemeyer thought a guardianship or trusteeship would create a buffer between the Soviet Union and areas to the south and thus confine Soviet influence. He afterward characterized this recommendation as "the most important element" of his report. Here was a notion as unrealistic as the Knox neutralization scheme of before the First World War.

When he passed in this impossible report Wedemeyer sat down in an office in the State Department and waited for President Truman and Secretary Marshall to accept it. He was vastly disappointed when they did not. "I had no doubt that my recommendations would be accepted and implemented." The general could not understand why the report should become top secret, why at least the leading officials in the Pentagon, and members of the Senate Foreign Relations Committee and the House Foreign Affairs Committee should not have full access to it. He could not understand, even eleven years later when he published his memoirs, that a report could not remain secret with such a list of readers. Nor could he

comprehend how it could embarrass China or the United States, since at least the Generalissimo was conversant with its ideas and recommendations. He could not believe that after the mission the Administration would continue the do-nothing policy toward China, and even carry that policy to such an extreme as to refuse to release his report. "I was just left to twiddle my thumbs in a spacious office at the State Department . . ." The chief of the Far Eastern division, Walton Butterworth, visited him occasionally but not to discuss the report and recommendations. In one meeting Butterworth broached the subject and said the Secretary of State wanted Wedemeyer to delete certain specific portions of the report. The Department could not publish it otherwise. Marshall, Butterworth said, might be angry if Wedemeyer refused to accede to this request. Wedemeyer telephoned Marshall's office, learned that the Secretary was attending the UN sessions in New York, put in a long-distance call, and told Marshall he could not cut up the report as requested. Far from showing anger, Marshall understood and respected Wedemeyer's position.[6]

"Why did you join in the suppression of the Wedemeyer report on China?" a critic asked during Marshall's confirmation as Secretary of Defense in 1950.

"I did not 'join in.' I personally suppressed it," said Marshall. "Throughout his report he made references to the proposition that Manchuria should be in a trusteeship. We were then in a struggle in Greece and this would have confused the issue very much. . . . Besides that, this was a report from a man I

had sent to find out something for me, and not for a public speech. Chiang had assured me he would resign before he would accept any relationship in which Russia or Britain had a part. But the report was suppressed by me."[7]

Wedemeyer committed another *faux pas*, in addition to writing an inappropriate report: at the end of the mission he gave a lecture to a group of the highest officials of the Chinese Government including Generalissimo Chiang and pointed out government delinquencies in the frankest terms, incensing many Kuomintang members and ruining whatever influence he might have had in China. It was not the Chinese way; and it hurt people personally, however true the criticism. Premier Chang Chun gave an interview to the American press on September 2 and charged that Wedemeyer had failed to understand the Chinese situation and had not sought his information impartially, the premier declared flatly that the Chinese Government would change neither its domestic or foreign policy as a result of the Wedemeyer mission. In extenuation one must say that it may well be, as Wedemeyer maintains in his memoirs, that Ambassador Stuart put him up to the speech. He asserts that Stuart told him no one could have a better chance of getting some home truths through to the Chinese, that there was every good reason to make a critical speech at what was a critical juncture in Chinese history. Ambassador Stuart's memoirs criticize Wedemeyer for indiscretion. According to the memoirs the speech shocked Stuart, like everyone else except Wedemeyer. It is difficult

to get to the root of this disagreement, except to say that, Leighton Stuart to the contrary, the speech does read suspiciously like a missionary endeavor. It did not matter anyway, as probably nothing could have reformed the Kuomintang government at that late date in its history.[8]

As luck had it, Wedemeyer's official mission was followed by junketing tours of the maverick Democrat, William C. Bullitt, and the dyed-in-the-wool Republican Congressman Judd, and both these visitors gave the Chinese advice à la Wedemeyer. Ambassador Stuart looked on in agony during this diplomacy.[9]

In November, 1948, the Chinese delegate to the United Nations meeting in Paris, Dr. T. S. Tsiang, called on Marshall with a message inquiring whether the United States would agree to appointment of US officers in command of Chinese army units under pretense of acting as advisers, and whether the US would appoint an officer of high rank to head a special mission. Marshall remarked to Tsiang the hopelessness of such a proposal.

On a forlorn chance of personal success Mrs. Chiang Kai-shek, who had so impressed Americans with her appearances during the war, asked transportation to the United States by Navy plane so that she might talk with officials of the American Government. Her request came in late November, 1948, giving the distinct impression that it represented a trip to Canossa, that the Chinese had counted on speaking to a different President after the election. Marshall in Cabinet raised the question as to whether

Mrs. Chiang should be allowed to come, and the President said yes. Marshall rejoined that he proposed to give her every possible facility as the wife of the head of a friendly state. She arrived on December 1 and stayed with Mrs. Marshall in Leesburg. She saw Marshall a couple of times, but he was going into the hospital for the operation that forced his retirement the next month. She was left cooling her heels waiting to see Truman, who put her off until a "tea" scheduled for December 10. The President was not exactly that busy, as he received all kinds of people including Elmer Davis, Maury Maverick the former Representative from Texas, and Toots Shor the nightclub entrepreneur. Eventually the tea came off, with Mrs. Chiang in company of Mrs. Marshall and Mrs. Truman. Unperturbed the wife of the President of China deserted her lady friends and talked business with the President. Margaret Truman watched with some interest: "She was very charming but very shrewd. She talked to Dad for a long time, seeking aid for her cause."[10]

2

Marshall's successor Acheson summarized the Truman Administration's defense of China policy in the letter of transmittal of the famous *China White Paper*: "Nothing that this country did or could have done within the reasonable limits of its capabilities could have changed that result; nothing that was left un-

done by this country has contributed to it. It was the product of internal Chinese forces, forces which this country tried to influence but could not. A decision was arrived at within China, if only a decision by default."[11] And while this comment was to be a red flag before anticommunist bulls in Congress and out for years thereafter it still has the look of truth. It seemed like self-righteousness but was it not true?

Examine the possibilities other than the policy Marshall (and Acheson) followed. Would an enlarged military mission in China and greatly increased funds have sufficed? Americans in the 1960s can look at their country's record in Indochina where in a far smaller area—with about one twentieth the population—exactly the prescription Wedemeyer had proposed was proving if not a failure then no smashing success.

As for outright American military intervention on a massive scale, few individuals in the United States, Democrat or Republican, ever wanted such a course. No responsible leader advocated it in the Truman Administration or in Congress. Senator Owen Brewster of Maine said: "I never proposed to send an army into China." Senator William F. Knowland stated without contradiction that "there has never been a proposal on the part of those who are critical of the policy we have pursued in the Far East to send an army to China." Representative Judd said in the House: "Not for one moment has anyone contemplated sending a single combat soldier in . . . So it is important to make clear when we speak of

military aid . . . it is supplies, training and advice, nothing further."[12]

Money would not do the trick, as Senator Connally pointed out in some classic oratory to his opponent Knowland who was

carrying on . . . and even demanding billions more for Chiang. After a while, I rose and chided him, "The senator wants to pour money down this rat hole." I repeated this statement three times, each time bending down more and more. After the third time, I pointed to an imaginary hole in the Senate floor and said, "And there at the bottom of the rat hole you'll find old Chiang, the generalissimo who never generalissimos. I do not think it is fair for the senator to be making speeches in an effort to stir up the ragged battalions of those who would pour two billion or three billion dollars more into the rat hole in China in order to resuscitate Chiang Kai-shek, who has deserted his people and has gone to Formosa with one hundred thirty-eight million dollars in gold in his pocket. It belonged to the Chinese Government, but he has absconded with it." Later on I apologized to him for having said Chiang absconded with $138,-000,000. "I should have said three hundred million dollars instead," I told him. Republicans frequently blamed Marshall himself for Chiang's loss of China. After hearing this nonsense several times, I told Senate Chiang-lovers, "Marshall could not wave a magic wand and convert to democracy all the Communists north of the Yangtze River. Nor could

he wave another wand and end the immense corruption and indifference of the Chinese Nationalists for the masses of the people. Nor could he wave a third wand and bring all the Nationalists into a love feast, with the Communists or the Communists with the Nationalists."[13]

President Truman privately made no bones about the defects of the Nationalists. He wrote Senator Vandenberg in 1950 that the unfortunate situation in the Far East came about as a result of the corrupt Chinese Nationalist government, "through no fault of ours that I have been able to discover." The Chinese, he said, were fundamentally anti-foreign and "we must be exceedingly careful to see that this anti-foreign sentiment is not turned in our direction."[14] In mid-1949 the President told David E. Lilienthal, chairman of the Atomic Energy Commission, that the "grafters and crooks" and their lot in China had no interest in the millions and millions of Chinese who did not have enough to eat. Two and a half billion dollars had gone into China in recent years and "I'll bet you that a billion dollars of it is in New York banks today." The President said "nothing can be done about China until things kind of settle down."[15]

Marshall in 1947-48 said the same, on many occasions, public and private. There are recurring comments in Forrestal's diary about China. Each time China came up in Cabinet, or in Marshall's private discussion, it was the same decision: no decision. It is clear that after Marshall came back to become

Secretary of State the following two years were barren of policy, for the Secretary had decided, and so had responsible members of the Administration, there was nothing to do. At the time of sending out Wedemeyer, Marshall said things in China showed every sign of disintegration and he had been searching for a positive and constructive formula to deal with the problem; but his solution was to send Wedemeyer: no solution. About this time he talked to a small group about the incompetence of Chiang's generals, some of the most incompetent military men he had ever known, whom Chiang would not dismiss because they were old military classmates. "I have tortured my brain," said the Secretary, "and I can't now see the answer."[16] The same commentary appeared when Marshall, out of office in 1949, spoke in October of that year at a roundtable discussion in the Department and talked eloquently of China problems; at hearings on his nomination as Secretary of Defense in 1950; and at the MacArthur hearings in 1951. He held this opinion until his death in 1959.

A recent student of America's policy in China, Tang Tsou of the University of Chicago, believes Marshall did miss an opportunity with the Wedemeyer report—that by suppressing it he lost a chance to publicize America's China problems and gain support for his do-nothing policy, regardless of its merits. This distinguished scholar maintains that Marshall's refusal to raise a public debate over China "led to a breakdown of bipartisanship and enabled the critics of the administration to charge it with sole responsibility for the China debacle."[17] But with all

credit to Tang Tsou's convincing and eloquent volume, a masterful analysis of America's China policy, one must say that bipartisanship over China never existed in the first place (so Senator Vandenberg claimed), and Marshall had to do his best not to raise complicating factors in the era 1947-48 during congressional passage of the Truman Doctrine and Marshall Plan.

CHAPTER TWELVE

ATOMIC WEAPONS?

SOMETIMES the most important aspects of life—personal, national, diplomatic—pass almost unnoticed, and such was true of the fairly quiet, humdrum diplomacy of atomic disarmament in the United Nations during the years 1947-48, perhaps the most important negotiation during the entire era. This diplomacy did not have the color and immediate danger of the Berlin blockade, nor did it involve appropriations of the magnitude of the Marshall Plan. No pressure of party politics appeared, as in recognition of Israel. None of the major diplomatic figures of the United States or its allies or Russia sat dramatically around a table, as at the Moscow Conference of Foreign Ministers in 1947. There was no dramatic failure, as in the case of China, no domestic oratory of opposition. The contemporary observer saw a series of reports and proposals and some acid arguments and once in a while a few theatrics, but always small-scale; nothing went dramatically wrong because not much dramatically happened. Yet some future historian, looking back at life on earth from a vantage point of Mars or the moon, might see this portion of Marshall's diplomacy as the leading challenge of the time, its failure presaging the final turndown of civilization.

It was a difficult diplomacy to analyze. Even today,

as earth-life has survived into the 1960s, it is not easy to understand what exactly happened to the carefully-made American proposal for disarmament in the early postwar years. At the end of the war the United States Government had begun ponderously to form its atomic energy policy, putting through Congress the Atomic Energy Act, signed by the President on August 1, 1946, after hearings and debates of about six months. It provided for civil control of atomic energy, with transfer of control from the wartime Manhattan Project of the War Department. The Act contained a possible organizational error, setting up a commission rather than an administrator, forcing discussion before decision of problems, but in view of the nature of those problems the commission perhaps was a justifiable if cumbersome device. Despite placing of atomic matters in the hands of a group of men, the Senate took from January until April 9, 1947, to confirm the commission, largely because Kenneth D. McKellar, one of the Senate's lesser statesmen, moved vindictively against David E. Lilienthal whom President Truman had nominated chairman of the AEC. Lilienthal had served as administrator of the Tennessee Valley Authority, and in that post committed the original sin of not getting along with Mc-Kellar. The Senator constituted himself a one-man purgatory. Lilienthal recalled that McKellar fiendishly "roared, the veins on his forehead stood out, his eyes were red and looked tiny and fierce as he came at me time and again." He raised all the doubts and tricky questions he could think of, which were quite a few. On the first day of the hearings McKellar said

that "Macedonian scientists" under Alexander the Great had been the first men to try splitting the atom, and the secret then had eluded mankind for 2,000 years until the wartime chief of the Manhattan Project, Major General Leslie R. Groves, rediscovered it; McKellar wanted to know why Groves could not remain in charge of it—why the Truman Administration wanted to give the secret to Lilienthal.[1] At last, almost a year after the Bikini atomic explosions, two years after Hiroshima, the AEC was ready for business.

Chairman Lilienthal headed a distinguished commission consisting in 1947-48 of Sumner T. Pike, Robert F. Bacher, Lewis L. Strauss, and William W. Waymack. President Truman supported them in every way. Once when Lilienthal was calling at the President's office Truman in his abrupt, jerky way of talking, said, "Come in to see me any time, just any time. I'll always be glad to see you. You have the most important thing there is. You must make a blessing of it or" (and a half-grin as he pointed to a large globe in the corner of his office) "we'll blow that all to smithereens."[2]

Meanwhile talk and some action had gone toward setting up an atomic weapons control program for the world. The Prime Minister of Canada, W. L. Mackenzie King, with Prime Minister Clement Attlee and President Truman produced the Truman-Attlee-King Declaration of November 16, 1945, under which the three countries would exchange information with other nations on peaceful use of atomic energy. Drawn by the wartime scientific adviser to the United States

Government, Vannevar Bush, the agreement by implication committed the United States to international
control of atomic weapons. It asked the United Nations to establish a commission to bring about an
open world of nuclear research, promote peaceful
atomic energy, eliminate nuclear weapons. The Foreign Ministers Conference in Moscow in December,
1945, proposed to the General Assembly the organization of a United Nations Atomic Energy Commission. Secretary of State Byrnes at the Assembly in
January, 1946, said no single nation could solve these
atomic problems: "They are the common responsibility
of all nations." The Assembly adopted the Foreign
Ministers' suggested resolution without change, January 24, 1946. The United States readied detailed
proposals for the new agency; the State Department
set up a committee which produced proposals attributed to its chairman, Undersecretary of State Acheson, and the chairman of the committee's board of
consultants, Lilienthal. These propositions went to
Bernard Baruch who was the first US representative
on the UNAEC. The proposals which he advanced
contained a contribution of his own: a veto-less UN
Security Council in case a nation broke the agreement; they became known as the Baruch Plan. There
followed Baruch's famous speech at the first meeting of UNAEC on June 14, 1946, held in New York
in the undiplomatic surroundings of the Hunter College gymnasium. In preparation Baruch consulted his
idea man, Herbert Bayard Swope, who called him
up on the phone one day and gave him the first
sentence ("I've got your opening line. It comes from

the best possible source—the Bible"). Baruch used some of the fine old seventeenth-century words in his opening statement, "We are here to make a choice between the quick and the dead."[3]

It seemed a reasonable plan, a good combination of the real and the ideal and therefore true to life— and did it not seek to uphold life? It was agreeable to the two opposing groups of American physicists. During the war American scientists had divided between those men who felt that all atomic weapons ought to go on the scrap heap and those who held that war required any available weapon. Scientists at the University of Chicago had drawn up a protest against atomic weapons, their leader being the Nobel laureate physicist James Franck. The Franck report did not halt the decision already taken in Washington by the so-called Interim Committee, the group of men in high government office who advised President Truman to order the bomb to be dropped on Japan. The Baruch Plan contained elements acceptable to both groups of physicists. Employing the proposals of the Acheson-Lilienthal report it asked an Atomic Development Authority which would have monopoly of all the world's "dangerous" fissionable materials and production plants. There would be rigid on-the-spot inspections. Any attempt by a nation to build atomic weapons would become known to the Authority which would report the attempt to the nations of the world for appropriate sanctions. The ADA also would have the right to develop peaceful atomic energy. "Reduced to its essence the Baruch Plan was a mechanism to prevent surprise attack, to

maintain an 'open world' in nuclear research, and to preserve the international *status quo* by freezing military technology at its World War II level. Although the proposed Authority would not actually have the power itself to prevent a nation from converting atomic energy into military weapons, at least it would guarantee that such conversion could not be done in secret."[4] Presumably a nation learning of a violation would have about a year—while the offending nation was readying its atomic weapons— to prepare for war. Secretary Marshall at a press conference on February 7, 1947, shortly after entering the Department, just before the ill-fated Moscow Conference, set out the American point of view with a clarity which might have impressed his Russian readers:

The international control of atomic energy with effective safeguards is of first importance. It is not a problem of disarmament in the conventional sense. . . . Also essential to the establishment of real security are solutions acceptable to the great powers of the tremendous issues which the peace settlement poses. It is difficult to see how any *real* disarmament, or even any substantial reduction of armaments, can take place until such solutions have been found. The United States Government, I am sure, will avoid with care a repetition of the tragic consequences of unilateral disarmament and the limitation of armaments as was done in 1921. The problem cannot be solved on an emotional basis. This time it has to be a practical basis.[5]

2

The plan nonetheless failed. The reason may have been in part the personality of its chief advocate which clashed with leading figures of the American Government. Baruch was no easy person, both because of too long an experience in and out of government (he had an acute sense of when someone was undercutting him and always strove to keep authority in his own hands) and because he was an egotist of no small proportion and could invent his own problems. He began as American delegate to UNAEC by tangling with Undersecretary Acheson, who for most people was a delightfully easy person to get along with. Acheson had indiscreetly mentioned to the British representative on UNAEC, Sir Alexander Cadogan, that Baruch was going to offer the Acheson-Lilienthal proposals as American policy. Baruch blow oky high, tolling Aohocon "plainly that ho would then have to find another messenger boy, because Western Union didn't take anybody at my age. I had never served as a messenger or mouthpiece before, and did not intend to start now." The irate US representative went to Truman who calmed him down, for when Baruch asked the President who was to draft the atomic proposals Truman replied: "Hell, you are." But there were continuing Baruchean episodes. Vannevar Bush told Baruch that because of sheer scientific ignorance he, Baruch, was the most unqualified man in the country for the task. "Doc, you couldn't be more right," was the unruffled answer.

The Lilienthal journals give humorous evidence of Baruch's egotistical qualities. One day Marshall told Acheson that "Really Baruch was all right if you knew how to handle him. For example, he was determined to get his bust in the War College. This wouldn't do; we only have Napoleon, Alexander and Caesar in there; didn't even have Pershing in. So I salved him up and that was that." Next day Acheson went into Marshall's office bearing a card and saying, "Read this." The card announced that the War College invited Acheson to attend the unveiling of a bust of Bernard Baruch. "You certainly know how to 'handle' him," Acheson said. "Yes," said Marshall, "and to top it off, it seems I am going to make a speech at the unveiling."[6]

The Baruch Plan, apart from the crotchets of its leading exponent, held out difficulty for the Russians, and this fact encompassed its defeat. To them its primary defect was that it would have destroyed the Russian atomic program. Because of espionage the Soviets knew a great deal about the American atomic effort and had resolved to have atomic weapons of their own; at the end of the war the Russian program went into high gear. By the time the USAEC and UNAEC got underway and serious American proposals began, the Russians were well along to success, much farther than the West knew (Western intelligence on this subject was "meager," Chairman Lilienthal admitted to his diary).[7] To Russian leaders it seemed impossible to erase this vast effort, as the Baruch Plan demanded. They may also have understood even then the great diplomatic advantage which

possession of atomic weapons would give—how any nation with the bomb could blackmail its relatively unarmed neighbors, how diplomacy in general would take on a new dimension with Russia and other nations in possession of the bomb.

There was another danger to Russia in scrapping the atomic weapons program and putting everything nuclear under an international umbrella: for inspection, essential to international control, might expose the USSR's vulnerability to attack by the United States Air Force at a time when the Russians had no large bomber force of their own. The Russians knew it and refused to agree to any provisions for inspection. Baruch's special contribution to the United States plan, the proviso for enforcement, probably made little difference, for inspection made the plan nearly impossible anyway.

The plan was not all against the Soviets, for it did promise them virtual control of Europe, short of a major American or European rearmament. If the Russians had accepted the plan, and the Americans carried it out, the Soviets would have succeeded in removing the nuclear striking power of the United States while still maintaining in Europe a strong army with conventional weapons.

Sufficient reasons moved the Soviets to refuse the Baruch Plan, but they had to couch refusal in careful terms, not saying just "no." As a later student analyzed Russian atomic "gamesmanship" in 1946, there were at least five ploys: (1), to reject the American atomic energy proposals without appearing to do so; (2), link Soviet policy with popular aspirations for peace

throughout the world; (3), portray policies of the Western block—the United States in particular—as aggressive; (4), prevent the United States Government from using its atomic superiority to gain political advantages; (5), stall for time.[8] And so the Russians, much as technicians would approach a problem in mathematics or physics, approached the negotiations in UNAEC and eventually in the Security Council and General Assembly.

As soon as Baruch made his speech the world, so to speak, awaited the Russian reaction, which amounted to a most skillful nitpicking of his proposals. The opposing Soviet plan called for an international convention outlawing production and use of atomic weapons and requiring destruction of all atomic weapon stockpiles. The Soviets opposed inspection, control, punishment, even surrender of the veto which, they said, threatened the sacred sovereignty of all nations, not merely themselves.

Baruch resigned in January, 1947, having come, as he put it, to the end of the furrow. His work passed to the United States representative on the Security Council, Senator Austin, whose deputy, General Frederick H. Osborn, picked by Secretary Marshall to replace Baruch (Osborn was wartime head of Army Special Services), took over most of the technical argument with the Russians on atomic energy. Austin was perhaps too sanguine a man for the job. He had determined not to exasperate the Russians; he felt they would come around. Undersecretary Acheson found him difficult: "Senator Austin terrifies me. 'I can handle the Russians.' God! Famous last

words."[9] But it didn't matter, as nothing was going to happen at the UN in connection with atomic energy. By summer of 1947 the Soviets on UNAEC were stalling tautologically for time. They asked for, indeed insisted on, strict international control. No one knew what that meant. Osborn asked the Soviet representative Andrei Gromyko: "What is this strict international control? Is it inspection?" Gromyko replied: "To the question, 'What is strict international control?' I answer: The proposals submitted by the USSR delegation. They relate to the principal questions and not to all of them. If adopted, these proposals would constitute a basis for the establishment of complete international control."[10] Six working groups and two committees of UNAEC labored through August, 1947, to complete a report before the September session of the General Assembly. The report stated "progress," no final result in sight

Stalin had talked about atomic energy in an interview with Harold Stassen on April 9, 1947, and threw out some hope for action, in the meaninglessly confident way in which he was a master with Western visitors. He said the "desire and conscience of the peoples of the world demanded that the use of atomic energy for warlike purposes be prohibited." He foresaw successful international control. "Things," he said mysteriously, perhaps with a sly tug at his mustache or a puff on his long cigarette, "are leading up to it."

Despite this tantalizing encouragement, the UNAEC through the winter of 1947-48 could reach no agreement, and at last by late spring of 1948 had dead-

locked. In a vote of May 17 the commission referred international control to the Security Council because in view of the majority the Soviet Union had determined never to agree to control. With the Berlin question coming up to crisis in the blockade, Gromyko on June 16 indulged a furious attack against the United States. The Americans, he said, wished "to convert the international control agency, which is to carry out the day-to-day functions of control and inspection, not only into a kind of trust controlling all the atomic facilities of the world, but into something like a police organization. The final touch would be to place at the head of that organization some retired American general." The Security Council passed this difficult problem back to the General Assembly. Gromyko's parting words before the Council on June 22 were prophetic, spoken two days before the Soviet Union began a total blockade of Berlin: "There is . . . no sense in referring the matter back from the Security Council to the General Assembly. It is obvious to all that this can lead nowhere, that nothing positive or useful can come of it."[11]

3

By the end of the year 1947 and in early 1948, when clearly nothing good was going to come of negotiations in the UN, the United States began in earnest to take atomic matters into its own hands, until such time as another nation should come on the "secret" of atomic weapons or, to put the case better, succeed in producing enough uranium and master-

ing the other technology of bomb construction. One of the first signs of a more nationalistic policy was the move to renegotiate the wartime Quebec (1943) agreement with Canada and Great Britain. The agreement had been a product of wartime secrecy and had not been explained to congressional leaders as late as the winter of 1947. Senator Vandenberg and members of the Joint Congressional Committee on Atomic Energy, then under chairmanship of the Republican Senator Bourke B. Hickenlooper, were doubtful of continuing the wartime pledge. There was fear of security arrangements with the British and also that too much atomic know-how too close to Europe and possible Russian seizure was not wise. Under a *modus vivendi* concluded on January 7, 1948, the United States obtained a larger portion of Congo uranium ore and clarified the non-weapon areas of technical information it would share with the other two nations. The British allowed abrogation of the wartime US pledge not to use the bomb without British consent.

A couple of problems arose with the British. Chairman Lilienthal of the AEC soon learned that the British were developing their own atomic bomb. This bothered him—both the idea that the bomb-producing factories might be open to seizure, and that at the very moment the Marshall Plan was getting underway the British were allocating terribly scarce materials and thousands of highly skilled workers to this project of duplicating the weapons of the United States. Lilienthal went to Undersecretary Lovett about the whole business and Lovett said the State Department knew what the British were up to and ac-

cepted it.[12] One of the members of the AEC, Strauss, worried over technical cooperation for peaceful use of the atom, believing that technology for peaceful use was essentially the same as for military use. He deplored sending radioactive isotopes abroad even for medical purposes. When Lilienthal was absent from Washington in the summer of 1948, Strauss took alarm and raised a small storm over possible discussion with the British of the basic metallurgy of plutonium. He consulted various people including Senators Hickenlooper and Vandenberg, fearing that there had been some leak of vital secrets. He went to great lengths to change the authorization of the scientist Cyril Smith, then in England for exchange of information; at last Sumner Pike, acting chairman of the AEC, found the man, and there had been no compromising discussions. All this two years before the case of Klaus Fuchs broke in 1950, a very bad case indeed, which strengthened arguments against releasing too much top-secret atomic technology even to Great Britain.

The year 1948 marked a new test of atomic weapons by the United States in Eniwetok, following the Bikini tests of two years before. The Russians had an observer at Bikini. The Eniwetok tests had no publicity, being kept strictly within the family of the armed services and the United States AEC; Undersecretary Lovett with Secretary of Defense Forrestal concurring vigorously protested the proposal of Lilienthal that there be publicity for the new tests. Not that the Russians remained in complete ignorance. A notation in Forrestal's diary, dated March 3, 1948, reads

as follows: "Word today from Eniwetok that there was affirmative identification of a non-U.S. submarine with schnorkel on the surface in the neighborhood of Eniwetok."[13]

Secretary Marshall felt no hesitation about the Eniwetok tests. When Lilienthal and some AEC colleagues called upon him some eight months before the tests, inquiring whether there might be diplomatic repercussions, Marshall's major thought was for the meeting of the Council of Foreign Ministers scheduled for London at the end of 1947: it would be unfortunate if the tests occurred then or just before or immediately after. "He smiled quietly as he said these things." Interestingly, the meeting with Lilienthal brought some memories as the Secretary of State sat conversing in a corner of his long, narrowish, beautiful office (the date of the meeting was June 11, 1947). He spoke with such gentleness, in his soft, husky voice. He was quite relaxed, very free, with a twinkle in his eye. Lilienthal wrote in his diary that Marshall was "Youthful-looking in color and demeanor. And with not one sign of tension or worry. I am not sure whether that is good or not, considering how much there is to worry about." The wartime Chief of Staff recalled the use of atom bombs on the Japanese, how neither the US Army nor anyone else had understood the shock effect of the bombs—that dropping these infernal weapons would give the Japanese an excuse to get out of the war without completely losing face. Marshall revealed to Lilienthal that the Army had planned to use twelve atom bombs on Japan to facilitate land-

ing American troops. Talk of the atomic bombs led the Secretary of State circuitously to discuss poison gas during the Second World War. The only reason the US Army had not used gas on the Germans, he said, was because Churchill and the British were afraid the Germans would use gas on the British Isles. The Secretary, having just proposed the Marshall Plan at Harvard and being perhaps full of economic information about Europe and especially Great Britain, expatiated on how the British were always terribly vulnerable to attack from the Continent, how their foreign policy so often reflected this fact; it was important for Americans to understand their feeling. Marshall recalled that the Army thought of using poison gas on the Japanese, after the costs of the Iwo Jima capture. The idea, he explained, was to force the inhabitants of Okinawa to move into a remote part of the island and to keep the defenders in gas masks. A week in masks would have so debilitated the Japanese troops that the US Army could have captured them with little loss of life. Lilienthal remarked to his diary uneasily how international covenants bound the United States not to use poison gas. General Marshall as Secretary of State did not seem worried about wartime advocacy of poison gas, despite treaties. Lilienthal recalled to Marshall that the Russian position on prohibition of atomic weapons was that all governments should sign a treaty promising not to use them, with no inspection or other measures to enforce the atomic-limitation treaty, and that the Russians were arguing that this was the way the nations had banned poison gas from warfare.[14]

Until the USSR exploded its first atomic device in August, 1949, nothing more could come of the hope of the United States and the world for enforced limitation and control of atomic weapons. When Lilienthal reported to Truman the results of Eniwetok the President rubbed his hand over the back of his neck: "Why," he said, "that's enough to wipe out a good part of the world. If we could just have Stalin and his boys see one of these things, there wouldn't be any question about another war." Lilienthal and the President knew things were not that simple. That day Truman looked hard at his AEC chairman and his face was terribly weary. "Of course," he added, "I don't like the idea of such things at all. I gave the order for the others, and I don't want to have to do that again, ever. What I hope you will work hard at is the peaceful things about it, not the destructive. But until we are sure about peace, there's nothing else to do."[15] Atomic diplomacy had to continue in the UN. The General Assembly shunted the problem back to UNAEC which reconvened on February 18, 1949. Discussions promptly degenerated into long repetitive speeches, haggling, name-calling, the worst kind of international talk.

It remained for a new set of problems (new weapons, new carriers, new nations possessing or wanting weapons and carriers, a developing quarrel between the USSR and Communist China), and also the technical ability to detect certain nuclear tests without on-the-spot inspection, to bring the slightest order, a partial nuclear test-ban treaty, into the competition for nuclear supremacy; and what would hap-

pen with both France and the Chinese outside the test ban was in the mid-1960s a highly moot point.

What might have made this saddening tale impossible or given it some other end was another government in the USSR, a regime of good will rather than, if not malevolence, narrow understanding of its national interest. In the Baruch Plan the United States had a workable technical instrument; the proposal contained some provisions unacceptable to the Soviet Union but offered American nuclear disarmament after great wartime expenditure. The Soviet Government preferred its own devices.

CHAPTER THIRTEEN

MILITARY REORGANIZATION

SECRETARY of State Marshall's tenure coincided with a notable reevaluation and reordering of American military forces. Problems and difficulties of this reorganization had considerable bearing on American diplomacy then and later. Marshall did not take much part in this change to what became the Military Establishment. But his attitude toward the change in 1947-48 is worth examining.

Military reorganization clearly was due by this time. The dominant reason for an Establishment was the continued intransigence of the Soviet Union, the evident wish of the Russian dictator to keep alive and exacerbate the issues dividing his country and the United States. There was also the fact that the numerical strength of the armed forces had gone down to an uneasily low level, from over sixteen million to below a million and a half. The military had failed to receive new equipment, so that the vestiges of the great wartime forces were drawing antequated items.

Likewise there was need for military reorganization because of the imminent independence of the Air Force. During the war the Air Force had been part of the Army but managed an autonomous existence. Independence of the Air Force raised the prob-

lem of coordinating the activities of what would be three military services: Army, Navy, and Air. It had been bad enough to have two vital services fighting each other; three squabbling military departments would be administratively intolerable. Unification of the services had found much support during the congressional investigation of Pearl Harbor in 1945-46. The forty volumes of evidence on the disaster of 1941 proved that the services needed cooperation beyond the golf course sessions of 1941 between Admiral Husband E. Kimmel and General Walter C. Short. Pearl Harbor made a Central Intelligence Agency seem imperative. Likewise a National Security Resources Board, to plan for allocations in crisis and prevent helterskelter administration as during the Second World War.

Another argument for reorganization was the sheer size of the postwar military budget, despite cutbacks to a supposedly peacetime force level. Even by most scrupulous calculation the annual military budget was going to take ten or twelve billion dollars, more than the cost of the entire Federal Government in prewar years.

The plan for an over-all Military Establishment took shape, with inevitable fuss over wording of clauses. In disgust the former Wall Street financier Forrestal, then Secretary of the Navy, soon to be Secretary of Defense, told Senator Leverett Saltonstall that "there were very few occasions that I could recall where the language of the mortgage had made the bonds good."[1] At last the legislation was ready. President Truman signed the unification act together

with an executive order defining the roles and missions of the services, and nominated Forrestal as Secretary of Defense. The Act set up a National Military Establishment, including a new Department of the Air Force which like the two old-line service Departments of the Army and the Navy would have its own Secretary and Undersecretary. The new Secretary of Defense was to have "general direction, authority and control" over the several services. The new law also set up a much needed National Security Council (NSC), and directly under it a Central Intelligence Agency;[2] War Council; National Security Resources Board, and under it a Munitions Board for procurement and a Research and Development Board for research. In subsequent years this structure required much change. The original idea to keep the Secretary of Defense's office a small place and avoid a new bureaucracy to coordinate the old eventually gave way to a new bureaucracy to coordinate the old. The National Military Establishment became the Department of Defense, with some downgrading of the service Secretaries (they gave up regular attendance at meetings of the National Security Council). The NSC had a varying history, not of so much importance under Truman, more under Eisenhower, less under Kennedy and Johnson. The Central Intelligence Agency had a checkered history. The War Council, composed of the service Secretaries and Chiefs of Staff, disappeared, being too much apparatus. The National Security Resources Board disappeared, its mobilization duties transferred. The Munitions Board and the Research and Development Board

changed their names and moved into the expanding
Department of Defense. Eventual ordering of boards
and titles turned out far different from the plan of
1947 but the latter was a good start.

The Senate promptly confirmed Forrestal's appointment on July 27, 1947. Although he did not go through
the swearing-in ceremony until September 17 he
soon was functioning in his new role. He approached
the task gingerly, keeping in mind his administrative
dictum that ninety per cent of work in high Federal
office consisted of soothing egos and obtaining cooperation—probably too dainty an approach for the
job he now undertook which required occasional
knocking of heads. Everything at first seemed to go
all right. The National Security Council held an
initial meeting on September 26, 1947, and heard
careful explanation from Forrestal that its task was
to advise the President and not make policy: "determination of and decisions in the field of foreign
policy would, of course, be his [the President's] and
the Secretary of State's."[3] The CIA gathered a staff
under Rear Admiral Roscoe H. Hillenkoetter. Vannevar Bush took over the Research and Development
Board.

2

The new military harmony ended when the communist coup in Czechoslovakia in early February,
1948, brought a feeling of crisis to the American
Government and people. The Military Establishment
with all its new organization proved inadequate. In

June, 1948, during the Berlin airlift crisis a Pentagon meeting of high-level military and civil officials completely bypassed the National Security Council, and made a recommendation to the President which was received at Blair House without much thought about its out-of-channels form.[4]

Apart from international crises military unification would have had trouble because of the exigencies of budget making: the business of drawing up the military budget for fiscal 1949 (July, 1948, through June 1949) reduced unification to a near-absurdity. Secretary of the Air Force W. Stuart Symington and his Chief of Staff, General Carl Spaatz, agitated for a seventy-group Air Force and did not hesitate to go over the heads of Forrestal and President Truman by taking their case to Congress. A meeting of the Chiefs of Staff at Key West in March, 1948, arranged by Forrestal to allow the busy generals and admirals to think in peace, failed to prevent the Air Force crisis. Soon everything was in disarray.

The Symington-Spaatz direct play to Congress is important to any study of American diplomacy in 1947-48 because it involved much more than appeared on the surface: it sought to perpetuate America's atomic power against Russia, to make sure that the United States could get its atomic bombs over Russian territory; this insurance ignored the appallingly weak US Army, the inability of the United States Government to send ground troops anywhere beyond the size of a division without partial mobilization. Army weakness had been the principal inhibiting factor in Marshall's diplomacy, and the Air Force

scheme would have done little or nothing to assist it. Actually it did the opposite, bolstering national confidence for the most serious and crucial diplomatic showdown possible, the kind of showdown Marshall was trying to avoid. Forrestal opposed the Symington-Spaatz proposal with all the arguments he could think of, but his was a lonely fight toward military-diplomatic sanity. The magnificent arguments on his side quickly became lost in the siren songs of the Air Force devotees, the budget and electoral worries of President Truman, and the peculiar military-diplomatic preoccupations of Secretary of State Marshall.

The Air Force under Symington got almost completely out of hand during Forrestal's era at the Military Establishment. Forrestal could do little to restrain the new third arm of the services. At one juncture Symington made a rousing speech to a group of aircraft engineers on the West Coast, and Forrestal thought of asking for his resignation, but thought twice and lost a golden opportunity. During a visit to an Air Force installation the sophisticated Secretary of Defense found himself shocked at the inexperience and self-confidence of the young officers who because of rapid growth of their service had gone up quickly to high command. Yet old-timers such as Spaatz and his successor as Air Force Chief of Staff, General Hoyt S. Vandenberg, were little more restrained than the youngsters. The Secretary of Defense had to deal with a group of men led by a fighting Secretary who believed air power the key to the military future of the world—who had failed both to understand the difficulties of wartime strategic

bombing, especially without fighter cover, and the horrendous new problems of atomic bombing: all they knew was that the Air Force had carried the bombs in each case and could do so again. It may be that the Air Force's remarkable showing in the Berlin airlift gave further confidence to the "fly boys," although their requests for more budget came well before the Berlin crisis.

The budget fight was a hot one. After the Czech crisis President Truman was willing to allow the Military Establishment a supplementary budget for fiscal 1949 of perhaps $3 billion over the already arranged military budget of about $11 billion. The Air Force then suddenly welshed from the Key West decision to support the supplementary appropriation and asked for a special fund all for itself, some $800,000,-000, which it claimed would raise its then strength of fifty-five groups to seventy groups, the latter being a new magic number. Forrestal countered that to keep the Military Establishment in kilter, in balance, would require not the fairly modest Air Force figure but closer to $15 billion in supplementary appropriation. Moreover, the cost of this new program would continue into subsequent budgets; it was no one-step proposition. The Air Force went to Capitol Hill. Congress, desirous of doing something after the Czech crisis, unassured by the Secretary of Defense's sober but unattractive proposition of a general increase in the military budget, gladly supported the Air Force. There also was a good bit of congressional and popular feeling, to which the Air Force catered, that an increase in the glamorous Air Force would

make unnecessary one of the most unattractive parts of the Military Establishment's supplementary program, namely, repassage of Selective Service and institution of Universal Military Training. The Air Force kept hammering its simple argument, with assistance from the fortuitous reporting of two boards of investigation at the time of the Czech crisis—the Finletter report of January, 1948, by a presidential Air Policy Committee chaired by Thomas K. Finletter; and the Brewster-Hinshaw Board's report of March, 1948, by a parallel Joint Congressional Aviation Policy Board under Senator Owen Brewster.

Forrestal beseeched the President for support, and found some help but mainly a desire to keep the military budget down. For fiscal 1949, Truman would go along on the supplementary $3 billion, but that was his limit. And he was less interested in how the Military Establishment cut its pie than in the pie's size which for fiscal 1949 and subsequent years, he felt, had to stay at about $15 billion: $11 billion for regular military budget in fiscal 1949 plus $3 billion supplementary (which he would allow into following years), plus an already-agreed-upon annual appropriation of $600 million for stockpiling raw materials. By nature the President was a fiscal conservative, despite his reputation as a liberal Democrat, whatever that means. Truman did not like to see the country turn to deficit financing when plants were running at full blast and employment moving toward Henry Wallace's once dreamy prophecy of sixty million jobs. It took no knowledge of Keynesian economics to convince the President that during great national pros-

perity something was wrong when the budget would not balance or yield a surplus. Some of the President's more conservative advisers, who made sense to him, told him it would set a bad example to Europe if the United States failed to balance its own budget in such good times. The President also was not insensitive to his needs in the election year 1948. Defection of the Wallace-ites, already evident in the spring of 1948, made the Democratic Party more conservative and this had meaning for the budget. Then there was a serious danger of inflation if with a big increase in budget the armed forces began competing for goods and services in the already-tight economy. The country had suffered a large postwar inflation, and more of it was politically as well as economically dangerous —demands by labor, resistance by industry, consumer dissatisfaction, etc. etc. etc. To impose controls on the economy and thereby allow the military to make new purchases was likewise politically dangerous, whether controls were selective or general. And anyway, the management of a great national economy is a fragile undertaking, and no President in his right mind during an election year would venture perhaps unnecessarily into treacherous terrain. When President Truman weighed all factors, known and otherwise, he decided to follow into the foreseeable future what he already knew, the military budget of fiscal 1949 which with additional Czech-crisis funds approximated $15 billion. When he conversed with his Director of the Bureau of the Budget, James E. Webb, who had resolved to hold fiscal 1949 and 1950 to their predetermined limits, he was talking to a man after his

own heart. Webb had little respect for Forrestal. "Forrestal has lost control completely," he told a friend.[5] Webb went over the Military Establishment with a microscope and after picking out some absurdities proposed cuts or delays in weapon procurement and force levels that alarmed Forrestal. The President seemed to take all of Webb's analysis with benign approval.

3

As if the Military Establishment did not have enough trouble, there were the special military-diplomatic interests of Secretary of State Marshall which did not help Forrestal's unceasing efforts to strengthen the Establishment. An outside observer would have thought that in the spring and summer and autumn of 1948, after the Czech coup, Marshall would have full awareness of the need for more exportable Army divisions. It had proved impossible to release more than a division for possible service in Palestine. Lack of troops had produced talk of pulling out of Korea. The German and Austrian garrisons were short. At the time of the Greek crisis, a year earlier, it had been impossible to send troops of almost any kind and the Administration in its inner councils had discussed weakly the sending of B-29 squadrons as a demonstration. Marshall knew all about this acute Army weakness and had talked publicly about it. In 1948 in the crucial months of weakness, when Forrestal was blowing what trumpets he could for more Army forces, the Secretary of State fastened his mind on

two programs which, estimable in themselves, would not have provided the immediate forces in being he so needed for a more effective diplomacy.

The Secretary for a long time had been a devotee of Universal Military Training, and UMT now engaged his thoughts to such extent that he could not see even the larger importance of other measures such as Selective Service which would help the immediate force levels. At the Secretary of State's virtual insistence UMT went into the Military Establishment's recommendations transmitted by President Truman in a special address to Congress on March 17, 1948. It soon appeared that UMT did not have a ghost of a chance of passage.

With its failure the Secretary began to look toward arming America's allies in Europe, another idea of momentarily secondary importance. The British and French in 1947 had concluded the Treaty of Dunkirk as a symbol of their continuing alliance. The Anglo-French in March, 1948, brought in the Benelux countries (Belgium, the Netherlands, Luxembourg) to form the Brussels Pact, a five-nation Western European Union, again more symbol than reality. WEU attracted Marshall, and when military ministers of the WEU countries approached him for weapons and new equipment for their largely unarmed armies he reacted impulsively in favor. These nations, he said, were in a particularly apprehensive state of mind, "completely out of their skin, and sitting on their nerves," and the United States had to recreate hope in them soon.[6] General Alphonse Juin worked some French logic on the Secretary, and Marshall came

back to Washington breathing fire about how Juin's million young Frenchmen were waiting only for American guns. To be sure, the Secretary knew the almost agonizing weakness of the Paris government, but he succumbed to the old allure of French greatness. There was talk of renewal of lend-lease. Forrestal had the largest difficulty getting the Secretary's attention away from this dream of rearming Europe, toward rearming the United States. When the Secretary of Defense told the Secretary of State about the low force levels, the aging wartime equipment, Marshall's mind moved back to 1940 and the terrible military weakness of that time and he told Forrestal that however bad things were in 1948 they were vastly better than in 1940.

The Secretary of State in these crucial months of 1948 repeatedly ignored hints for support thrown out by the Secretary of Defense, even refused to draw himself into the Air Force controversy. Marshall knew that on February 1, 1948 the total armed-forces strength stood at 1,374,000, and by October 1 had risen to 1,531,881; increase would continue through the first half of 1949, but thereafter because of operation of the Truman budget ceiling the force level would have to go down (at outbreak of the Korean War in June, 1950, the Establishment would be down to 1,465,000). Marshall showed no alarm. He seems also to have converted Truman to his point of view, if that was necessary, or at least he avoided presenting the other more alarming point of view.

In the highest circles of the American Government at this time a fascinating drama was being played

out. Here was an era of clear international danger. First the Czech crisis. Then General Clay's famous cable of early March, 1948, relating uncertainty of Soviet peaceful intentions, his feeling that the Russians might strike with dramatic suddenness. Everyone remembered Pearl Harbor, and Clay's brooding comments in March-April brought consternation in official Washington. The new Central Intelligence Agency on March 16, 1948, gave a combined State-Army-Navy-Air estimate that war was not probable within sixty days. Not for another two weeks would CIA extend this tenuous forecast of peace, and then without concurrence of the Air Force. Affairs simmered down, although military planners dourly looked to American possession of the atomic bomb as their only fighting hope. At a Joint Chiefs of Staff meeting on May 5 the staff planners "presented a plan for emergency war by Russia which was completely dependent upon full use of atomic bombs for success." Next day the President ordered an alternate plan because (1) bombs might not be available because they might at that time be outlawed and (2) the American people might not permit use of the bombs for aggressive purposes.[7] Selective Service passed Congress in June, 1948. The start of the airlift saw numerous discussions in Washington, and incessant teletype conferences with civil officials and military commanders abroad, so much conferring that it wore out many individuals because of the late hours and concentration. Hopes for a Russian backdown from the blockade disappeared in September and October, and Forrestal was querying casual visitors to his office

whether they thought the American people would agree to use the atomic bombs in event of war with Russia. The President himself at one point, September 13, 1948, was scared: "Have a terrific day. Forrestal, Bradley, Vandenberg (the General, not the Senator), Symington brief me on bases, bombs, Moscow, Leningrad, etc. I have a terrible feeling afterward that we are very close to war. I hope not. Discuss situation with Marshall at lunch."[8]

That day now long past, Monday, September 13, 1948, is a day for the historian to remember with some thought for the kindness of fate or Providence, thankfulness for the long historical obscurity of the private crises of the world since the end of the Second World War. The chairman of the Atomic Energy Commission, Lilienthal, wrote in his diary that day about a conversation with the Director of the Bureau of the Budget, Webb:

Jim Webb came to see me today. The situation in Berlin is bad, he reports. The Russians seem prepared to kick us in the teeth on every issue. Their planes are in the air corridor today, and anything could happen. "Anything—they might walk in tomorrow and shoot Gen. Clay." The President is being pushed hard by Forrestal to decide that atomic bombs will be used, but the National Security Council, Jim has reason to believe, will advise the President that there is no occasion to decide that question right now. "The President has always been optimistic about peace. But he is blue now, mighty blue. . . ."[9]

Somehow the crises always relaxed, and perhaps naturally so, although in retrospect one has the feeling that not merely the nation but the Truman Administration failed to learn the most possible from this episodic war crisis of 1948. The trouble may have been that the Administration had lived with crisis too long: it was beginning to appear that the country would muddle through. Pearl Harbor did not recur. The President, steadier than most men, began to concentrate on getting himself reelected, continuing his domestic and international program against what he saw darkly as a Republican Restoration. Forrestal kept talking about a bigger Military Establishment and the President wrote him off as a tense and preoccupied if efficient individual, concerned like all officers of the Cabinet with his own bailiwick. It was the President's job to reduce department budgets and mediate the parochialisms of executives.

The peculiar proposition about it all, as mentioned, was that Secretary of State Marshall, who usually had such keen perception of military-diplomatic realities, in this case failed to see Forrestal's problems and dwelled on UMT and rearming WEU. The President regarded the aging Secretary of State as steady as a rock; Marshall would not scare. Forrestal was getting a slightly harassed look on his too-tense face, the President carefully observed. In early spring of 1949 Forrestal was to begin rubbing a spot on his head to rawness, carrying a characteristic gesture into illness, and his departure from office, hurried by the President, soon ended in his tragic suicide.

By that time a new executive, Louis Johnson, was running the Military Establishment, and had forced the budget into the Truman $15 billion ceiling with all that meant for military-diplomatic imbalance. Marshall had left the Secretaryship of State, an ill man in need of medical care and rest. The course of events was inviting the Korean War.

CHAPTER FOURTEEN

THE PROPOSED VINSON MISSION

THE unsuccessful plan to send Chief Justice Vinson to Russia in the autumn of 1948 stands out as a final failure in the immediate postwar effort to get along with the Soviet Union. After three years of deterioration of peace, or unwillingness of the USSR to allow establishment of peace, here was a proposed mission to Moscow by one of the leading men of the United States Government, an individual whose position was by law nonpartisan, without tincture of personal or party advantage. It was to be a journey to reduce tension, to restore sanity in Russo-American relations. Vinson did not leave the United States.

Envisaged as a trip of good will, the journey never came off and hence failed to achieve its large purpose. It failed also in a smaller, political purpose, enhancement of Truman's presidential election campaign against Governor Dewey. Truman was in a tight spot and needed the boosting of a successful trip to Russia, or at least a trip that showed genuine concern for peace with Russia. The Wallace-ites were trumpeting their feelings and desires for peace and Henry Wallace persistently had been stating a personal willingness to go to Russia.

There was a third failure. The Department of State and in some respects Secretary Marshall erred in not

understanding Truman's political problems in the autumn of 1948. Marshall had not proposed the mission and when he heard of it he strongly and effectively opposed it. But the Secretary had gotten so embroiled in diplomatic concerns, admittedly important in the closing months of 1948, that he forgot the difficult and almost impossible political troubles of Truman. The Secretary went about his business and almost saw it ruined because the President in a desperate move gave evidence of infirmity in United States foreign policy. The Secretary had political acumen, as in his statements at the outset of his secretaryship both to the press and President that he was not available for a presidential draft in the election of 1948. Marshall also was one of the few high officials in Washington who had enough loyalty, not to mention political good sense, to go down to the Washington Union Station in the autumn of 1948 and see the President off when Truman was going out on his long whistlestopping tour in the campaign against Dewey. There was never any question of Marshall's loyalty during that impossible time when all signs pointed to Truman's defeat, despite presidential willingness to go to the far reaches of the nation, traveling 31,700 miles and delivering 356 speeches, as many as sixteen speeches in one day, talking to between twelve and fifteen million people. Where Marshall made his mistake, again, was not to realize Truman's intense personal difficulty having to support an aggressive foreign policy in the midst of a political campaign.

It was probably natural that the President's po-

litical troubles would lead to diplomatic trouble. Truman had a party doubly split—disaffection in the South led by Senator Strom Thurmond of South Carolina, and resuscitation of the old Progressive Party now led by Wallace and including a medley of fellow travelers and communists. The Wallace-ite Progressives were the more embarrassing; they threatened Democratic votes in the North, in particular New York State, and they eventually took New York out of the Democratic camp and gave the state's big electoral vote to the Republicans. The stock in trade of the Wallace-ites was blind love of peace, reinforced by explanations that the Administration was dividing the world with the Truman Doctrine and the Marshall Plan and producing a third great war in the twentieth century. Despite the national resolve to stand up to the communists, evidenced in the decisive foreign policies of the year 1947, there was just enough residual popular belief in the need to negotiate, enough fear that the Truman Administration was not negotiating, enough evidence that normal diplomatic channels had become almost impossible and the United Nations Assembly and Security Council were merely sounding boards for propaganda, to give point to the Wallace-ite assertions that at the very least the United States Government should make one more effort to send a special mission to Moscow. There had been all the missions in the past, not merely during the Second World War; and it was easy to argue without knowledge of reasons behind events that some of the Second World War missions had succeeded—such as Harry Hopkins' mission to Stalin 1945 when the UN Charter was stymied at San Francisco. The Amer-

ican people anyway had great belief in reasoned argument, implicit in the ideas of their democracy. Stalin had seemed reasonable, listening to Westerners with his quiet mien, smoking and doodling as envoys talked Western logic.

Such was the situation in which two of Truman's speech writers, David Noyes and Albert Z. Carr, apparently conceived the idea of sending Chief Justice Vinson to Moscow, just as Chief Justice John Jay had gone to London in 1794 and concluded a treaty ending somewhat similar quarreling between the United States and England, and as (so Truman recalled in his memoirs) the Chief Justice of England, Viscount Reading, had come to the United States during the First World War and quietly galvanized Anglo-American amity.[1] Noyes and Carr wrote a speech which Truman was to give over a nationwide radio hookup. The idea attracted Truman and he called in Vinson and asked him to go. He told Vinson of trouble over control of atomic energy, at that time a wrangling in the UN about the key point of inspection. He said he wanted Vinson to play it by ear but let Stalin see the sincerity of the American people. Vinson after some meditation in the presidential office, and a statement that the Supreme Court's function was not to engage in politics, agreed to go. The Chief Justice consented on Sunday, October 3, in two talks. The President told his press secretary Charles G. Ross to request free time on the networks. Meanwhile he decided to talk with Secretary of State Marshall, then in Paris, by teletype on Tuesday, October 5.

Difficulties inherent in this presidential approach to

Russia became clear on the fateful Tuesday, in conversation with Marshall wherein the Secretary said a special mission would cut the ground under his negotiations at the UN General Assembly meeting in Paris over the Berlin blockade. Marshall said also that the Security Council had just started to consider the American-British-French resolution condemning the Soviets for the blockade. The Secretary raised the issue of consultation with America's allies—which, of course, the President could do only with risk of a leak and ruination of what Truman hoped would be a surprise move. According to Jonathan Daniels who then was a White House aide the President emerged from the communications room crestfallen, having promised Marshall he would not send Vinson. Daniels and some of the White House staff argued with the President, both as advisers on policy and on the election campaign. According to Daniels, Truman just listened, and his owl-like eyes, magnified by the thick lens of his glasses, seemed almost slate gray. Then he said quietly, "I have heard enough. We won't do it." Daniels watched in silence while the President got up and went out of the glass-paned door of the office onto the terrace by the rose garden and walked back toward the White House alone, very much alone. No dramatics, no remarks about rather being right than being President. Next time Daniels saw Truman he was laughing with reporters and politicians and the police at the railway station "as he got back on that long train which everyone seemed so sure was taking him nowhere."[2]

The presidential decision of Tuesday stuck, but not

before Truman showed some signs of indecision to two Senators, Connally and Vandenberg. Their separate accounts published some years later are in general agreement.[3] The President summoned both men to the White House that Tuesday evening for a quiet off-the-record meeting. When Connally got there first he found Truman still undecided about the Vinson mission. "He was still trying to work up his courage to send Vinson to Moscow." Waiting for Vandenberg they talked generally about policies. At one point he asked the Senators what they thought of his making a person-to-person telephone call to Stalin. Connally and Vandenberg at once opposed. "You don't know any Russian and he doesn't know any English," Connally recalled saying. "Besides there's the question of authenticity. After you finish talking, what will you have? No witnesses or documents. And there's no possible way of telling about commitments agreed upon or promises made regarding the future." Truman looked disappointed. After the two Senators left, Vandenberg said to Connally, "He must be feeling desperate about the campaign." Connally recorded himself as saying nothing.

It was after this that the fat fell into the fire, because Charlie Ross felt it incumbent upon himself to explain to a network why he was asking for free time—so the President could explain the proposed Vinson mission. After the inevitable network leak there seem to have been comments by State Department officers to newspaper correspondents, presumably "for background only."[4] Word of the mission got into the papers on Friday, October 8, and pro-

duced a large to-do, a good part of it political. The President had made a mistake. Truman had given appearance—so dangerous in public life—of indecision. When he knew the affair was going to get into the papers he tried to repair the damage by calling Marshall home for the nominal purpose of a report on the Paris proceedings. In a communiqué of the meeting between him and Marshall which took place on Saturday, October 9, Truman chose his words on the Vinson mission as carefully as possible: "Secretary Marshall described to me the situation which we faced in Paris, and, in the light of his report and the possibilities of misunderstanding to which any unilateral action, however desirable otherwise, could lead at present, I decided not to take this step." Marshall also in a communiqué that Saturday sought to cover over any troubles, making his sudden appearance in Washington seem a natural and regular meeting: "The President called me home . . . We settled on this week end as being the time most convenient to both of us to get together. I did not know until I got off the plane this morning of the statements in the press regarding the matter of Chief Justice Vinson making a direct approach to Generalissimo Stalin." That, then, was the end of things.

Truman's memoir commentary on this Vinson confusion is puzzling, if only because it required several pages of explanation—being obviously something still preying on his mind. His account does not altogether jibe with those of other participants and observers and one suspects that the former President, writing his memoirs in retirement in Kansas City, liked to recall the more successful aspects of his

Administration and discount commentary of the opposition. The memoirs assert that the President would have consulted the Allies before sending Vinson, but print the communiqué of Saturday, October 9, which embarrassingly refers to "unilateral action" as what Truman had in mind.[5] The memoirs also state, quite erroneously, that a newspaper leak preceded Truman's abandonment of the mission:

> But before the complicated international machinery could be coordinated and all clearances obtained, there was an unfortunate leak to an unfriendly newspaper, and a big outcry of "appeasement," "politics," "unilateral action" was picked by other newspapers and press services. The Vinson mission was severely embarrassed before it could even be fully explored with all the powers concerned. . . . Following the premature publication . . . a number of complications set in that compelled me to reconsider the advisability of this mission. I had a talk with Secretary Marshall in Paris. . .[6]

The record is clear that Marshall's immediate opposition, given three days before the newspaper publication, killed the proposal. And it is interesting to see in the Truman memoirs a frank avowal that the mission had a political purpose. The President was pleased to relate that he obtained political mileage out of the proposal, even though Vinson didn't go to Russia. In a campaign speech before the American Legion in Miami he contended that the mission had sought to dispel "the present poisonous atmosphere of distrust . . . My emissary was to convey the

seriousness and sincerity of the people of the United States." A great many people, he explained in his memoirs, "now began to realize that the prospects for peace were to be best served in the hands of this Democratic administration."[7]

In the autumn of 1948 political rumor continued to circulate about an Administration trip to Russia, and some days after the Vinson affair, on October 22, James Reston of the New York *Times* telephoned Senator Vandenberg, then in Grand Rapids, about a rumor that had reached Reston's colleague Krock that Truman had in mind a new version of the Vinson mission and this version had Vandenberg's approval. The Senator cryptically telegraphed Truman's aide in Washington, Matthew J. Connelly, that he, Vandenberg, did not approve a phone call to Stalin. Connelly sent the message to the presidential campaign train. Truman wired back to Grand Rapids: "Nothing will be done without consultation with you."[8]

It was an unfortunate affair, whatever political advantage Truman obtained or could have obtained. No one probably ever will be able to penetrate the recesses of the mind of the then ruler of Russia, and Stalin may or may not have taken the President's confusion amiss. At that precise time the Berlin airlift was getting underway, and promised success, but shortly came the bad weather during November and December, 1948, and Stalin may have recalled the presidential indecision and wondered if by hanging on a little more the Russians might force the Americans to retreat from the city.

CHAPTER FIFTEEN

LATER YEARS

G EORGE C. Marshall lived for a little more than
ten years after his resignation as Secretary of
State on January 20, 1949. Ill health compelled his
retirement after a kidney operation in December,
1948. He had remained in office during the last months
only out of loyalty to President Truman who was in
the hectic election campaign.

Upon receiving Marshall's resignation Truman
could do little other than accept it, for clearly the
general, as everyone called him, could not continue
as Secretary of State. The President commented once
more on Marshall's many services to the country.
He was deeply grateful for the general's work at the
Department. [1] Marshall held equal affection for Harry
S. Truman who he felt was not a politician but a
statesman. The general could remark in honesty that
"the full stature of this man will only be proven by
history, but I want to say here and now that there has
never been a decision under this man's administration,
affecting policies beyond our shores, that has not been
in the best interest of this country. It is not the courage
of these decisions that will live, but the integrity of
them." [2]

The loyalty that held Marshall and Truman together is worth examination in detail, because theirs
was no ordinary friendship and because also it oc-

curred at a time when the President needed a man in the Department, his first Cabinet officer, whom he could trust and rely upon. The times required confidence between the two men, and great confidence there was. Truman doubtless liked the general's nonpartisanship, Marshall's desire to make the secretaryship a job above or outside of politics. It was not merely that Marshall by following out this desire made his own path and that of Truman easier in Congress, especially such a Republican Congress as assembled in 1947 and remained in office until Marshall left the Department. Marshall's desire to run a nonpartisan Department also kept the general out of the covert enumerations which went on during 1947 and part of 1948 with the purpose of replacing Truman as the Democratic presidential nominee in 1948. There was plenty of disloyalty in the Democratic Party, with the boss of Chicago, Jack Arvey, in almost open disaffection, the Mayor of New York, William O'Dwyer, out of line, and many other politicos moving uneasily against the President's projected nomination and campaign. It seemed as if Truman could not win, and it must have been a great source of security to know that General Marshall, for one, was not trying to undercut him or willing to stand by while others undercut him. Marshall was one of the few leaders in Washington, as mentioned, who saw Truman off at the Union Station. Nonpartisanship did not keep the general from demonstrating his affection for a fellow fighter and Truman enormously appreciated it.

Before, during, and after Marshall's secretaryship the lives of the two men were replete with indica-

tions of Truman's and—after the general became well acquainted with the President—of Marshall's esteem. When following the kidney operation Marshall was recuperating in Pinehurst, North Carolina, and lay in bed sleeping one afternoon, a cavalcade pulled up outside the cabin and there was the President of the United States, on hand to visit his esteemed Secretary of State. The President had slipped unobtrusively out of Washington, failing purposely to take any credit through publicity for what was a kindly visit. There later was some twitting of Mr. Truman by the reporters, for the President went down to nearby Fort Bragg in the Air Force constellation plane unofficially named the "Dewdrop," the aircraft that the manufacturers had intended as the official ship for Governor Dewey when the latter entered the presidency. "This one rides very well," he told the newsmen who had inquired about the "Dewdrop," "but the 'Independence' is better." But apart from this joshing, which the President indulged with glee, his purpose had been to see Marshall, and the Secretary of State was indeed pleased.[3]

Time after time Truman showed his liking for Marshall, and vice versa. The President gave a speech about Marshall and afterward wrote to Paul G. Hoffman on June 7, 1949: "Thanks a lot for your note of the sixth. I enjoyed the meeting very much and I was talking from the heart—the General is at the top in my book."[4] That Christmas from Pinehurst there issued a cordial greeting in the rounded script:

My dear Mr. President: Mrs. Marshall and I send you and Mrs. Truman, and Margaret, our

affectionate holiday greetings. And I add my gratitude and keen appreciation for all you have done in my behalf, with assurances of my deep feeling of loyalty to you and yours. May 1950 bring you all you wish for and continued good health. G. C. Marshall. Pinehurst, N. C. 12/23/49[5]

For Marshall there was still to be another stint of public service, for after outbreak of the Korean War in June, 1950, President Truman on September 21 called back "the greatest living American" to be Secretary of Defense. Again the friendship and trust. To Mrs. Marshall the President wrote jocularly after going through some of the congressional mechanics of Marshall's appointment:

As you are the General's superior officer I send you a personal souvenir which you may wish to koop. Not attompting to oottlo tho ancicnt ques tion as to which is mightier, the pen or the sword —the General is facile in the use of both—I am forwarding the implement with which I had the pleasure of approving today H.R. 9646, "An Act to authorize the President to appoint General of the Army George C. Marshall to the office of Secretary of Defense." I wish for your sake and for the General's that this meant less instead of more work for him.[6]

The general found occasion for appreciation to the President on Truman's birthday, May 8, 1951, and sent him a fine note:

I wish that your birthday could have fallen this year on a more peaceful and less critical day. However, I tender my congratulations along with great satisfaction in the fact that you are hale and hearty with both feet on the ground.

That was a fine speech you made last night. I wish I could do equally well before the committees of Congress this morning. However, I will do my best. It probably will be a rather warm affair.

With great respect and warmest personal congratulations.[7]

Marshall enjoyed being Secretary of Defense, for he instinctively knew his way around in that area. He had experienced the embarrassment of being Secretary of State during the nadir of America's military power. He had done well at diplomacy, proving the right man for the work in 1947 and 1948, but in the Department of Defense the former Chief of Staff was putting his hands on levers he fully understood. He knew staff work, and the job at the Pentagon was by 1950 and 1951 second nature.

Once the Korean mobilization was moving easily, and command difficulties in the Far East had found settlement, and he had testified in favor of the Administration during the sensational "MacArthur hearings" of Congress in the spring and summer of 1951, the time came for permanent retirement: September 12, 1951.

Affection between Truman and Marshall continued unabated. Ferdinand Pecora asked Truman to address a dinner of the Four Freedoms Foundation when it

would present its annual award to Marshall. The President could not go, and he was deeply disappointed. He jotted a note to his secretary, William D. Hassett: "Mr. Hassett: give them an all out message—whistles, stops all out etc. Wish I could go HST."[8] A high school principal from Wheeler, Indiana, caught the President's fancy when he inquired what people had impressed him most—Stalin, Churchill, Queen Elizabeth, etc. The answer was: "I have met a great many distinguished people of this age since I have been President. I have been closely associated with General George C. Marshall, whom I consider one of the great men of this age." In the next sentence of what proved a long letter Truman mentioned President F. D. Roosevelt.[9]

Marshall on November 6, 1952, sent a handwritten letter to the President before Truman's own retirement from politics, a remarkable letter considering the supposedly reserved nature of the general:

> For you I will always have the deepest of gratitude, and, I think, of understanding more possibly than any other man. Always you supported me to the full. Always in International and National Defense matters you took the courageous stand; and for that I am sure history will mark your record clearly as having met the great world problems of the past eight years with initiative, courage and wisdom.
>
> I hope your health has not suffered from the severity of the campaign.

With my love to Margaret and my affectionate regards to Mrs. Truman and you personally.

With great respect.

Faithfully yours,
G. C. Marshall[10]

The general spent his final years, except for the months just before his death, in the quiet and comfort of Dodona Manor in the summer, Pinehurst in winter. For the most part his health stood up in good shape. But he was in his seventies and feeling his age; the strenuous forty-five years of active Army service, not to mention his diplomatic career in 1947-48, and later service as Secretary of Defense, had worn down his resistance and energy. In this twilight of his life he continued to make numerous appearances—excursions into the capital or to New York, speeches as he accepted awards of one kind and another. He received the Nobel Peace Prize in December, 1953, the first professional soldier ever to obtain it. On public occasions the general often spoke extempore. He would point out the necessary connection between diplomacy and military power, recall the battles and campaigns in the several combat theaters of the Second World War, ending these discourses with remarks about the abiding strength and decency of the American people. In his extraordinary fashion he managed to lift his auditors out of whatever mental ruts they had been traveling and show them the splendors of the world as, under peace and justice, their countrymen might help to organize it in the future.

There was a magical wholesomeness in Marshall's speeches. Marshall was a true gentleman, had been so all his life, and he evoked the same character in the minds and hearts of his listeners.

The general had developed a great sense of history, and took pride in the historical importance of the Marshall Plan, his greatest achievement as Secretary of State. In a ceremony on June 5, 1949, honoring him on the second anniversary of his speech inaugurating the plan, he told his listeners that

> There is a great difference between reading history and actually living it. For generations, ever since the birth of this Republic, our people have not only felt very remote in distance from Europe but many of them are descendants of people who fled from Europe to escape the peculiar trials and limitations that fell upon people from time to time in the changing fortunes of that crowded but divided continent. Yet, seemingly in a moment, our American people found themselves in a position of not only the most intimate relationship with western Europe, but called upon to make more and heavy contributions to the welfare of your people. To me, the impressive fact is that these people of the United States made an overwhelming and unhesitating decision to do their best to bring western Europe back to peace and prosperity.[11]

He saw the American people in the role of leaders of the world. He often repeated the following peroration (as in a speech of March, 1948):

We have an acknowledged position of leadership in the world. We have been spared the destruction of war which literally flattened Europe. We are enjoying a high degree of prosperity. These things being so, the character and strength of our leadership may well be decisive in the present situation.[12]

He refused to write his memoirs, declaring that to be of any historical importance such a book would have to be very accurate. "That is, you mustn't omit and make it pleasant reading."[13] He feared that if he spoke the truth he would have to say unpleasant things about many men still living, that by being honest he could almost ruin the reputations of at least some people he had known, and yet if one did not mention the unpleasant sides of people—whose personal reputations were tied almost inseparably into the course of public events—it was not history. He said he would have no part in this sort of business during his lifetime. He left his papers to the George C. Marshall Research Foundation, formed in 1953, which constructed a fitting modern library in Lexington between the campuses of Washington and Lee University and VMI, where historians could use the papers and publish books about him after his death. He did consent to a large three-volume projected biography by the skilled military historian Forrest C. Pogue and willingly granted Pogue a series of interviews, many of them taped, in which he recalled his career in long detail, especially his years as a youth and beginning soldier—the time when he failed to keep papers and the record was

obscure. The taped interviews, like his papers of later times, were to be under lock and key until Pogue published the biography and until, of course, the general passed on.

At last the end came—after a lingering illness the general died in Walter Reed Army Hospital on October 16, 1959, at the age of seventy-eight. There were military obsequies *de rigueur*, but without special ceremony, as he had requested. His former subordinate, President Eisenhower, attended the short service in the chapel at Fort Myer. So did former President Truman. Reporters noted that the two men, reputed to be at outs, shook hands on this first time since they had come together since the funeral of Chief Justice Vinson in 1953. At the chapel there was no eulogy. The family and honorary pallbearers accompanied the hearse to the burial plot in Arlington.

Tributes to Marshall poured in, many showing genuine grief.[11] Former President Truman, whose face appeared sadly drawn at the funeral, produced an extravagant but altogether sincere appraisal. "He was the greatest general since Robert E. Lee. He was the greatest administrator since Thomas Jefferson [*sic!*]. He was the man of honor, the man of truth, the man of greatest ability. He was the greatest of the great in our time." Paul Hoffman, administrator of the Marshall Plan, in a public letter declared him to have been "the most selfless man I have ever known." Dean Acheson produced a finely wrought "Homage to General Marshall" in which he recalled the fond if formal relations between "Acheson" and "General Marshall." George Kennan, by this time a senior observer of

American foreign policy and its major figures, made a measured commentary in a letter to the New York *Times*. The functions and traditional procedures of the Department of State, Kennan said, had been mostly a mystery to Marshall, as were those of the Foreign Service. The general had taken on the secretaryship out of a sense of duty rather than personal inclination. He brought a refreshing directness and organization to his work, and willingness to make decisions without agonizing over them. He had failed in China not because of any illusions or hallucinations but because the problem was too large and the possibilities for helpful American action too slender. And he had left office wearing the same personal qualities with which he came. Having occupied an office that sometimes broke its holders, Marshall did not break or change. He was ever "the image of the American gentleman at his best—honorable, courteous, devoid of arrogance, exacting of others but even more of himself, intolerant only of cowardice, deviousness and cynicism." It was a tribute from an individual who liked to describe himself as a realist in world affairs. Kennan, like almost all of Marshall's countrymen, recognized the nearly perfect matching of the real and ideal, in some sense the general and the diplomat, in this man who had come a long way in history from that distant era of his birth one December day in the year 1880 when Rutherford B. Hayes was President of the United States and little boys could grow up in Uniontown, Pennsylvania, in blacksmith shops and organ lofts and attend VMI with its memories of the Civil War, then the only real war.

GLOSSARY OF ABBREVIATIONS

ADA	Atomic Development Authority
AEC	United States Atomic Energy Commission
CEEC	Committee of European Economic Cooperation
CIA	Central Intelligence Agency
EAC	European Advisory Commission
ECA	Economic Cooperation Administration
GATT	General Agreement on Tariffs and Trade
JCS	Joint Chiefs of Staff
NSC	National Security Council
OAS	Organization of American States
OEEC	Organization for European Economic Cooperation
UMT	Universal Military Training
UNAEC	United Nations Atomic Energy Commission
UNRRA	United Nations Relief and Rehabilitation Administration
UNSCOP	United Nations Special Committee on Palestine
VMI	Virginia Military Institute
WEU	Western European Union

NOTES

GEORGE C. MARSHALL

CHAPTER ONE

1. Mrs. Fred Martin to Truman, n.d., OF 20, Harry S. Truman MSS, Truman Library, Independence, Mo.

2. Forrest C. Pogue, *George C. Marshall: Education of a General* (New York, 1963), pp. 30-31.

3. Robert Payne, *The Marshall Story: A Biography of General George C. Marshall* (New York, 1951).

4. Katherine Tupper Marshall, *Together: Annals of an Army Wife* (New York, 1946), p. 135.

5. Forrest C. Pogue, *George C. Marshall*, pp. 123-124.

6. Katherine T. Marshall, *Together*, p. 18. Also Forrest C. Pogue, *George C. Marshall*, pp. 281-282.

7. For Pershing's efforts to assist Marshall, see Pogue, *George C. Marshall*, pp. 293-297, and Pogue's "General Marshall and the Pershing Papers," *Quarterly Journal*, vol. 21 (1964), 1-11. The conversation between Hagood and Dern appears in William Frye, *Marshall: Citizen Soldier* (Indianapolis, 1947), p. 234.

8. Robert Payne, *The Marshall Story*, p. 118.

9. Arthur Bryant, *Triumph in the West* (New York, 1959). The Chief of the Imperial General Staff, Sir Alan Brooke, carried on a long strategic argument with Marshall, as did Churchill.

10. Remarks of former President Eisenhower in *Addresses Delivered at the Dedication Ceremonies of the George C. Marshall Research Library, May 23, 1964* (Lexington, Virginia), p. 14.

11. *Ibid.*, p. 15.

12. Samuel Eliot Morison, *Strategy and Compromise* (Boston, 1958). This volume reports conversation by the author with Marshall.

13. Marshall's remarks on relations with Roosevelt are in Forrest C. Pogue, *George C. Marshall,* pp. 323-324. Dean Acheson heard only Mrs. Marshall address him as "George." *Sketches from Life* (New York, Harper and Row, 1960), p. 147. Senator Arthur H. Vandenberg wrote Mrs. Vandenberg on July 26, 1948 that Robert A. Lovett, then Marshall's Undersecretary of State, "was in for his usual Sunday rendezvous. He said he never knew Marshall to call any but four special people by their first names—his wife, his stepdaughter, Bob's wife and you. He never calls a man by his first name." Arthur H. Vandenberg, Jr., and Joe Alex Morris, eds., *The Private Papers of Senator Vandenberg* (Boston, Houghton Mifflin Co., 1952), p. 449.

14. Frank McNaughton and Walter Hehmeyer, *This Man Truman* (New York, 1945), pp. 55-56. Hehmeyer handled publicity for the wartime Truman Committee.

15. Henry L. Stimson and McGeorge Bundy, *On Active Service in Peace and War* (New York, 1948), p. 661.

CHAPTER TWO

1. Albert C. Wedemeyer, *Wedemeyer Reports!* (New York, 1958), p. 295.

2. Parker La Moore, *"Pat" Hurley: The Story of an American* (New York, 1932); also Don Lohbeck, *Patrick J. Hurley* (Chicago, 1956).

3. Diary entry of Nov. 27, 1945, in Walter Millis and E. S. Duffield, eds., *The Forrestal Diaries* (New York, 1951), p. 113. My thanks to Princeton University for permission to quote from the published Forrestal diaries. "Pat's fiasco did not confer any credit upon him," wrote the chairman of the Senate Foreign Relations Committee to a friend. "All we had to do

was let him rave." Tom Connally to Harry B. Hawes, Dec. 17, 1945, Connally MSS deposited in the Library of Congress.

4. For the episode of the President's call and Marshall's answer, *Together*, p. 282.

5. *Addresses Delivered at the Dedication Ceremonies of the George C. Marshall Research Library, May 23, 1964*, p. 17.

6. See the careful account in Herbert Feis, *The China Tangle* (Princeton, 1953), pp. 413-430.

7. Dept. of State *Bulletin*, vol. 13 (Dec. 16, 1945), 946.

8. Letter of Dec. 18, 1945, OF 150, Truman MSS.

9. Tillman Durdin, in *New York Times Magazine*, Jan. 19, 1947. This entry and subsequent references or quotations to the *Times*, copyright 1947-50, 1959, by The New York Times Company. Reprinted by permission.

10. US Sen., 82d Cong., 1st Sess., *Institute of Pacific Relations: Hearings before the Subcommittee to Investigate the Administration of the Internal Security Act and Other Internal Security Laws of the Committee of the Judiciary* (15 vols., Washington, 1951-53), V, 1656.

11. *Loc. cit.*

12. *Op. cit.*, p. 1653.

13. Dept. of State *Bulletin*, vol. 15 (Dec. 29, 1946), 1179-1183.

14. *Bulletin*, vol. 16 (Jan. 19, 1947), 83-85.

CHAPTER THREE

1. Diary of Fleet Admiral William D. Leahy, deposited in the Library of Congress. Entry of Jan. 8, 1947.

2. New York *Times*, Jan. 8, 1947.

3. *Ibid.*, Jan. 9.

4. *Loc. cit.*

5. New York *Times*, Jan. 12, 1947.

6. Arthur H. Vandenberg, Jr., and Joe Alex Morris, eds., *The Private Papers of Senator Vandenberg*, pp. 337-338.

7. Leahy diary, Jan. 21, 1947.

8. New York *Times*, Jan. 22, 1947.

9. Leahy diary, Jan. 21, 1947.

10. Joseph W. Martin, Jr., as told to Robert J. Donovan, *My First Fifty Years in Politics* (New York, 1960), p. 179. This and subsequent quotation from the above volume by kind permission of Representative Martin.

11. Arthur H. Vandenberg, Jr., in *The Private Papers of Senator Vandenberg*, p. xv.

12. Tom Connally, as told to Alfred Steinberg, *My Name is Tom Connally* (New York, Thomas Y. Crowell, 1954), p. 311.

13. Marshall to Davies, Feb. 19, 1947, OF 20, Truman MSS.

14. James Reston, New York *Times*, Feb. 15.

15. Goss to Truman, Jan. 24, 1946, Truman to Goss, Feb. 2, OF 20, Truman MSS.

16. Robert T. Oliver, "Our Ailing Diplomacy," *Christian Century*, vol. 64 (Mar. 26, 1947), 398.

17. *Lying in State* (Garden City, New York, Doubleday, 1952), p. 145.

18. 80th Cong., 1st Sess., *Congressional Record*, vol. 93, p. 5296.

19. Dept. of State *Bulletin*, vol. 18 (Apr. 11, 1948), 489-490.

20. Diary entry of Mar. 9, 1947, in *The Journals of David E. Lilienthal* (2 vols., New York, Harper and Row, 1964), II, 158-159.

21. Diary entry of June 13, 1947, in Walter Millis and Eugene S. Duffield, eds., *The Forrestal Diaries*, p. 279.

22. Interview of Dean Acheson with Mrs. St. John Garwood, Nov. 2, 1958, Oral History Research Office, Columbia University.

23. Harry S. Truman, *Memoirs: Years of Trial and Hope, 1946-1952* (New York, 1956), p. 112. Quotations from both volumes of the Truman memoirs by kind permission of LIFE Magazine (c) 1956 Time Inc. All rights reserved.

24. Dean Acheson, *Sketches from Life*, p. 148.

25. New York *Times*, May 19, 1949.

CHAPTER FOUR

1. *The Marshall Story*, p. 289.

2. Speech of Feb. 22, 1947, in Dept. of State *Bulletin*, vol. 16 (Mar. 2, 1947), 391.

3. Lucius D. Clay, *Decision in Germany* (Garden City, N.Y., Doubleday, 1950), p. 152.

4. *War or Peace* (New York, 1950), pp. 110-111, 168.

5. "On the other hand, when on the second night we went to see 'Swan Lake' at the Ballet Theatre, we entered an entirely different world of astounding artistic beauty and performance. The 'Bolshoi' was crowded to suffocation. The dancers are among the very highest paid of the Russian comrades and the people of Moscow told me that in many cases weeks and months elapse before they are able to obtain ballet seats. The depression of the trip was almost insignificant as compared with the charm of this one evening." Stanton Griffis, *Lying in State*, p. 189.

6. *As It Happened* (New York, 1954), p. 237.

7. Dean Acheson, *Sketches from Life*, pp. 2-3. See also Lord Strang, *Home and Abroad* (London, 1956), ch. 11, "Ernest Bevin," pp. 287-300; Francis Williams, *Ernest Bevin* (London, 1952), pp. 244-247.

8. Walter Bedell Smith, *My Three Years in Moscow* (Philadelphia, Lippincott, 1950), pp. 215-216.

9. Robert D. Murphy, *Diplomat among Warriors* (New York, Doubleday, 1963), p. 306.

10. Lucius D. Clay, *Decision in Germany*, p. 148.

11. Mark W. Clark, *Calculated Risk* (New York, 1950), p. 487.

12. Walter Bedell Smith, *My Three Years in Moscow*, p. 216.

13. James Reston in the New York *Times*, Apr. 30, 1947; Lucius D. Clay, *Decision in Germany*, pp. 148-149.

14. The following account relies on Walter Bedell Smith, *My Three Years in Moscow,* pp. 217ff.

15. Diary entry of Apr. 28, 1947, in Walter Millis and Eugene S. Duffield, eds., *The Forrestal Diaries,* pp. 266-267.

16. James Reston in the New York *Times,* Apr. 25, 1947.

17. Speech in Pittsburgh of Jan. 15, 1948, in Dept. of State *Bulletin,* vol. 18 (Jan. 25, 1948), 108.

18. Forrestal to Trenholm H. Marshall, Feb. 20, 1948. James V. Forrestal MSS deposited in Princeton University Library.

19. Quoted in Tang Tsou, "Civil Strife and Armed Intervention: Marshall's China Policy," *Orbis,* vol. 6 (1962), 89-90.

CHAPTER FIVE

1. New York *Times,* Mar. 12, 1947.

2. Walter Lippmann, *Isolation and Alliances* (Boston, 1952), pp. 31-32.

3. Winston S. Churchill, *Triumph and Tragedy* (Boston, 1953), p. 227.

4. William H. McNeill, *The Greek Dilemma: War and Aftermath* (Philadelphia, 1947); and especially McNeill's *Greece: American Aid in Action, 1947-1956* (New York, 1957).

5. Arthur H. Vandenberg, Jr., and Joe Alex Morris, eds., *The Private Papers of Senator Vandenberg,* pp. 338-339.

6. Leahy diary, Mar. 7, 1947. The admiral did feel that the new American stand if necessary for good military reasons was in a larger sense bad policy, "a reversal of the traditional American policy to avoid involvement in the political difficulties of European States." Diary, Mar. 10, 1947.

7. In a letter of May 21, 1952 to Harold Moody, principal of Wheeler High School, Wheeler, Indiana, Truman put the "decision to prevent Greece and Turkey from becoming satellites of the Soviet Union" as second after the atomic bomb, and on a par with "the decision to prevent Berlin from becoming a part of East Germany." PPF 6068, Truman MSS. For other points in this extraordinary letter see the present volume, p. 264.

8. Harry S. Truman, *Memoirs: Years of Trial and Hope,* p. 105.

9. Details of drafting the Truman Doctrine speech appear in Joseph M. Jones, *The Fifteen Weeks (February 21-June 5, 1947)* (New York, 1955).

10. Undated memorandum, Joseph M. Jones MSS, Truman Library.

11. Joseph M. Jones, *The Fifteen Weeks,* p. 159.

12. To Loring Pickering, Mar. 18, 1948, OF 1170, Truman MSS.

13. Joseph M. Jones, *The Fifteen Weeks,* pp. 178-179.

14. Clipping in Truman MSS; Smith to Truman, June 18, 1947; N. E. Martin to Truman, Elm Creek, Nebr., Apr. 16; Boykin telegram, Apr. 9; resolution of the Texas House of Representatives and President's reply, Truman MSS; Truman to Melton, Apr. 15; Truman to Starr, Apr. 16, and Starr correspondence and copy of the Allen column: above material all in OF 1170, Truman MSS.

15. Letter of Apr. 15, OF 1170, Truman MSS.

16. Leahy diary, Apr. 15, 1947.

17. Husted McCullough Meyer to Truman, Apr. 7, 1947, OF 426, Truman MSS.

18. Diary entry of Mar. 23, 1947 in *The Journals of David E. Lilienthal,* II, 163-164.

19. Leahy diary, Feb. 27.

20. *Ibid.,* Mar. 10.

21. Joseph M. Jones, *The Fifteen Weeks,* p. 195.

22. *Rocky Mountain News,* Apr. 11, 1947, OF 426, Truman MSS.

23. Joseph W. Martin, Jr., as told to Robert J. Donovan, *My First Fifty Years in Politics,* p. 193.

24. *My Name is Tom Connally,* p. 319.

25. Dept. of State *Bulletin,* supplement, "Aid to Greece and Turkey: a Collection of State Papers," vol. 16 (May 4, 1947), containing the 111 questions and answers in pp. 866-895.

26. Arthur H. Vandenberg, Jr., and Joe Alex Morris, eds., *The Private Papers of Senator Vandenberg,* pp. 344-345.

27. *Ibid.*, pp. 347, 350.

28. Joseph M. Jones, *The Fifteen Weeks*, p. 197. For an interesting analysis of the congressional temper during passage of the Truman Doctrine see Albert R. Sellen, "Congressional Opinion of Soviet-American Relations: 1945-1950," thesis at the University of Chicago, 1954, pp. 76-87. Also H. Bradford Westerfield, *Foreign Policy and Party Politics: Pearl Harbor to Korea* (New Haven, 1955), ch. 10, pp. 221-226.

29. Undated draft of presidential press release in Clark Clifford Files, Truman Library.

30. *Greece: American Aid in Action*, p. 23.

31. The Democratic State Chairman, William Ritchie, said publicly: "The Democrats of Nebraska were not consulted in this matter, and we wonder if the Republican party of Nebraska was." J. H. Norris wrote to Truman, Nov. 20, 1947. The President answered a few days later that he had known Griswold since the two men had gone to school together at Fort Sill during the First World War. Moreover, Griswold was "always, in my opinion, a good administrator, although I never agreed with him politically. The job he has is not a political job, but an administrative job, and a very difficult one at that, and he is doing it very well. It is necessary for me on some occasions to pick men for the job, not because they are politically correct from my viewpoint, but because they can do the job, and that is the reason Griswold is in Greece." Truman to Norris, Nov. 25, 1947, OF 206E, Truman MSS.

CHAPTER SIX

1. Press release of Feb. 14, 1947, OF 426, Truman MSS.

2. Will Clayton believed that the British did not take proper precautions—as they could have done under the loan agreement—to prevent conversion of war debts held in India and Egypt, and that a great deal of the pressure on sterling came thereby, via Amsterdam and Brussels. W. L. Clayton Reminiscences in the Oral History Research Office, Columbia

University, 1962. For the loan consult Richard N. Gardner, *Sterling-Dollar Diplomacy* (Oxford, 1956), pp. 188-254, 306-347.

The embarrassments of 1947 were all a saddening come-down for the British who probably had been dreaming ever since the war that their country might resume its place in world affairs; the convertibility fiasco, coupled with other clear signs of Britain's economic weakness and dependence on the United States, raised to public view the facts of British economic life. Not least of the troubles, moreover, was the comment of many Americans, some (such as Secretary Forrestal) in high public life, that socialism was the chief problem in Britain—that the doctrinaires of the Attlee Cabinet had forced the country toward ever more socialistic measures, despite economic costs. There was talk that only American capitalism could generate economic statesmen, that the British doctrinaires were hopeless in the face of economic complexity and general need for common sense. D. C. Watt, *Personalities and Policies* (Notre Dame, Ind., 1965), ch. 3, "American Aid to Britain and the Problem of Socialism, 1945-51."

3. Alfred J. Rieber, *Stalin and the French Communist Party: 1941-1947* (New York, 1962).

4. Theodore H. White, *Fire in the Ashes: Europe in Mid-Century* (New York, 1953), p. 53.

5. Hoyt Price and Carl E. Schorske, *The Problem of Germany* (New York, 1947).

6. Harry S. Truman, *Memoirs: Years of Trial and Hope*, p. 113.

7. Memorandum by F. H. Russell, Apr. 8, 1947, Jones MSS.

8. Jonathan Daniels, *The Man of Independence* (Philadelphia, Lippincott, 1950), p. 323.

9. Interview of Paul Nitze with Mrs. St. John Garwood, Nov. 4, 1958. Oral History Research Office, Columbia University.

10. William L. Clayton, "GATT, The Marshall Plan, and OECD," *Political Science Quarterly*, vol. 78 (1963), 493-503.

11. Harry B. Price, *The Marshall Plan and Its Meaning* (Ithaca, 1955).

12. It appears as if this "memo" by the Staff had much less influence in the Department than the ideas of Will Clayton; the Marshall Plan took its inspiration and detail from Clayton rather than the Kennan memorandum. Clayton had become ill before returning from Europe on May 19; upon arrival in the United States he went to bed under doctor's orders, with a slight attack of pneumonia; so he did not formally present his memorandum to Marshall until May 27. It is true that the Kennan paper bears the date of May 23. But the Undersecretary for Economic Affairs sent his own memorandum to the Department in advance of formal presentation, and it is entirely possible that Secretary Marshall read it before asking Kennan for a paper. Moreover, on this question of the influences of the two memoranda, Kennan's paper was tentative and vague, whereas Clayton's set out the problems of Europe and their solution in clear detail.

One of Clayton's assistants in 1947, Ambassador George C. McGhee, recalls carrying Clayton's memorandum of May 27 to the Department during Clayton's sickness, that is, before May 27, and adds in a letter to the author of March 29, 1965: "As you know, it is a controversial subject, but there is no question in my mind that Clayton should be recognized as the real father of the Marshall Plan."

Assessing Clayton's influence, one must consider—in addition to the Clayton memorandum dated May 27—another paper of his bearing the date of March 5. (Ellen Clayton Garwood, *Will Clayton: A Short Biography* [Austin, Tex., 1958], pp. 115-118, prints the memorandum of March 5.) This earlier memorandum contained some of the ideas of his paper of two and a half months later. Acheson apparently remembers this earlier memorandum: "I know Clayton's memo about the breakdown of relations between town and country in Europe

was written before the May 27 memo that is of record."
(Interview of Dean Acheson with Mrs. St. John Garwood,
Nov. 2, 1958, Oral History Research Office, Columbia University.) Harry Price says that Kennan in writing the Planning
Staff memo of May 23 had before him "a disturbing firsthand
report" prepared by Clayton. (*The Marshall Plan and Its
Meaning*, pp. 21-22.) Thinking that there might have been
some other Clayton memorandum (not that of May 27, not
of March 5), the Department of State recently searched the
working files of the Policy Planning Staff, but failed to find it.
But was not the March 5 memorandum the paper in question? Clayton did not communicate this March memorandum
to Secretary Marshall, who was just going off to the Moscow
Conference. Clayton himself believes Acheson had in mind,
and Kennan read, the memorandum of March 5. In a recent
letter to the author of October 28, 1964, he writes:
"Referring to your mention of my memorandum of March 5
and the fact that the Department had been unable to locate
the other memorandum that I was supposed to have written,
will say that I think your statement that this was probably the
March 5 memorandum is very likely correct. As a matter of
fact, long before I went to Geneva for the GATT Conference,
I had been thinking very seriously of the situation in Western
Europe and the fact that these countries would require financial assistance from the United States in enormous amounts,
otherwise some of them would undoubtedly succumb to Communist threats and offers of material help."

13. Memorandum by Joseph M. Jones, July 2, 1947, Jones
MSS.

14. Joseph M. Jones, *The Fifteen Weeks*, pp. 255-256.

CHAPTER SEVEN

1. Dean Acheson, *Sketches from Life*, p. 2.
2. Hugh Dalton, *High Tide and After: Memoirs, 1945-
1960* (London, 1962), p. 256.

3. Dalton diary, quoted in *Conference of Scholars on the European Recovery Program, March 20-21, 1964, at the Harry S. Truman Library* (Independence, Mo., 1965), p. 26.

4. Harry S. Truman, *Memoirs: Years of Trial and Hope,* p. 116.

5. Joseph M. Jones, *The Fifteen Weeks,* p. 253.

6. Interview of Dean Acheson with Mrs. St. John Garwood, Nov. 2, 1958.

7. The Swiss in March, 1948, signed the convention creating the Organization for European Economic Cooperation (OEEC) but refused to accept Marshall Plan aid.

8. Arthur H. Vandenberg, Jr., and Joe Alex Morris, eds., *The Private Papers of Senator Vandenberg,* p. 376. For congressional reaction see Albert R. Sellen, "Congressional Opinion of Soviet-American Relations: 1945-50," pp. 96-116; H. B. Westerfield, *Foreign Policy and Party Politics,* pp. 379-380.

9. Leahy diary, Nov. 17, 1947.

10. *The Private Papers of Senator Vandenberg,* pp. 379-380.

11. Editorial comment in OF 426, Truman MSS.

12. David J. Evans to Truman, Dec. 30, 1947, OF 1170, Truman MSS; J. R. Wallace to William D. Hassett, secretary to the President, Mar. 20, 1948, OF 1170; Herbert L. Davis to Truman, Mar. 31, 1948, OF 1170; New York *Times,* Mar. 18, 1948.

13. Letter to Mrs. Vandenberg, *c.* Nov. 13, 1947, in *Private Papers of Senator Vandenberg,* p. 379.

14. New York *Times,* Jan. 9, 1948.

15. *Loc. cit.*

16. Dean Acheson, *Sketches from Life,* pp. 55-57.

17. Dept. of State *Bulletin,* vol. 17 (July 13, 1947), 84; vol. 1 7(Oct. 26, 1947), 828; vol. 17 (Nov. 23, 1947), 972; vol. 18 (Jan. 18, 1948), 72.

18. *Bulletin,* vol. 17 (Nov. 2, 1947), 857.

19. John Leighton Stuart, *Fifty Years in China* (New York, 1954), p. 236.

20. Dept. of State *Bulletin,* vol. 18 (Mar. 21, 1948), 374.

21. *Ibid.*, p. 381. The fall of Czechoslovakia also sparked the beginning of American military rearmament, for which see below, pp. 237 ff.

22. For the effort to name Acheson see the interesting remarks of Senator Vandenberg to Lilienthal, diary entry of Apr. 24, 1948, *Journals of David E. Lilienthal*, II, 329.

23. Officials of the occupying powers represented the three Western zones of Germany until October 31, 1949, when Western Germany became a full member of the OEEC: delegates of the Federal Republic took their places. The Anglo-American Zone of the Free Territory of Trieste was admitted on October 14, 1949. In June, 1950, the United States and Canada became "associates" but not members.

24. Figures from Statistics and Reports Division, Agency for International Development, Nov. 13, 1963. (The incarnations of the assistance program are hard to keep in mind: Economic Cooperation Administration, then Mutual Security Agency, then Foreign Operations Administration, then International Cooperation Administration, then Agency for International Development.) It is difficult to get precise statistics on Marshall Plan aid; contemporary and later figures show remarkable disagreement. The above figures, which probably are as close to final as one can come, differ from those in Harry B. Price, *The Marshall Plan and Its Meaning*, the official ECA history.

25. US Sen., 82d Cong., 1st Sess., *Institute of Pacific Relations: Hearings before the Subcommittee to Investigate the Administration of the Internal Security Act and Other Internal Security Laws of the Committee of the Judiciary*, V, 1652.

CHAPTER EIGHT

1. Frank L. Howley, *Berlin Command* (New York, 1950), pp. 7-8.

2. FDR to Hull, Oct. 20, 1944, in *The Memoirs of Cordell Hull* (2 vols., New York, 1948), II, 1621.

3. "After I came to know Bevin well, what had happened was as clear as day to me." Dean Acheson, *Sketches from Life*, p. 1. For Marshall's remark at the time of adjournment see Lucius D. Clay, *Decision in Germany*, pp. 347-348. Upon return to the United States, Marshall told President Truman's Cabinet of the hesitation of Bevin and Bidault to call for adjournment of the sessions. Diary entry of Dec. 19, 1947, in Walter Millis and Eugene S. Duffield, eds., *The Forrestal Diaries*, p. 353.

4. Lucius D. Clay, *Decision in Germany*, p. 400.

5. *Berlin Command*, p. 10.

6. Philip E. Mosely, *The Kremlin and World Politics* (New York, 1960), p. 188. See also William M. Franklin, "Zonal Boundaries and Access to Berlin," *World Politics*, vol. 16 (1963-64), 1-31.

7. General Howley kindly read the present chapter in draft and suggested this addition.

8. Major General George P. Hays, in New York *Times*, Jan. 13, 1948, cited in Eugene Davidson, *The Death and Life of Germany* (New York, 1959), p. 185.

9. Comment by General Howley.

10. Lucius D. Clay, *Decision in Germany*, p. 354.

11. "Top secret" cable in Walter Millis and Eugene S. Duffield, eds., *The Forrestal Diaries*, p. 387.

12. *Ibid.*, p. 411.

13. Lucius D. Clay, *Decision in Germany*, p. 361.

14. Robert D. Murphy, *Diplomat among Warriors*, p. 316.

15. Eugene Davidson, *Death and Life of Germany*, pp. 202-203, citing an interview.

16. The press statement is in Dept. of State *Bulletin*, vol. 19 (July 11, 1948), 54. For the note of Marshall to Ambassador Panyushkin dated July 6, 1948, see *Bulletin*, vol. 19 (July 18, 1949), 85-86.

17. ". . . Went to Pershing's funeral in the marble amphitheatre. An impressive ceremony. This is the fifth time I have prepared to attend the General's funeral. It came off this

time." Diary note of July 19, 1948, in William Hillman, ed., *Mr. President* (New York, 1952), p. 140. Kenneth C. Royall was Secretary of the Army, having replaced Robert P. Patterson on July 24, 1947. William H. Draper was Undersecretary of the Army.

Speaking of Pershing's funeral, Margaret Truman Daniel recalls the following meeting between Truman and Secretary Marshall: "General Pershing's body lay in state in the Rotunda of the Capitol and Dad went there to pay his respects. The police on duty didn't recognize Dad and wouldn't let his driver park. 'Just move over,' the policeman said. 'General Marshall's car is going to be parked here.' Dad leaned over and looked at General Marshall and grinned and General Marshall's face registered his horror. The policeman nearly fainted." *Souvenir* (New York, 1956), p. 217.

18. Robert D. Murphy, *Diplomat among Warriors,* p. 318.

19. Willy Brandt, *My Road to Berlin* (New York, 1960), p. 203.

20. Eugene Davidson, *Death and Life of Germany,* p. 221.

21. *Berlin Command,* pp. 246-247.

22. Walter Bedell Smith, *My Three Years in Moscow,* pp. 237ff.

23. *Ibid.,* p. 253.

24. Harry S. Truman, *Memoirs: Years of Trial and Hope,* pp. 130-131.

25. W. Phillips Davison, *The Berlin Blockade* (Princeton, 1958), p. xi: "The objective of the Berlin blockade was to prevent West German economic recovery and formation of a West German government or, failing this, to incorporate the population and resources of West Berlin into East Germany, thus depriving the democracies of a valuable outpost behind the iron curtain and invaluable prestige throughout the world."

26. Comment by General Howley in reading a draft of this chapter.

27. *Diplomat among Warriors,* pp. 317, 321.

CHAPTER NINE

1. Bernard M. Baruch, *The Public Years* (New York, 1960), p. 357.

2. OF 20, Truman MSS. Perón told the American Ambassador: "As an Argentine, I must resent Mr. Braden's intervention in our internal affairs and in the election; as Juan Perón, I am deeply grateful to him." George S. Messersmith to William D. Pauley, US Ambassador in Rio de Janeiro, Feb. 26, 1947. Messersmith MSS deposited in the University of Delaware library.

3. Memorandum by Norman E. Towson to Messersmith, Dec. 4, 1946, Messersmith MSS. For the conversation with Truman see the draft memoir in the Messersmith MSS; with Leahy, the Leahy diary, Jan. 10, 23, 1947; conversation with Marshall, the Messersmith memoir.

4. O. Edmund Smith, Jr., *Yankee Diplomacy: U.S. Intervention in Argentina* (Dallas, 1953), pp. 143-168. The Messersmith MSS give details of the resignation. Announcement was made in Washington without consulting the Ambassador, who cabled Truman and Marshall on June 6, 1947: "As I have not submitted any resignation to the President, has my 'resignation' been accepted by him?" Messersmith felt that Undersecretary Acheson did not like him, but that his resignation was accepted because President Truman had to give James Bruce the job—all in an effort to get a vice presidential candidate for the election in 1948. The Ambassador believed that the whole affair embarrassed President Truman who had only good will for Messersmith. Upon return to Washington, Messersmith spent an hour with Secretary Marshall who was very courteous but spoke only about Europe—not one word about Latin America or Argentina, Messersmith's resignation, or his retirement from the Foreign Service.

5. *Souvenir*, pp. 179-180.

6. Sol Bloom, *Autobiography* (New York, 1948), pp. 281-291.

7. Arthur H. Vandenberg, Jr., and Joe Alex Morris, eds., *The Private Papers of Senator Vandenberg,* p. 366.

8. Joseph W. Martin, Jr., as told to Robert J. Donovan, *My First Fifty Years in Politics,* p. 187.

9. New York *Times,* Apr. 16, 1948.

10. The following account of the conference relies upon Beaulac's *Career Ambassador* (New York, 1951), chs. 29-32, pp. 226-256.

11. *Ibid.,* p. 238.

12. Dept of State *Bulletin,* vol. 18 (Apr. 11, 1948), 470.

13. Matthew B. Ridgway, *Soldier* (New York, 1956), p. 181.

14. Willard L. Beaulac, *Career Ambassador,* p. 253.

15. R. Hart Phillips, *Cuba: Island of Paradox* (New York, 1959), pp. 293-294.

CHAPTER TEN

1. For the larger picture of American-Middle Eastern relations since 1945 see my "United States Policy in the Middle East," in Stephen D. Kertesz, ed., *American Diplomacy in a New Era* (Notre Dame, Ind., 1961), pp. 270-296.

2. Letter to Virginia C. Gildersleeve, Oct. 15, 1945, OF 204, Truman MSS.

3. Letter of Dec. 10, 1945, OF 204, Truman MSS.

4. For the commission of inquiry see the accounts by three members: William Phillips, *Ventures in Diplomacy* (Boston, 1952), pp. 420-456; Bartley C. Crum, *Behind the Silken Curtain* (New York, 1947); Richard Crossman, *Palestine Mission* (New York, 1947).

5. The remainder of the present paragraph is from the letter by Epstein to Dr. Nahum Goldman who was in the Jewish Agency for Palestine in London, Oct. 9, 1946. Chaim Weizmann MSS deposited in the Truman Library. As for identity of the Jewish Agency's friend in the White House, it may have been the presidential assistant David K. Niles.

See the sketch of Niles in Alfred M. Lilienthal's *What Price Israel* (Chicago, 1953), pp. 93-95.

6. Letter to Leo E. Levinson, Oct. 11, 1946, John W. Snyder MSS deposited in the Truman Library.

7. Undated memorandum for the President initialed by GCM, OF 771, Truman MSS.

8. Anonymous memorandum, Oct. 23, 1947, Snyder MSS.

9. Walter Millis and Eugene S. Duffield, eds., *The Forrestal Diaries*, p. 411.

10. A copy of the letter reached Weizmann, and circuitously came back to the Truman Library in the Weizmann MSS.

11. Jacobson's friend and lawyer, A. J. Granoff, gave an interview to Sidney L. Willens which appeared in the Kansas City *Times*, May 13, 1965. The Jacobson quotations are from a letter in possession of Granoff. Together with Jacobson's widow and granddaughter, Granoff on May 22 attended a dedication ceremony in Tel Aviv, of a 600-seat auditorium in a new $700,000 B'nai B'rith building; the auditorium was named in honor of Jacobson.

12. See Harry S. Truman, *Memoirs: Years of Trial and Hope*, pp. 160-165; Jonathan Daniels, *The Man of Independence*, pp. 317-320.

13. Leahy diary, Mar. 20, 1948.

14. OF 204, Truman MSS.

15. *The Man of Independence*, p. 319.

16. Weizmann MSS.

17. *Memoirs: Year of Decisions* (New York, 1955), p. 69. In 1959 at Columbia University, Truman said there still was anti-Semitism in the State Department. *Truman Speaks* (New York, 1960), p. 84.

18. James G. McDonald, *My Mission in Israel: 1948-1951* (New York, Simon and Schuster, 1951), pp. 6-7; Walter Millis and Eugene S. Duffield, eds., *The Forrestal Diaries*, pp. 440-441.

19. *My Mission in Israel*, pp. 7-8, 18.

20. In response to British military executions, Jewish terrorists garrotted and hung two British sergeants near Nathanya, an act that appalled British public opinion.

21. *My Mission in Israel*, pp. 24-26.

22. Letters of Aug. 6 and Nov. 29, 1948, Weizmann MSS.

23. *Memoirs: Years of Trial and Hope*, pp. 168-169.

24. Walter Millis and Eugene S. Duffield, eds., *The Forrestal Diaries*, p. 508. In the winter of 1947-48 Forrestal conducted an unsuccessful personal campaign to keep the Palestine question out of politics. Pp. 309-310, 344, 346-348, 357, 359, 361, 363.

25. Letter of June 16, 1948, Forrestal MSS.

26. William A. Eddy, *F.D.R. Meets Ibn Saud* (New York, 1954), p. 37. Colonel Eddy, then American Minister to Saudi Arabia, had been a professor of English at the American University at Cairo, professor of English at Dartmouth, and president of Hobart and William Smith Colleges. He served as interpreter between Roosevelt and Ibn Saud at the famed meeting in 1945 on Great Bitter Lake in the Suez.

27. *Years of Trial and Hope*, p. 158.

28. Truman's assistants in the White House conducted a study of the Palestine correspondence and drew up detailed statistics running from 1946 to 1951. Memoranda from Andie Knutson for Philleo Nash, July 24, Aug. 6, 1951, Nash Files, Truman Library.

29. For the President's quoted remark, *Inside the Democratic Party* (Indianapolis, 1958), p. 149. Also pp. 104-105, 120, 127, 137, 146-147, 166, 215.

30. William D. Hassett, secretary to the President, to Myron C. Taylor, Feb. 15, 1947, OF 86 Misc., Truman MSS.

31. For the election of 1948 and Zionism see H. Bradford Westerfield, *Foreign Policy and Party Politics*, pp. 234-237; and in particular the excellent new account by Louis L. Gerson, *The Hyphenate in Recent American Politics and Diplomacy* (Lawrence, Kansas, 1964), pp. 153-156. A friend who sometimes accompanied Eddie Jacobson to the White House assured President Truman on one occasion that neither

he nor Jacobson would ever ask him to do anything against the best interests of the United States. "I'll never forget that moment," A. J. Granoff remembered. "The President, grim and obviously irritated over the remark, answered, 'You guys wouldn't get to the front gate if I thought any different. You needn't have said it.'" Interview in Kansas City *Times*, May 13, 1965.

32. *Years of Trial and Hope*, pp. 166-168.

CHAPTER ELEVEN

1. Guy Wint, *Spotlight on Asia* (London, 1955), p. 78.

2. Quoted in Tang Tsou, *America's Failure in China: 1941-50* (Chicago, 1963), p. 483.

3. Leahy diary, July 7, 1947. An entry of July 12 relates that Captain Mullaney, USN, recently on duty in China, believed that Ambassador Stuart, the Minister-Counselor at the Nanking Embassy W. Walton Butterworth, and Raymond Ludden were trying to aid the Communists. Also entry of Dec. 13: "It is my belief that from a purely military point of view a non-Communist China is of more importance to the security of the United States than a rehabilitated Western Europe."

4. *Wedemeyer Reports!*, p. 358.

5. US Sen., 82d Cong., 1st Sess., *Military Situation in the Far East: Hearings before the Committee on Armed Services and Committee on Foreign Relations* (5 vols., Washington, 1951), III, 2312.

6. *Wedemeyer Reports!*, pp. 396-398.

7. Testimony of Sept. 19 in New York *Times*, Sept. 20, 1950.

8. John Leighton Stuart, *Fifty Years in China*, pp. 186-187. *Wedemeyer Reports!*, pp. 387-389. Upon return home Wedemeyer suggested Stuart's relief. Leahy diary, Oct. 21, 1947. But this suggestion was no novelty; Stuart's health was not good, and Marshall in July, 1947, just before Wedemeyer went on the mission to the Far East, had said that

Stuart's ill health had made him insufficiently forceful and again asked Wedemeyer to become Ambassador; this time Wedemeyer refused. *Wedemeyer Reports!,* p. 382.

9. *Op. cit.,* p. 187.

10. Diary entry of Nov. 26, 1948, in Walter Millis and E. S. Duffield, eds., *The Forrestal Diaries,* p. 533; New York *Times,* Dec. 10, 1948; Margaret Truman, *Souvenir,* p. 284.

11. *United States Relations with China* (Washington, 1949), p. xvi.

13. Tom Connally, as told to Alfred Steinberg, *My Name is Tom Connally,* p. 316.

14. Letter of Mar. 27, 1950, OF 384, Truman MSS.

15. Diary entry of May 11, 1949, in *Journals of David E. Lilienthal,* II, 525.

16. Diary entry of June 12, 1947 (relating a meeting of the Business Advisory Council of the Dept. of Commerce), in *ibid.,* pp. 200-201.

17. *America's Failure in China,* p. 399. Also the same author's "Civil Strife and Armed Intervention: Marshall's China Policy," *Orbis,* vol. 6 (1962), 101.

CHAPTER TWELVE

1. Diary entry of Mar. 4, 1947, in *Journals of David E. Lilienthal,* II, 155. In addition to this source the present chapter is under heavy debt to Richard G. Hewlett and Oscar E. Anderson, Jr., *The New World: 1939-1946* (University Park, Penna., 1962), the first volume in the official history of the AEC. The Hewlett and Anderson work is a major piece of historical scholarship—as will certainly be the second volume of the official history, not yet released.

2. Diary entry of Apr. 3, 1947, in *Journals of David E. Lilienthal,* II, 166.

3. Bernard M. Baruch, *The Public Years,* p. 369.

4. Robert Gilpin, *American Scientists and Nuclear Weapons Policy* (Princeton, 1962), p. 54.

5. Dept. of State *Bulletin*, vol. 16 (Feb. 16, 1947), 286.

6. Diary entry of Nov. 18, 1947, in *Journals of David E. Lilienthal*, II, 258. For the Baruch conversations with Acheson, Truman, and Bush, set out above, see *The Public Years*, pp. 361-364. For his difficult qualities, also Margaret L. Coit, *Mr. Baruch* (Boston, 1957).

7. Entry of June 30, 1948, in *Journals of David E. Lilienthal*, II, 376.

8. Joseph L. Nogee, *Soviet Policy towards International Control of Atomic Energy* (Notre Dame, Ind., 1961), p. 264. Nogee entitles his last chapter "The Gamesmanship of Negotiations." Also John W. Spanier and J. L. Nogee, *The Politics of Disarmament: A Study in Soviet-American Gamesmanship* (New York, 1962).

9. Diary entry of Jan. 17, 1947, in *Journals of David E. Lilienthal*, II, 132.

10. Joseph L. Nogee, *Soviet Policy towards International Control of Atomic Energy*, p. 105.

11. *Ibid.*, pp. 135-137.

12. Diary entries of July 5, 7, 1948, in *Journals of David E. Lilienthal*, II, 380-381.

13. Walter Millis and Eugene S. Duffield, eds., *The Forrestal Diaries*, pp. 330, 386. Also diary entries of Feb. 21, Mar. 3, 1948, in *Journals of David E. Lilienthal*, II, 296, 301.

14. Diary entry of June 12, 1947, in *ibid.*, 196-200. The United States position on use of poison gas is not easy to relate. Technically no agreement binds the American Government, for the United States representative signed the Geneva Gas Protocol of June 17, 1925, but the Senate never consented to ratification. As late as 1952 the Senate cited what it considered the agreement's inadequacies. The whole issue of gas came to public notice early in 1965 when the United States employed nonlethal gas in Vietnam. At that time the American position seems to have been that although the nation had not ratified the Protocol of 1925 it shared the general abhorrence of "inhuman" forms of warfare. New York

Times, Mar. 23, 1965. Some international lawyers have contended that ratification by more than forty of the signatories or adherents of the Protocol has brought it into the law of nations as part of customary precedent. This argument is open to doubt.

15. Diary entry of May 18, 1948, in *Journals of David E. Lilienthal,* II, 342.

CHAPTER THIRTEEN

1. Diary entry of July 22, 1947, in Walter Millis and Eugene S. Duffield, eds., *The Forrestal Diaries,* p. 294.

2. With the President as chairman the NSC included the Secretary of State, Secretary of Defense, the three service Secretaries, the chairman of the new National Security Resources Board, and such other department or agency heads as the President might from time to time add.

3. Diary entry of Sept. 26, 1947, *Forrestal Diaries,* p. 320.

4. *Forrestal Diaries,* pp. 452-454. During these months "The effect of NSC is not prominent; NSC no doubt considered the staff papers, debated policy and arrived at recommendations, but every glimpse we have been given of the actual policy-making process in this period shows Defense, State, the Budget Bureau, the White House, making the independent determinations—usually on a hasty if not extemporaneous basis—which really counted." Walter Millis, *Arms and the State* (New York, 1958), p. 223.

5. Diary entry of May 25, 1948, in *Journals of David E. Lilienthal,* II, 351.

6. Diary entry of Oct. 10, 1948, in *Forrestal Diaries,* p. 500.

7. Leahy diary, May 5, 6, 1948.

8. Diary entry of Sept. 13, 1948, in William Hillman, ed., *Mr. President,* p. 141.

9. *Journals of David E. Lilienthal,* II, 406.

CHAPTER FOURTEEN

1. Jonathan Daniels, *The Man of Independence*, pp. 361-362; Harry S. Truman, *Memoirs: Years of Trial and Hope*, pp. 212ff. Also Albert Z. Carr, *Truman, Stalin, and Peace* (New York, 1950), pp. 119-120. Carr worked for a while in the White House and recounts Truman's reaction to gloomy prophecies from his advisers concerning the election, after failure of the Vinson scheme; according to him the President listened and then said in a pleasant voice, "Well, maybe it isn't that bad," and left the room.

2. *The Man of Independence*, pp. 28-29.

3. *My Name is Tom Connally*, p. 331; A. H. Vandenberg, Jr., and Joe Alex Morris, eds., *The Private Papers of Senator Vandenberg*, pp. 456-458.

4. H. Bradford Westerfield, *Foreign Policy and Party Politics*, p. 318.

5. " 'I intend,' I explained, 'to discuss the purpose of this mission and mean to have the full agreement of our allies before you leave for Moscow.' " (This was part of the President's explanation to Vinson.) *Memoirs. Years of Trial and Hope*, p. 215.

6. *Ibid.*, p. 216.

7. *Ibid.*, p. 219.

8. A. H. Vandenberg, Jr., and Joe Alex Morris, eds., *The Private Papers of Senator Vandenberg*, pp. 458-459.

CHAPTER FIFTEEN

1. See such typical comments as on Feb. 18, 1947; May 7, 1948; undated, 1948. William Hillman, ed., *Mr. President*, pp. 137, 219, 150.

2. Quoted in Alexander De Conde, "George Catlett Marshall," in Norman A. Graebner, ed., *An Uncertain Tradition* (New York, 1961), p. 265.

3. New York *Times,* Jan. 13, 1949. The visit took place on Jan. 12.

4. PPF 4901, Truman MSS.

5. PPF 2996, Truman MSS.

6. Sept. 18, 1950, PPF 2996, Truman MSS.

7. PPF 2996, Truman MSS.

8. Undated penciled note on Pecora telegram of Feb. 5, 1952, PPF 8-E, Truman MSS.

9. Harold Moody, principal and US history teacher of Wheeler High School, to Truman, Apr. 3, 1952, Truman to Moody, May 21, PPF 6068, Truman MSS.

10. PPF 2996, Truman MSS.

11. New York *Times,* June 6, 1949.

12. Speech of Mar. 19, 1948 at the University of California at Berkeley, in Dept. of State *Bulletin,* vol. 18 (Mar. 28, 1948), 423.

13. New York *Times,* Mar. 13, 1950.

14. *Ibid.,* Oct. 21, 1959; Paul Hoffman, letter to *ibid.,* Oct. 20; Dean Acheson, "Homage to General Marshall," *Reporter,* Nov. 26 (*Sketches from Life,* pp. 147-166, is an elaboration); George Kennan, letter to New York *Times,* Oct. 18.

BIBLIOGRAPHICAL ESSAY

I. *Biographical*

Marshall refused to assist would-be biographers, with two exceptions, and so he never received the literary garlands and bouquets in honor of his life and work which many leading Americans in recent years have secured, so to speak. The Marshall literature is spare and shows no large information until one reaches the most recent volume, the beginning installment of Forrest C. Pogue's authorized biography. Katherine Tupper Marshall, *Together: Annals of an Army Wife* (New York, 1946) sets out the experiences and knowledge of the second Mrs. Marshall in the period 1930-45, especially the Second World War when she presided over Quarters Number One at Fort Myer and sought in every possible way to make her husband's life decently relaxed at home. Mrs. Marshall is a discerning woman and her short memoir has large historic value. William Frye, *Marshall: Citizen Soldier* (Indianapolis, 1947) surveys its subject until the general's resignation as Chief of Staff in 1945; a careful volume, it relies on some interviews with Marshall's associates and upon open sources. When Marshall became Secretary of State there were several interesting essays such as John Hersey, "Mr. Secretary Marshall," *Collier's,* Mar. 29, Apr. 5, Apr. 12, 1947; and Robert T. Elson, "New Strategy in Foreign Policy: A General and a Banker Bring Order and Method to the U.S. State Department," *Fortune,* Dec. 1947, on Marshall and Undersecretary Lovett. Catching popular interest once the general returned to public life as Secretary of Defense, Robert Payne's *The Marshall Story: A Biography of General George*

C. Marshall (New York, 1951) reveals the hand of a master writer, author of literally dozens of books. One can find here an excellent sense of the long upward striving of Marshall's career, fine feeling for times and contemporaries. There is also a tendency to write up episodes in an allusive literary style, and some effort to guess through the empty places of the subject's life where material was unavailable. Occasional inaccuracies enlist the reader's caution: as when Payne from reading Mrs. Marshall's memoir discovered that the general met his future second wife in a town named Columbus and concluded that it was Columbus, Ohio instead of Columbus, Georgia. Joseph R. McCarthy, *The Story of General George C. Marshall* (n.p., 1952) has most of the Senate speech of June 14, 1951, with asides cut out and with some new material including press comment; based on commonly available sources, this famous diatribe draws out and elaborates the material's critical portions or seeming disagreements; but if one reads carefully he has a feeling that it is a milk-and-water attack, nothing libelous, not even real abuse, a much overrated or overremarked piece of nonsense. The general's death in 1959 led to a few publications such as John P. Sutherland, "The Story General Marshall Told Me," *U.S. News and World Report,* Nov. 2, 1959, some things the general said with injunction not to quote him until after he had passed on; there is not much here of interest as Marshall knew better than to say the things which, apparently, his contemporary General Douglas MacArthur could remark to newspaper friends with the same injunction. More interesting for analysis of the Marshall personality is Dean Acheson's "Homage to General Marshall," *Reporter,* Nov. 26, 1959, elaborated in Acheson's *Sketches from Life* (New York, 1960), pp. 147-166. Alexander De Conde's "George C. Marshall," a judicious sketch in Norman A. Graebner, ed., *An Uncertain Tradition* (New York, 1961), pp. 245-266, sets out the general's diplomacy in engaging manner. The book to end Marshall books is Pogue's *George C. Marshall,* a multivolume biography of which the first volume, *Education of a General*

(New York, 1963) takes Marshall to installation as Chief of Staff on August 1, 1939. Pogue has first use of the archives in the George C. Marshall Research Center at Lexington, Virginia. He has engaged in over three hundred interviews with Marshall's contemporaries, and a series of twenty-five interviews with Marshall himself in 1956-57 before illness ended the discussions. The Pogue work will run to three volumes.

II. *Memoirs*

One of the best books to emerge from the immediate scene of postwar American and world diplomacy was James F. Byrnes' *Speaking Frankly* (New York, 1947), a best seller still worth close reading. Byrnes did not speak as frankly as he would later in his autobiography (*All in One Lifetime* [New York, 1958]) but considering the closeness of his early book to events, and the high authority of its author, *Speaking Frankly* is a remarkable production. It is essential introduction to Marshall's diplomacy, though it does not describe anything beyond its author's tenure at the Department. During Marshall's first year as Secretary not much else of memoir nature appeared on American diplomacy except two books on the same subject, Palestine. Bartley Crum, *Behind the Silken Curtain* (New York, 1947) and Richard Crossman, *Palestine Mission: A Personal Record* (New York, 1947) give American and British interpretations of the joint Anglo-American commission from a pro-Israel point of view (for a more judicious opinion on the commission see the later account by another member, William Phillips, *Ventures in Diplomacy* [Boston, 1952], pp. 420-456).

The ebullient Sol Bloom published his *Autobiography* (New York, 1948) shortly after return from the Rio Conference in 1947, offering wonderful description of the conference's arrangements, a diplomatic cameo to tempt contemporaries to look to memoirs by participants in more important conclaves.

Publication then moved forward notably in the year 1950 when the defining of the cold war prompted several leading participants to set out their experiences. Mark W. Clark, *Calculated Risk* (New York, 1950) describes a little of the bleak atmosphere at the Moscow Conference in 1947, to which Clark went to help in discussion of the Austrian question. Lucius D. Clay, *Decision in Germany* (New York, 1950) deals with major German issues of the past five years, including for Marshall's era the breakup of the Allied Control Council, blockade, and formation of a West German Government. Clay also brought out his *Germany and the Fight for Freedom* (Cambridge, Mass., 1950), discursive lectures. His assistant in Berlin, Brigadier General Frank L. Howley, *Berlin Command* (New York, 1950) writes with éclat of encounters with the Russians; no one can read General Howley's crisp prose without a sense of the purposefulness of the author and his excellent performance during the blockade: Clay apparently did not like Howley too well at the outset but came to see that Howley's techniques and traits were exactly what the doctor ordered in a time of trouble. The Howley volume is based on a diary. A quite different work is John Foster Dulles, *War or Peace* (New York, 1950), the future Secretary of State's random thoughts probably put together in dictation to a secretary or tape recorder. Much of this volume is statesmanlike utterance. There are a few reminiscences, such as about the Moscow Conference of 1947. Falling between the books by Howley and Dulles is Walter Bedell Smith's *My Three Years in Moscow* (Philadelphia, 1950), careful setting out of the general-turned-ambassador's life in the Russian capital, with occasional witty remarks.

One of the most extraordinarily revealing diplomatic publications (and military, of course) of the post-1945 years has been Walter Millis and Eugene S. Duffield, eds., *The Forrestal Diaries* (New York, 1951), casual diary entries, jottings, and documents, brought together by skillful editing. The interesting aspect of this publication is inclusion of what must have been much "top secret" material, a more expeditiously

declassified body of prose seldom having left the archives so early after its composition. It seems fairly clear that down to the present writing (March, 1965) no government in the Western world, including the United States, has allowed similar publication from its files—and Forrestal, as mentioned, had the habit not merely of reporting Cabinet discussions and other highly interesting talks but inserting documents in his so-called diary. The historian can feel, however, that the national interest did not suffer from publication of the diaries, and that publication indeed has been a clear public service, as so much of what happened in Forrestal's time became ancient history, almost, what with outbreak of the Korean War—which event sealed, at least for fifteen years, the division of East and West, communist and noncommunist worlds.

Two interesting diplomatic memoirs are Willard L. Beaulac, *Career Ambassador* (New York, 1951), on the Bogotá Conference of 1948; and James G. McDonald, *My Mission in Israel: 1948-1951* (New York, 1951), an outspokenly partisan account by the late Ambassador, filled with criticism of the Department of State.

Arthur H. Vandenberg, Jr., and Joe Alex Morris, eds., *The Private Papers of Senator Vandenberg* (Boston, 1952) has a great deal about American domestic politics but also records the Senator's conversion to bipartisanship and general American participation in world affairs, and there are sidelights on people and events, though much less revelation on matters of high policy than appears in the *Forrestal Diaries*. Whatever Vandenberg's lack of intellectual attainment, or at least ability to state thoughts without cliches and mixed metaphors, he provided a near-essential link between the Truman Administration and its Republican Congress in 1947-48.

A diplomatic memoir of quality, the witty Stanton Griffis's *Lying in State* (Garden City, N.Y., 1952), could never—one can say with certainty—have been written by anyone but an American: Europeans would cringe at the very title. Still, the author's cynicism must have been helpful in the postwar world, and his comments on just about anything are worth

pondering, including organization of the State Department which he found bureaucratic and old-maidish.

John Leighton Stuart, *Fifty Years in China* (New York, 1954) has a grand chapter on the Marshall mission and is almost magisterial in description of the breakdown of the Nationalist Government. There may be passages of naiveté in the diplomatic parts of this missionary-educator's memoir, but they strike fire even in their simple explanations. Again, it is easy for a cynic to say that Stuart had little understanding of diplomacy or the communist mind, so-called, but he had great understanding of China and the Chinese which may well have been more important. Two quite different memoirists, Senator Connally (as told to Alfred Steinberg), *My Name is Tom Connally* (New York, 1954) and Clement R. Attlee, *As It Happened* (New York, 1954) are difficult to juxtapose other than because of their near-simultaneous publication, except that both Connally and Attlee were politician-statesmen under the skin, despite different habitats, and it is no accident that they agreed on foreign policy during the Marshall period. Connally discussed events and came to conclusions with Texas exaggeration and humor, and Attlee set out in his only relevant chapter ("Foreign Affairs," pp. 237-248) the same issues and conclusions with good British restraint.

Out of office the Democrats wrote their memoirs and brought them out in the mid-1950s, and the principal work of this genre was Harry S. Truman, *Memoirs: Year of Decisions* (New York, 1955) and *Years of Trial and Hope* (1956). This well-known work shows major evidence of its author's participation, and in our ghost-ridden time this remark is not as silly as it sounds. Composition of this work must have taken place largely on the desk of the former President, for the paragraphs with their careful logic and sometimes awkward shifts and phrases sound authentically like their subject. Mr. Truman did obtain help from Dean Francis H. Heller of the University of Kansas who checked references and occasionally drafted detailed analyses, but major work

was that of the author of record. Short of Churchill's memoirs, which often resort to dull quoting of documents, there is no recent memoir of such quality, and if the Truman prose is not in Victorian epic style it may be more historically accurate, one might say less tendentious. There are some inaccuracies in the Truman memoirs, of necessity, and sometimes Mr. Truman has placed himself in the best light as any good memoirist ought to do. But the memoirs are a masterful production, first resort—and likely a reliable one—for diplomacy of his time. The account of 1947-48 shows the deep admiration of Truman for the general in charge of the Department of State.

On a different level is Margaret Truman Daniel's *Souvenir* (New York, 1956), a gossipy "as told to" volume which relates that General Marshall was "My Hero." The then Miss Truman had great fondness for the gallant General Marshall. There are some interesting sidelights here on diplomatic matters, such as Mrs. Chiang Kai-shek talking politics to "Dad" during the tea of December, 1948. The book has no index.

Lord Strang, *Home and Abroad* (London, 1956) offers a first-rate sketch (pp. 287-300) of Ernest Bevin, for whom "Bill" Strang worked in the Foreign Office. Matthew B. Ridgway, *Soldier* (New York, 1956) relates "Bogota in Riot Time," experiences at a presumed diplomatic conference.

Colin Cooke, *The Life of Richard Stafford Cripps* (London, 1957), dealing with the Chancellor of the Exchequer after Lord Dalton (for whom see below, p. 315), is based unfortunately on speeches and public statements.

As mentioned, former Secretary Byrnes published his autobiography in 1958, *All in One Lifetime*, partly to correct the version of his secretaryship offered in the Truman memoirs. Lieutenant General Albert C. Wedemeyer's *Wedemeyer Reports!* (New York, 1958) examines China experiences and the special mission of 1947, pp. 275-404. John M ("Jack") Redding, *Inside the Democratic Party* (Indianapolis, 1958) has foreign policy sidelights on the campaign of 1948, notably Truman's refusal—Redding says—to take advantage of the Palestine issue in the campaign. Dean Acheson, *Power and*

Diplomacy (Cambridge, Mass., 1958) is more a tract for the times, analysis of the plight of the United States since 1945, than discussion of diplomacy under Marshall's or Acheson's secretaryship. Mr. Truman recently published two books, *Mr. Citizen* (New York, 1960) concerning his transition to the life of a private citizen beginning in 1953, with little about his foreign policy as President; and *Truman Speaks* (New York, 1960), lectures at Columbia University in 1959 which have a few remarks on policy, such as the comment that the State Department, anti-Semitic in 1945-48, was still anti-Semitic.

An antidote to the Democratic memoirs is Joseph W. Martin, Jr., as told to Robert J. Donovan, *My First Fifty Years in Politics* (New York, 1960), full of bitterness because of Martin's displacement as Republican Party leader in the House, but offering clever party views about issues and political problems of the Truman and other eras. Martin's explanation as to why the GOP found it easier after the war than before to be bipartisan on foreign policy is a masterpiece of domestic political calculation.

Bernard M. Baruch, *The Public Years* (New York, 1960) shows the Baruch egotism and ability and deals in small part with atomic questions. Leslie R. Groves, *Now It Can Be Told* (New York, 1962) offers experience of the chief of the Manhattan Project, displaced by civil control beginning in 1947. Lewis L. Strauss, *Men and Decisions* (New York, 1962) gives the point of view, sometimes conservative, of the Truman era commissioner in 1947-48 and later chairman of the Atomic Energy Commission.

Two notable English memoirs are Clement Attlee, *Twilight of Empire: Memoirs of Prime Minister Clement Attlee* (New York, 1962), more revealing than *As It Happened* of nearly a decade before but still a restrained book; and Hugh Dalton, *High Tide and After* (London, 1962), by the Chancellor of the Exchequer until November, 1947, based partly on Dalton's diaries.

William M. Rigdon, *White House Sailor* (Garden City,

N. Y., 1962), by Truman's assistant naval aide, publishes some of the human-interest episodes of Truman's presidency, such as an account of the ocean voyage back to the United States after the Rio Conference of 1947.

Two recent publications give evidence of the generally increasing historical quality of memoirs with passage of time. Robert D. Murphy, *Diplomat among Warriors* (New York, 1963) tells a great deal of its author's experience as troubleshooter for the Department and often diplomatic aide to generals. The book has some factual errors and unsupported opinion, and time may prove that Murphy's volume has been overrated because of a careful publisher's promotion, but it deals with a long diplomatic era of tremendous change and its author was at the center of many events. A different kind of book is *The Journals of David E. Lilienthal* (2 vols., New York, 1964), the most extraordinary diary published in the past generation by an American public man. The first volume concerns the Tennessee Valley Authority, but the second deals with the AEC and, in addition to setting forth the most fascinating details of that important enterprise, is full of commentary by and about leading figures of the government —what Marshall said to Acheson and vice versa, Acheson on Marshall, Truman on the atomic bomb. A work of major historical importance.

III. *Monographs*

For any student of American foreign policy in recent times the first resort for factual information is the Council on Foreign Relations series entitled *The United States in World Affairs,* edited for the Marshall period by John C. Campbell. This account has careful checking for factual accuracy, and within limits of prudence is as forthright and open as one might wish, much like its analogue in Great Britain, the annual *Survey* published by the Royal Institute of International Affairs. The Council volumes, apart from understand-

able hesitation to reveal "inside" material perhaps known to the compilers, avoid personal commentary and any show of the major rivalries within governments which sometimes appear during the making of policy.

Another Council publication was Hoyt Price and Carl E. Schorske, *The Problem of Germany* (New York, 1947), result of a study group that worked over the winter of 1946-47 prior to announcement of the Marshall Plan. Analysis of another troublesome place in Europe is in William Hardy McNeill, *The Greek Dilemma: War and Aftermath* (Philadelphia, 1947), which gave opportunity for a later volume by McNeill, *Greece: American Aid in Action, 1947-1956* (New York, 1957) sponsored by the Twentieth Century Fund and relating the success of American assistance. For the latter see also C. A. Monkman, *American Aid to Greece: A Report on the First Ten Years* (New York, 1958). Also Leften S. Stavrianos, "The United States and Greece: The Truman Doctrine in Historical Perspective," in Dwight E. Lee and George E. McReynolds, eds., *Essays in History and International Relations* (Worcester, Mass., 1949), pp. 36-59, a well-footnoted study on Greek-American relations from the 1820s to 1947; and Stephen G. Xydis, *Greece and the Great Powers, 1944-1947: Prelude to the "Truman Doctrine"* (Thessaloniki, 1963), a detailed diplomatic study.

An encyclopedic work stressing formal development is Graham H. Stuart's *The Department of State: A History of Its Organization, Procedure and Personnel* (New York, 1949), with some account of Marshall administration.

Jonathan Daniels, *The Man of Independence* (Philadelphia, 1950) offers judgments on the Truman Administration from the vantage point of a White House aide, and includes some of Truman's strictures on former Secretary of State Byrnes. It has novel material on recognition of Israel, apparently from the presidential assistant Clark Clifford, not complimentary to the State Department. Albert Z. Carr, *Truman, Stalin, and Peace* (New York, 1950) discusses the Vinson mission, also from association with the President, though with a good deal

less authority on this smaller subject; one has impression that the author overwrote a fairly small amount of material. A book by another participant in history, though as a student encountering a revolution sometimes attributed to the foreign policy of the United States, Derk Bodde's *Peking Diary: A Year of Revolution* (New York, 1950) offers more on the Chinese revolution than almost any memoir except that of Ambassador Stuart.

Elias Huzar, *The Purse and the Sword* (Ithaca, 1950) sets out two nondiplomatic items which affected foreign policy in the era of small defense budgets and the Air Force rebellion in favor of more budget and a quick solution to international problems.

William Diebold, Jr., *Trade and Payments in Western Europe: A Study of Economic Cooperation, 1947-1951* (New York, 1952) is a technical study, probably too technical for the average student of foreign policy. On another subject is Francis Williams, *Ernest Bevin* (London, 1952), an interim biography—awaiting completion in the 1960s of the authorized two-volume work by Alan Bullock; Williams knew Bevin and can write with authority.

Theodore H. White, *Fire in the Ashes: Europe in Mid-Century* (New York, 1953), an impressionistic, beautifully written account of Europe's revival, was a best seller as the Korean War came to an uneasy end and attention returned to Europe, by one of America's finest reporters. For the spirit of the early postwar years this book has great merit. Herbert Feis analyzed *The China Tangle: The American Effort in China from Pearl Harbor to the Marshall Mission* (Princeton, 1953) in one of the volumes of his masterful five-volume work on American diplomacy during the Second World War. O. E. Smith, Jr., *Yankee Diplomacy: U.S. Intervention in Argentina* (Dallas, 1953), a rather superficial and short book done from printed sources including textbooks, tries to discuss what admittedly was an unsuccessful American intervention. A good piece of controversial literature and a point of view not often heard is Alfred M. Lilienthal, *What Price Israel* (Chi-

cago, 1953), a careful effort to analyze the politics of Israeli independence (on the same subject see the masterful new work by Louis L. Gerson, *The Hyphenate in Recent American Politics and Diplomacy* [Lawrence, Kansas, 1964], pp. 153-156). Lilienthal has completed a trilogy on Israel, the other volumes being *There Goes the Middle East* (New York, 1957) and *The Other Side of the Coin* (New York, 1965).

John P. Armstrong's "The Enigma of Senator Taft and American Foreign Policy," *Review of Politics*, vol. 17 (1954-55), 206-231, brought out the twists and turns of "Mr. Republican" on issues of foreign policy, and tantalized his readers in hope of a book to come—not yet published. See also William S. White, *The Taft Story* (New York, 1954). Leon D. Epstein, *Britain: Uneasy Ally* (Chicago, 1954) discusses uncertainties of the British when facing the Eightieth Congress and some of the vacillations of American policy then and in successive years. Albert R. Sellen, "Congressional Opinion of Soviet-American Relations: 1945-50," thesis at the University of Chicago, 1954, very ably presents the shades and shadings of policy toward Russia, as does also H. Bradford Westerfield, *Foreign Policy and Party Politics: Pearl Harbor to Korea* (New Haven, 1955) for a larger time period and somewhat wider scale. See also Holbert N. Carroll, *The House of Representatives and Foreign Affairs* (Pittsburgh, 1958). James A. Robinson, *Congress and Foreign Policy-Making* (Homewood, Ill., 1962) has a few pages on 1947-48 from obvious sources.

Turning to the Truman Doctrine and Marshall Plan, one has the book by an able speech writer in the Department of State, Joseph M. Jones, *The Fifteen Weeks (February 21-June 5, 1947)* (New York, 1955). Jones helped compose the Truman speech to Congress announcing aid to Greece and Turkey. Harry B. Price, *The Marshall Plan and Its Meaning* (Ithaca, New York, 1955) is the official ECA history; Price held more than three hundred interviews, nearly two hundred in the thirteen European countries taking part in the Marshall Plan. An unpublished study is Ross J. Pritchard, "Will Clayton: A

Study of Business-Statesmanship in the Formulation of United States Economic Foreign Policy," thesis at the Fletcher School of Law and Diplomacy, 1955; this essay used Clayton's papers and also benefited from conversation with its subject. For a technical analysis see Richard N. Gardner, *Sterling-Dollar Diplomacy* (Oxford, 1956), which uses some Clayton papers and deals with many subjects other than the Marshall Plan. William C. Mallalieu, *British Reconstruction and American Policy: 1945-1955* (New York, 1956) has a chapter on the Marshall Plan and benefits from Clayton and other material. See also Mallalieu's "The Origin of the Marshall Plan: A Study in Policy Formation and National Leadership," *Political Science Quarterly*, vol. 73 (Dec., 1958), 481-504, general commentary which remarks that its sources include hitherto unpublished archival material from the Department of State. The authoritative work on Will Clayton is by his daughter Ellen Clayton Garwood, *Will Clayton: A Short Biography* (Austin, Texas, 1958), an interesting volume based on reminiscence and a series of interviews with men involved in the Marshall Plan and other of Clayton's activities. See also the convenient compilation by Robin Winks, *The Marshall Plan and the American Economy* (Boston, 1960), a booklet of readings for college students. Will Clayton, "GATT, The Marshall Plan, and OECD," *Political Science Quarterly*, vol. 78 (1963), 493-503 reprints the crucial memorandum of May 27, 1947, which stirred the Department toward what became the Marshall Plan. An interesting mimeographed booklet, just released (March, 1965) is *Conference of Scholars on the European Recovery Program, March 20-21, 1964, at the Harry S. Truman Library*, published by the Harry S. Truman Library Institute for National and International Affairs, Independence, Missouri. The present author and Jerry N. Hess edited the transcript, and the author was discussion leader of the conference which included thirty individuals, mostly diplomatic historians. The published transcript runs to fifty-nine pages of singlespace typescript, and contains some quotations from the Dalton diaries together with scholarly conclusions about the Marshall Plan.

Margaret L. Coit's *Mr. Baruch* (Boston, 1957) has two chapters on atomic energy, Baruch's concern for some months at the end of the war. This is a fulsome biography critical of Baruch's enemies. Miss Coit writes in a breathless, epic style which does not fit the human outlines of her subject.

W. Phillips Davison, *The Berlin Blockade* (Princeton, 1958) is a massive study, the best available and probably to become available until declassification of records of the Department of State and Department of Defense. Walter Millis, *Arms and the State* (New York, 1958) has material on American re-armament after the Second World War. Eugene Davidson, *The Death and Life of Germany* (New York, 1959) sets out the American occupation from 1945 until organization of a German Army ten years later, in beautiful prose with skillful judgment; see ch. 8, "The Year of the Blockade." Philip E. Mosely brought together some of his essays under the title of *The Kremlin and World Politics* (New York, 1960) including the often-quoted essay concerning the wartime European Advisory Commission, on which Mosely served.

On questions of atomic policy there was a bulge in the literature in 1961-62, for reasons that defy analysis. An able doctoral thesis turned into a book, Joseph L. Nogee's *Soviet Policy Towards International Control of Atomic Energy* (Notre Dame, Ind., 1961) shows the gamesmanship of Soviet negotiation on this issue. John W. Spanier combined with Nogee in *The Politics of Disarmament* (New York, 1962), a popularization and updating. An intriguing analysis, showing how what once would have been described as the farthest thing from diplomacy—physics—now has an altogether un-easily-close relation, is Robert Gilpin, *American Scientists and Nuclear Weapons Policy* (Princeton, 1962), excellently written. A wonderful source, evidence of the high quality of U.S. Government historical research, is Richard G. Hewlett and Oscar E. Anderson, Jr., *The New World: 1939-1946* (University Park, Penna., 1962), the first volume of the official history of the AEC.

The historian Tang Tsou of the University of Chicago

recently has discussed China problems in "The Historians and the Generals," *Pacific Historical Review*, vol. 31 (Feb., 1962), 41-48; "Civil Strife and Armed Intervention: Marshall's China Policy," *Orbis*, vol. 6 (spring, 1962), 76-101; and the authoritative *America's Failure in China: 1941-50* (Chicago, 1963). Muddying the waters was a simultaneous book-length publication by Anthony Kubek, *How the Far East Was Lost* (Chicago, 1963), which used—without discernible result—the papers of Ambassador Hurley.

Recent works dealing with the Marshall years and policy are Jean Edward Smith, *The Defense of Berlin* (Baltimore, 1963), which unfortunately discusses the Berlin blockade from a few well-known sources; William M. Franklin, "Zonal Boundaries and Access to Berlin," *World Politics*, vol. 16 (1963-64), 1-31, an expert setting-out of the politics and policy leading to the Berlin predicament; Herbert Nicholas, *Britain and the U.S.A.* (Baltimore, 1963), the Albert Shaw lectures by a distinguished British historian; Arnold A. Rogow, *James Forrestal: A Study of Personality, Politics, and Policy* (New York, 1963), about an undoubtedly highly-strung man; A. Doak Barnett, *China on the Eve of Communist Takeover* (New York, 1000), by a student of Chinese affairs who traveled into almost every mainland region; Cordell A. Smith, "The Marshall Mission," thesis at the University of Oklahoma, 1963, containing only about fifty pages on the mission of 1946, written almost entirely from the *China White Paper* and other well-known published documents and memoirs; and *The American Review*, vol. 2 (1962-63), the March issue of which deals with the Marshall Plan, publishing papers of a conference in Cambridge, in summer, 1962, of the European Association of American Studies. D. C. Watt's *Personalities and Policies* (Notre Dame, Ind., 1965) reprints his article in the *American Review*, "American Aid to Britain and the Problem of Socialism, 1945-51." See also Watt's excellent new volume touching (pp. 53-98) on the Marshall era, *Britain Looks to Germany: A Study of British Opinion and Policy towards Germany since 1945* (London, 1965).

IV. *Periodicals*

Major reliance of all scholars must continue to be the New York *Times,* which with passage of years has become ever more complete and authoritative. Its coverage, both in sheer space for news and in numbers of correspondents all over the world, is so far beyond that of other newspapers that there is no comparison. Its index allows easy access to its pages.

In the papers of the Democratic National Committee and in its regular manuscript collections (for which see below) the Truman Library has masses of newspaper clippings from around the country on almost any subject during the Truman Administration, boxed and easily available.

Journals discussing diplomacy of 1947-48 are likely sources —*Foreign Affairs,* and *International Affairs.* Also the *Economist* and *New Republic* and *Nation.* The American weekly news magazines are useful for color and mood.

V. *Printed Sources*

The best printed source on American diplomacy and foreign policy is the Department of State *Bulletin,* published in weekly installments running to a volume each six months. Not merely the most important policy pronouncements appear almost automatically in the *Bulletin,* but distinguished members of the Department often publish articles discussing problems of major concern. It would be possible to draw together from the *Bulletin* a revealing series of scholarly articles on American foreign policy which would describe that policy from year to year almost without break. The *Bulletin,* incidentally, printed such an interesting item as the 111 questions and answers, asked by Congress and offered by the Department, on "Aid to Greece and Turkey: A Collection of State Papers" (vol. 16 [May 4, 1947], 866-895).

A printed source well worth examination is the *Public*

Papers of the Presidents: Harry S. Truman, 1947 (Washington, 1963); *Harry S. Truman, 1948* (Washington, 1964). The new series in which these volumes appear began in 1957, and contains public messages, speeches, and statements. The well-known compilation by James D. Richardson covered 1789-1897 and was published between 1896 and 1899, but after that time the government had no such organized publication. The National Historical Publications Commission recommended a new series, and at the present writing the Eisenhower volumes and two years of the Kennedy Administration have appeared. Among other things for the Truman years—sheer convenience of such a compilation—the series publishes Truman's press conferences verbatim. His custom at the time was to authorize quotation only in special cases.

William Hillman, ed., *Mr. President* (New York, 1952), an authorized volume of diaries, memoranda, and correspondence, is a sort of documentary publication bearing on American policy during Marshall's years. This volume was highly political, coming in a presidential year, but prints revealing material including some account of the President's falling out with Secretary Byrnes

For Germany, a prime diplomatic topic in 1947-48, see Department of State, *Germany, 1947-1949: The Story in Documents* (Washington, 1950); and *Documents on Germany: 1944-1961* (Washington, 1961), including material on the international agreements concerning air access to Berlin.

Another prime topic produced the most controversial documentary publication of the postwar years, the so-called *China White Paper*: Department of State, *United States Relations with China: With Special Reference to the Period 1944-1949* (Washington, 1949). This volume came out in August, 1949, just after Ambassador Stuart left for the United States, and printed dispatches of his which, he believed, deeply embarrassed his confidences with Nationalist officials. It is true that the Department published the volume to prove the rightness of policy toward China which, at time of publication, had clearly failed; and critics then and later were to say

that the White Paper was an ex parte document believable only insofar as one could trust the Department of State in 1949. There is no way to disprove such judgment, although the present writer believes the compilation fair-minded, the record plain. Final judgment will have to await publication of regular volumes in the Department series *Foreign Relations of the United States* (see below). Early in the 1950s Congress encouraged publication in *Foreign Relations* of special volumes on China which would take the documentary story to 1949 and come out ahead of regular *FR* volumes. Secretary of State Dean Rusk in 1962 decided, and the non-Department scholarly Advisory Committee to *FR* concurred, that the China volumes not yet published should come out along with the other volumes for each year. Until *FR* has covered the remainder of the 1940s the *China White Paper* will have to suffice.

US Sen., 82d Cong., 1st Sess., *Institute of Pacific Relations: Hearings before the Subcommittee to Investigate the Administration of the Internal Security Act and Other Internal Security Laws of the Committee of the Judiciary* (15 vols., Washington, 1951-53), V, reprints the conference on problems of United States policy in China which assembled at the State Department on October 6, 7, and 8, 1949. At this crucial time about two dozen experts on Far Eastern affairs met at the Department and voiced their views, including Marshall, Kennan, Stuart, John K. Fairbank and Edwin O. Reischauer of Harvard, Bernard Brodie of Yale. This notable discussion, which well deserves special reprinting as a volume of source materials, shows American knowledge, opinions, and moods at the time of the Chinese Communist takeover.

The Department of State documentary series, *Foreign Relations of the United States,* is presently (1965) into the year 1944, and there is every indication that the series if bulging will move soon into the postwar era. But there is a continuing shortage of funds which may well see the *Foreign Relations* volumes, invaluable to the historian, appearing farther and farther behind what the Department and Secretary Rusk have

hoped would be a twenty-year line between event and publication. "Hold the Twenty-Year Line" has proved difficult, and the series—without pressure on Congress from interested scholars and the general public—may move toward a twenty-five-year line. This is a saddening possibility, considering the marked propaganda advantage the German Government of the 1920s achieved with publication of *Die Grosse Politik der Europaischen Kabinette* well before the Allied governments brought out their own documents bearing on the origins of the First World War, and the advantage that the Government of the United States has been obtaining until the present time through prompt publication of its own documents, often years before any documentation from other governments.

VI. *Manuscript and Other Sources*

The George C. Marshall Research Center materials now in the library at Lexington, Virginia, are not available to researchers until Forrest Pogue's volumes appear, and for the era 1947-48 this may be quite a while as the first volume in the biography, *Education of a General,* published in 1963, takes Marshall to 1939. One would assume that most of the Marshall papers concern the Second World War. Pogue's interviews with the general dealt with "high points of the postwar period," among other subjects, but the Research Center materials when open for 1947-48 may consist largely of documents from other collections, brought down in microfilm—such as pertinent files of the Department of State, or from the Truman Library in Independence.

The Harry S. Truman Library has a tremendous collection of papers of the former President, to which the director of the library, Dr. Philip C. Brooks, kindly allowed access. Files are in excellent order; there is no technical problem getting to them. The files are often revealing, as Mr. Truman is an interesting writer of letters and wrote a great many. No one need look for personal items, as the President like all great public figures is a cagey correspondent, but he often set out his views on public matters with frankness and detail. It is a testimony to the American sense of history that such

magnificent materials are now in so beautiful a library, open to the researcher; no such facilities exist in Europe—nor possibly will exist in the immediate future, say, in Great Britain where public authorities revere the Fifty-Year Rule (see D. C. Watt, "Restrictions on Research—the Fifty-Year Rule and British Foreign Policy," *International Affairs*, vol. 41 [Jan., 1965], 89-95). The only British collection now opening to scholars is the Hugh Dalton MSS, including a diary, at the London School of Economics and Political Science, but at the present writing the Dalton material for 1947-48 is not yet in order.

As mentioned, the Truman Library contains the Truman MSS, and also papers relating to members of the Administration which divide into two categories. When the original collection of Truman materials arrived from the White House, papers included in the collection which related to other individuals became known as "files": hence the Philleo Nash files were, in a sense, a section of the Truman materials, as also the David Lloyd files and Clark Clifford files. Collections added to the Truman Library, given after the main body of materials was in the library, are known as "papers" (denominated in the present book as MSS). The Joseph M. Jones MSS (papers) are a small collection of two or three boxes which Jones sent to the library; they do not contain a great deal, but there are successive drafts of the Truman Doctrine speech and Acheson's Delta speech and some material on drafting Marshall's address at Harvard. The John W. Snyder MSS (papers) contain interesting material on the British loan, the Marshall Plan, and other matters including customs regulation of ships plying illegally to Palestine in 1945-48. The Chaim Weizmann MSS (papers) are photographs of material in Israel, sent over to the library; some of it is interesting for inside information on the independence of Israel, especially the work of the Jewish Agency.

Dr. Brooks of the Truman Library spent several weeks in Europe in 1964 interviewing individuals who took part in the Marshall Plan. His interviews are now being typed and

checked, after which the donors of interviews may well put conditions on them. The interviews are not available at the present time.

The James V. Forrestal MSS in the library of Princeton University are in excellent order and have numerous boxes of correspondence etc. for 1947-48. Although a good bit of this material is routine and social, there are occasional letters of interest. The Forrestal diaries in manuscript, including material not in the published volume, are now at Princeton, but probably will not be open to researchers until the Department of State opens its archives for the same period. According to a new Department of State rule the restricted period for access to Department archives (restricted to researchers who are United States citizens and who can pass a security check, who are studying purely historical subjects, and who are willing to turn in their notes for Department scrutiny) will move forward with publication of volumes in the *Foreign Relations* series; volumes are now being published for the year 1944; there is an increasing lag in publication; access to unpublished Forrestal diary materials for 1947-48 hence may not come for some years. Dr Rudolph Winnacker of the Department of Defense assures me that the diaries contain little information of importance for Marshall's diplomacy in 1947-48.

The manuscripts division of the Library of Congress is now amassing holdings in the post-1945 era and will open its collections after a grant of literary rights to the public or upon special conditions stipulated by owners of papers or, if the papers contain Department of State materials, upon clearance with the Historical Office of the Department. Clearance will mean that collections cannot open in the manuscripts division until the Department's archives for the period in question are open (or relatively open, as for papers in the Department restricted period which usually is ten years in advance of completely free access). The Laurence A. Steinhardt MSS in the manuscripts division are open to scholars; Steinhardt was Ambassador to Czechoslovakia in 1945-48

and his papers have some interesting correspondence with fellow envoys. The Tom Connally MSS offer comments of the former chairman of the Committee on Foreign Relations. Connally was a good correspondent when he took the time to answer a letter carefully, but his papers in the Library of Congress seem to be a huge collection of junk—offhand letters, or routine answers to constituents' smallish problems. The diaries of Fleet Admiral William D. Leahy, now in the manuscripts division, are open to scholars with permission of Rear Admiral William H. Leahy. The Leahy volume, *I Was There* (New York, 1950), goes only until the year 1945, and volumes of unpublished diary run through the rest of the decade.

The Oral History Research Office at Columbia University has a memoir by Will Clayton, and also interviews by Clayton's daughter, Mrs. St. John Garwood, with eleven individuals connected with the work of her father. The Clayton memoir has literary rights dedicated to the public.

Some other collections of personal papers of individuals on the periphery of American foreign relations are now available, and I have made every effort to examine such collections in hope that these individuals might have collected items of interest. The papers of the late Senator Robert Wagner of New York are in the Georgetown University Library; but Professor J. Joseph Huthmacher, presently engaged in a biography of the Senator, assures me that ill health in 1947-48 allowed Wagner to attend only one Senate debate, on the Taft-Hartley Bill, and that there is nothing of interest on American foreign policy. The papers of Senator Alben Barkley at the University of Kentucky Library have almost no items of interest on foreign relations, although Barkley was a member of the Committee on Foreign Relations of the Eightieth Congress. Papers of Representative Sol Bloom, who attended the Rio Conference, are in the New York Public Library, but close examination of pertinent general correspondence files showed little of importance; they were full of letters about veterans' pensions, changes of Army assignment, and procure-

ment of immigration visas. Because of Bloom's prominence in the House Committee on Foreign Affairs—for some years he was the chairman—it is difficult to believe that all his personal papers went to the library. Ambassador George Messersmith left a collection of papers to the library of the University of Delaware in Newark, and in addition to a fair-sized correspondence they contain a huge manuscript memoir, perhaps half a million words, hurriedly dictated from memory not long before his death, setting out among other things the details of his ambassadorship to Argentina and his "row" over policy with Assistant Secretary Braden.

INDEX

Acheson, Dean, 22, 35, 49-53, 75, 81-82, 84, 91, 104-106, 109-110, 132, 140, 156, 205, 210-211, 222-223, 268. *See* Acheson-Lilienthal report
Acheson-Lilienthal report, 219-220
Agriculture, Dept. of, 48, 102
Air Force, US, 29, 32, 149, 178, 224, 234-236, 238-241, 243, 245-247, 261
Air Policy Committee, 241
Alaska, 73
Alexander the Great, 217-218, 223
Allen, Robert S., 88
Allied Control Council for Germany, 137, 142-143, 145-146, 155-156
American Legion, 257-258
American Revolution, 74
Anderson, Clinton P., 26
Anderson, Clayton and Company, 107
Anglo-American Committee on Palestine, 182-183
Argentina, 78, 116, 161, 163-167, 169
Army, British, 17, 66-67; Chinese, 27; Colombian, 177-178; French, 66-67; German, 9; Greek, 79, 97; Portuguese, 2; Soviet, 65-66; Turkish, 77, 79, 98; US, 1-2, 6-20, 32-33, 35, 44, 47, 66-67, 161-162, 177, 186-187, 230-231, 234-249
Arvey, Jack, 260
Atlantic Charter, 38
Atomic Energy Commission (AEC), 48, 213, 217-218, 223, 228-230, 232
Attlee, Clement, 58-59, 100-101, 115. *See* Truman-Attlee-King Agreement (*1945*)
Austin, Warren, 188-189, 225-226
Austria, 47-48, 63-64, 67, 80, 103-105, 122, 124, 139, 175, 243

Bacher, Robert F., 218
Baghdad Pact. *See* Central Treaty Organization

Baldwin, Hanson W., 103, 196
Baldwin, Stanley, 72
Baltimore *Sun*, 125
Barr, David G., 203
Baruch, Bernard M., 54, 89-90, 107, 219-227, 233
Baruch Plan. *See* Baruch, Bernard M.
Beaulac, Willard L., 173, 175
Beitzell, Mrs. C. L., 88
Belgian Congo. *See* Congo
Belgium, 122, 244
Bell, J. Franklin, 7-8
Benes, Eduard, 121
Berle, Adolf A., 51
Berlin Air Safety Center, 143
Berlin blockade, 135-160, 173, 200, 216, 227, 237-238, 240, 246-248, 254, 258
Berlin, Free University of, 153
Bernadotte, Folke. *See* Bernadotte Plan
Bernadotte Plan, 199-200
Bevin, Ernest, 67-69, 74-75, 110, 139-140, 194-195; portrait, 58-59. *See* Marshall Plan
Bidault, Georges, 60, 67-69, 139; portrait, 59. *See* Marshall Plan
Biffle, Leslie L., 109
Bisgyer, Maurice, 188
Bloom, Sol, 167-168
Bogotá Conference (*1948*). *See* International Conference of American States, Ninth
Bohlen, Charles E., 110
Bolívar, Simon, 174, 177
Boykin, Frank, 87
Braden, Spruille, 164-167
Bradley, Omar, 247
Brady, Diamond Jim, 168
Brazil, 161. *See* Inter-American Conference for the Maintenance of Continental Peace and Security (*1947*)
Brewster, Owen, 211, 241
Brewster-Hinshaw Board, 241
Brussels Pact (*1948*), 244
Bulgaria, 76
Bullitt, William C., 209

319

DATE DUE

GAYLORD

PRINTED IN U.S A.